A LIFE OF

Rashmi is married into the Palkhivala family who were amongst Yogacharya B.K.S. Iyengar's earliest students in Mumbai and shared a warm relationship with the Iyengars. Her family now has three established teachers of yoga: her husband, Jehangir, her mother-in-law, Dhan, and her brother-in-law, Aadil, and perhaps some more in the making.

Rashmi Palkhivala has always been an itinerant at heart...with the eventual dream of settling in a house up on a hill, preferably surrounded with mist and mango trees. She has diverse skills that hold very slight credibility in the real world, like building houses of mud, helping birth babies and being able to zap a headache out of existence with some dextrous foot reflexology. In real life, she teaches English to high school kids. She enjoys writing and directing plays for older teens and has worked with several Mumbai schools for their annual dramatic productions. She has written a delightful book on the history of Mumbai for children, called *Samundari City*.

As the home on the hill hasn't materialized yet, she presently lives with her family in Mumbai, in an apartment on the seventeenth floor.

A LIFE
OF
LIGHT

THE BIOGRAPHY OF B.K.S. IYENGAR

RASHMI PALKHIVALA

HARPER
element

First published in India in 2017 by Harper Element
An imprint of HarperCollins *Publishers*

P-ISBN: 978-93-5264-173-4
E-ISBN: 978-93-5264-174-1

2 4 6 8 10 9 7 5 3 1

HarperCollins *Publishers*
A-75, Sector 57, Noida, Uttar Pradesh 201301, India
1 London Bridge Street, London, SE1 9GF, United Kingdom
Hazelton Lanes, 55 Avenue Road, Suite 2900, Toronto, Ontario M5R 3L2
and 1995 Markham Road, Scarborough, Ontario M1B 5M8, Canada
25 Ryde Road, Pymble, Sydney, NSW 2073, Australia
195 Broadway, New York, NY 10007, USA

Typeset in 12/15 Garamond Premier Pro at
Manipal Digital Systems, Manipal

Printed and bound at
Replika Press Pvt. Ltd.

Contents

Since this book was conceived after Guruji's passing in 2014, it is constructed from books that have been left behind and the memories of those who have been associated with him who were willing to share their experiences. The italicized sections of the book are fictionalized parts of Guruji's story based on fragments of fact, pieced together with the author's imagination.

Guruji has been variously addressed through the book as Sundara, Iyengar, Mr Iyengar, Anna and Guruji depending on the phase of his life and whom he is interacting with at that point. So, though he was Sundara to his family, he was Mr Iyengar to his early western students, and later in his life, Guruji to everyone.

AN IMPOSSIBLE BIRTH

Bellur, Karnataka
The night of Saturday, 14 December 1918

P *lumes of wood-scented grey smoke emerged from the house and merged with the charcoal sky. The silence of the night amplified the sounds of mourning coming from several homes in the village. Inside the house, water boiled angrily in a fat-bellied copper cauldron placed on a crackling wooden fire.*

Seshamma's sister-in-law covered her with every blanket they possessed. They placed warm foments on her lungs and belly. But nothing could stop the shivering, the coughing and the deadly wheeze in her lungs. Besides the fever, there were the contractions to contend with, now coming unrelentingly, every three minutes.

Bellur had not felt the winter so intensely in more than a hundred years of living memory. It was rumoured to be one of India's coldest winters of all time with 16 December 1918 being the coldest recorded day in Karnataka's history, an unprecedented 2.4°C.

What made the chill of the winter of 1918 even harder to bear was the *jvara*, or the flu. The jvara had swept through the village, probably from Bangalore, a cantonment city 50 kilometres away. It may have come on the infected breath of a soldier returning home from the Great War. It may have come in with a mineworker who had gone to Bangalore on vacation and returned afflicted with the Great Scourge. It may have travelled with a pilgrim on his way to the Kolaramma Temple from the big city. However it had arrived, it was there, and it was spreading fast.

India was used to disease. The country had suffered through smallpox, cholera and the plague over the centuries, with only a minor furrow in her brow to show for it. The flu, which no one felt the need to take seriously, was traditionally treated with *kashaya*, a vile-tasting concoction of spices and herbs. And this innocuous 'jvara', which normally did not even warrant a visit to the local Ayurved, had turned out to be India's nemesis!

Though the flu pandemic of 1918 was possibly triggered by World War I, the speed and scale with which it raced through the world, and the decimation it left in its wake, were infinitely more terrifying than the effects of the war. The flu infected 500 million people across the world and killed approximately 70-100 million people. India was the worst affected with a death toll of about 17 million people. With one-fifth of the world population infected by the flu, it was very difficult to remain unaffected. Even US President Woodrow Wilson was said to be suffering from influenza as he signed the Treaty of Versailles to end World War I.

This contagion had the dubious distinction of being the most deadly pandemic to have afflicted the world. Four years of the Black Death and the Bubonic Plague combined had not wreaked as much havoc as the influenza pandemic did in just one year, 1918.

Most of India's doctors were away, serving in the war. Fleming's discovery of penicillin, the first antibiotic, was still a decade away.

Hospitals were simply not equipped in terms of manpower or medication. Doctors would watch helplessly as their patients struggled to breathe through a blood-tinged froth that gushed from the nose and mouth. Many doctors themselves succumbed to the disease. This was, of course, in towns that were lucky enough to have doctors and hospitals. Bellur had neither.

But how did it all begin? Travelling on soldiers' breaths across France, Spain, Germany, the USA and into India, it burned its way from crowded military barracks through prisoner-of-war camps, troop ships and mine shafts. One sneeze containing 40,000 influenza-laden drops could infect thousands of people within a few seconds. With people forced together into confined spaces by the exigencies of war, each sneeze ended up being more lethal than a bullet.

The virus struck quickly and remorselessly. A chilling story of the time tells us about a group of four women who planned to play bridge till late into the night. By the next morning, three of the four were dead from influenza.

The English, with their droll sense of humour and a penchant for creating nursery rhymes on very inappropriate subjects, had reason enough to be inspired. It was not unusual to find kids of the time skipping rope to this ditty:

> *I had a little bird,*
> *Its name was Enza.*
> *I opened the window,*
> *And in-flu-enza*[1]

Starting slowly, the virus mutated several times, gaining strength with each mutation. The initial strain of the virus, though it affected a lot of people, did not have as many fatalities as the later

---

1   https://virus.stanford.edu/uda/

mutation did. 'Nearly every house...has some of its inmates down with [influenza] fever and every office is bewailing the absence of clerks,' announced the *Times of India*, Bombay, June 1918. [2]

By August 1918, however, the virus had mutated into something much more dangerous and deadly. It was now a virus with the capacity to penetrate deep into lung tissue, leaving its victims gasping for breath with viral pneumonia and severe respiratory distress. The lack of oxygen caused a bluish discoloration of the skin called cyanosis, or it set the stage for a potent form of pneumonia. Either way, it was not pleasant. The victim would begin to find it difficult to breathe, and then a characteristic, crackling wheeze would emanate from the lungs. This would be followed by a racking cough and the breath would develop a pungent odour, which often signified the end.

The flu had several far-reaching effects. It left its victims debilitated, with their lungs and other vital organs severely impaired and made them more susceptible to other seemingly unrelated diseases like meningitis, nephritis and Parkinson's.

The 'most likely to die' list of the 1918 Influenza Pandemic was topped by pregnant women. Next on the list were the babies in their bellies at the time they contracted the disease.

In the family home, Seshamma's older children comforted the younger ones. The family was prepared to lose both Seshamma and the little baby but they weren't prepared to give up on them. So they nursed her carefully through the influenza that she had contracted, like so many others in the village.

It had been a difficult labour; the mother was enervated both by the pain of labour and the fatigue of the deadly influenza. She gave

---

2   Killingray, David and Phillips, Howard, *The Spanish Influenza Pandemic of 1918-19: New Perspectives (Studies in the Social History of Medicine)*, United Kingdom: Routledge, 2003

birth to a baby boy. They nursed the baby through, his influenza, all the while marvelling that mother and baby had made it through, when so many others, with seemingly stronger constitutions, had succumbed. When they later found out that the jvara had claimed more than seventy million lives all over the world, they were deeply grateful.

It seemed, from the start, that God was on their side.

THE YOUNG SUNDARARAJA

The little boy born that day was called Sundararaja – the King of Beauty. The family called him Sundara. Maybe it was a portent for the future. For the present, he could not have been more inappropriately named. By his own admission, Bellur Krishnamachar Sundararaja Iyengar was an unprepossessing child; a head too heavy for his body, a sunken chest, a protruding belly, and skin that retained an unhealthy cyanotic hue from his early wrangle with death. Sundara, the eleventh of thirteen children, became an obvious target for the painful teasing of his siblings.

Sundara's father, Bellur Krishnamachar Iyengar, was the headmaster of a local school in the neighbouring village of Bhudalkotte. His mother, Seshamma, was the wonder woman who had made it alive with her infant son through the influenza that had threatened to wipe out the village.

Generations ago the Iyengars had left their native state in the Southeast and ventured westward. They were part of a Tamilian Brahmin community who are known for being fiercely attached to their culture. What could have prompted them to make this move into a strange land where they knew no one?

The Iyengars traced their origins to Nathamuni, a Vaishnav saint and scholar of the tenth century who spent his life collating the songs and poetry written by Nammalvar and the other Alvars, who were considered divine emanations of Lord Vishnu.

Nammalvar, the most revered of them all, was born into a
Shudra family in 3102 BC. According to legend, Nammalvar was
born fully enlightened. As a baby, he neither cried nor suckled
nor opened his eyes. As a child, he purportedly responded to
no external stimuli. His parents heard a voice ordering them to
leave the child in a tamarind tree. They left him there and the tree
became his home.

Sixteen years later, a Tamil poet saint,[3] Madhurakavi Alvar, was
travelling through north India. Attracted by a bright light in the
south, he felt drawn towards it and began walking southwards till he
reached the tamarind tree. Nammalvar was sitting in the hollow of
the tree, deep in meditation. Having been in meditation for sixteen
years, his body was radiant with light. Madhurakavi tried to rouse
him, but he remained undisturbed. Finally, he asked Nammalvar
a theological question, 'If the subtle soul is embodied in the gross
body, what are its actions and thoughts?' Nammalvar broke his
silence and responded, 'If the soul identifies with the body, it will
be the body, but if it serves the divine, it will stay in Vaikunta (where
the Lord resides) and think of God.' From his answer Madhurakavi
understood that the youth was a realized soul.

Nathamuni, born in the tenth century, was already a highly
respected teacher and a spiritual adept when he came across some
travelling mystics singing chants that called to his soul. Approaching
them, he found out that these were the ten extant verses of the
Divya Prabandam composed by Nammalvar. One of the mystics
told him, however, that if he went to the tamarind tree where
Nammalvar had meditated and he was sincere in his meditation
and in seeking, he might find the lost 3,990 verses. So Nathamuni
went there, his heart filled with spiritual resolve and determination

3   Desikachar, Kausthub, *The Yoga of the Yogi: The Legacy of T.
Krishnamacharya*, New York: North Point Press, 2011

to recover the rest of the beautiful composition. His sadhana was so strong that Nammalvar apparently appeared before him and taught him the rest of the *Divya Prabandam*. This was not the least of Nathamuni's accomplishments. He had attained mastery over various subjects, including yoga. He was the author of a text called the *Yoga Rahasya*, which is considered one of his most precious contributions. It included many classical and practical teachings of yoga and how yoga could be used at various stages in life, including for women in pregnancy and in healing disease.

Ramanuja, born in 1017 CE, was the one who interpreted the texts left behind by Nathamuni. In his early life, Ramanuja debarred women and lower castes from learning the sacred texts, but later changed his stand and became more inclusive, even allowing 'outcastes' to enter temples.

His broadness of vision was not looked upon kindly by his compatriots who hounded him out of Tamil Nadu. This forced him and some of his followers to shift to Melukote in Karnataka in 1137 CE. From Melukote, his disciples branched out to other places in Karnataka to spread the word of Ramanuja. This is how the Iyengar family, who are originally from Tamil Nadu, came to settle in Bellur, in the Kolar district of Karnataka.

Kolar district, famous for its gold mines, is inhospitable country. The landscape is strewn with low, flat-topped, rocky outcrops that do not allow for farming. Bellur is a little village in Kolar district, which in 1918, and for decades after, had no school, no college and no hospital. Sundara's father, Krishnamachar, had to walk a fair distance to the next village, Narsapur, where he worked as the school headmaster. When Sundara turned five, his father retired from this position. Out of thirteen children, ten had survived. He and his wife took the family to twelve. It was many mouths to feed for a family that did not subsist on agriculture for their livelihood. Agriculture is one of the primary sources of income in Karnataka, and since they were migrants to Bellur, the Iyengars had no land to call their own.

This forced Krishnamachar to take his family, which included the five-year-old Sundara, and venture into the big city, Bangalore, to find a job.

In Bangalore, Krishnamachar was employed as a clerk in a huge provision store owned by a Muslim gentleman named Abdullah. Abdullah, happy with the diligence of his new employee, treated him well, often helping him out with extra money. Krishnamachar's meagre salary as a clerk could not cover the inevitable emergencies that crop up when one has such a large family to look after.

When Sundara turned nine, tragedy cast a grey cloud over the family again. His father was struck by a bout of appendicitis that proved fatal. As he struggled with the malady, Krishnamachar called the nine-year-old Sundara to his side. He prepared the young one for his death by telling him that his own father had died exactly when he was nine, as Krishnamachar believed he was about to do. He also predicted that his young son would have a life fraught with difficulties in his youth but he would be very happy thereafter. Scant comfort for a nine-year-old watching his father die.

Left rudderless, now it fell upon the older brothers to take over the financial responsibility of bringing up the younger siblings. There were four older brothers: Doreswami Iyengar, an accountant in Bangalore, Raja Iyengar, a school teacher in Bangalore and Vedantachar Iyengar, a railway clerk in Madras. The fourth brother, Ramaswami, after fruitlessly trying to wrap his head around the complexities of Math, English and Biology, failed his school-leaving exam and gave it all up to become a tailor.

None of them could afford to take on the burden of their mother and the unmarried siblings. As often happened in this kind of situation, the dependents were separated and tossed about from one home to the other. Sundara's younger brother, Cheluvarajan, stayed with their older sister, Rukkamma, and Sundara's younger sister, Jayamma, lived with their oldest sister, Namagiriamma. Sundara shifted from home to home. Since all the older siblings now had families of their own, the added burden of looking after their younger siblings weighed heavily upon them.

The influenza that Sundara had contracted at birth cast a long shadow on his health. Even as a teenager, his immunity was low and he often succumbed to illness. Describing himself later as an 'anti-advertisement for yoga', Sundara was plagued at different points in his youth with bronchitis, pneumonia, tuberculosis, typhoid and malaria.

At thirteen, after an attack of malaria, he suffered a prolonged bout of fever that could not be diagnosed. Suspecting typhoid, the doctor advised that the child be admitted to hospital.

Sundara was kept in the general ward of the Victoria Hospital in Bangalore for a month. The doctor probably felt that the child would be provided a nutritious diet and rest, which he was deprived of at home. The elegant stone building with its airy rooms and well-lit corridors would give the sickly child a chance of recovery. After spending a month in hospital, the persistent fever was cured, but it took more than a year for Sundara to fully recover his energy.

As a result of his illness, he missed so many days of school that this put a damper on his academic life. In Karnataka at the time, education was free till the eighth grade. Sundara managed to continue school despite his long absences and the family's dire pecuniary position.

In the next academic year, he failed in English. This did not bode well for the Lower Secondary School Exam, which he needed to pass to be eligible for high school. The problems with his health were still plaguing him, but he managed to finish most of his exams without event. However, on the last day, as he was cycling to his Biology and Hygiene paper, a combination of exhaustion, weakness and malnourishment made him fall unconscious on the street. By the time he recovered and reached the examination hall, he was late for the exam. He tried to answer the paper, but his mind drew a blank for the first half hour. Then slowly collecting himself, he summoned up whatever he could dredge out of his subconscious and hurriedly put it all down. Luck was on his side, because the examiner found his scribblings adequate to pass him in the subject. He was now eligible to enter high school.

Now the big hurdle before Sundara was how he would raise enough money to pay his high school fees.

Sundara went to stay with his eldest brother, Doreswami Iyengar. Though his older brothers looked after Sundara's basic needs of food and clothing, it was impossible for them to stretch their resources to include his fees. In those days, children had to only pay for eight months of the year of high school. To an impoverished student, the fees still seemed and out of reach.

Using one of his father's connections, Sundara thought he should procure a letter of recommendation from an influential lawyer K.T. Bhasyam who had defended Abdullah, his father's ex-boss, in a commercial litigation.

It was with great trepidation that the adolescent Sundara, and Raja Iyengar, his older brother, approached K.T. Bhasyam in his home at Cottonpet. The manicured garden and the whitewashed walls spoke of the severity of its occupant. K.T. Bhasyam was one of the foremost leaders of the freedom movement in Bangalore and was also responsible for spearheading the Congress Party in the city. He had a formidable reputation as a brilliant lawyer, legislator and political leader. Had he not joined the Congress, people predicted that he could have been the chief justice of Mysore or even the chief minister of the state. Respected for his integrity and simplicity, he was known to be incorruptible and not interested in giving or taking favours. Perhaps K.T. Bhasyam was moved by the plight of this fatherless boy, also an Iyengar like himself, or perhaps he saw the promise of greatness. Whatever it was that moved the great lawyer's heart, Sundara got his letter.

The Iyengar brothers then requested some business acquaintances of their father for the remaining sum. Being merchants who had a good relationship with the senior Iyengar, they chipped in all of the eight rupees needed to finance the remainder of Sundara's education for the year.

Bhasyam's letter enabled him to get a half scholarship. Bolstered by this, and the eight rupees collected from the merchants, Sundara was finally ready to enter the elusive portals of high school.

But just as he was about to start, Sundara had a visitor. It was a visit that was to change the course of his destiny.

Sundara's sister Namagiriamma had married T. Krishnamacharya in 1927. In 1934, when Krishnamacharya came to visit, Sundar was fifteen. Krishnamacharya was on his way to the Kaivalyadhama Yoga Institute in Lonavla.

En route to Bombay, Krishnamacharya stopped in Bangalore to visit his wife's family. Sundara was then staying with his brother, Doreswami. Krishnamacharya had been anxious about leaving his young wife alone in Mysore to fend for herself. He realized that it would be a good idea for one of her brothers to go to Mysore and keep Namagiriamma company till he returned from his travels.

As it was summer vacation time, Sundara agreed to go to Mysore to be with his sister. He thought it would be like a free holiday, as his brother-in-law was happy to pay his train fare. Sundara was excited. He had always wanted to explore the Mysore Palace and imbibe some of the rich cultural experiences that the city promised.

Sundara had no idea that he was supposed to be honoured by an invitation into the home of one of the most learned minds of the time in spirituality, the Vedas and yogic texts. He was lured by the thought of a free holiday. He did not question the fact that his other siblings had refused to go.

Mysore, as a city, was very unlike Bangalore. The rulers of Mysore were established patrons of the Arts and the city reflected the culture and pomp of its rulers.

Sundara had an eventful holiday in Mysore. The Mysore Palace, the gardens, the forests – he explored them all. Soon his brother-in-law returned. Having run through the gamut of experiences the city of Mysore had to offer, Sundara was ready to leave.

Bangalore was full of all his favourite nephews and nieces, the children of his brother Raja Iyengar and the children of his sister Seetamma, who were closer to him in age than his siblings were. Despite the fluctuations in his health, he had enjoyed the time spent with his nephews and nieces. Their games of football and cricket and the joy of sharing the precious few treats that came their way had all made him feel like he was part of a family.

In comparison, the spartan T. Krishnamacharya household did not hold much appeal. At the time, the couple had two infant girls. Sundara had no incentive to stay on in Mysore, but when T. Krishnamacharya asked Sundara to stay and complete his schooling there, Sundara was forced to agree. A poor boy, without a father to look after him, he did not have the luxury of choice.

The letter he had acquired with such difficulty from K.T. Bhasyam would make him eligible for a part-scholarship to school in Mysore as well. While his heart may not have been completely in it, this decision to stay back in Mysore began the most influential part of Sundara's life.

HIS GURU'S JOURNEY

T. Krishnamacharya was born to Srinivas Tatacharya and Ranganayakiamma[4] on 18 November 1888. He had five siblings – two brothers and three sisters. In a gurukul-like atmosphere, Srinivas schooled the children in the knowledge of the Vedas and other religious texts.

Though this sounds idyllic, life in this gurukul was neither beautiful nor easy. It was rigorous and rough on these young minds, and only the most committed benefitted from it. The teachings were all-important and had to be respected. Tatacharya woke the children up at 2 a.m. to learn the Vedic chants and practise their yoga asanas. Besides this, they had to master the religious rites and procedures.

When Krishnamacharya was ten, his father died and he was enrolled into the Parkala Math (ashram), which is like the Vatican for the Vishnu worshippers of South India. The pontiff of Parkala

---

4   Desikachar, Kausthub, *The Yoga of the Yogi: The Legacy of T. Krishnamacharya*, New York: North Point Press, 2011

Math was Srinivas Tatacharya's grandfather. Besides the religious importance of the position, it wielded considerable political power as well, as the pontiff of this *math* was, by convention, the teacher of the king of the land.

Under the tutelage of his great grandfather, and later his great grandfather's successor, the bright young man began to absorb the intricacies of Vyakarana (Sanskrit grammar), Vedanta, and Tarka (logic). As a teenager, he was already beginning to engage in debates with visiting scholars and teachers.

When he was barely sixteen, Krishnamacharya had a dream. He was asked to go to Alvar Tirunagari, where Nammalvar had meditated in the tamarind tree hollow for many years. It was an arduous journey for a sixteen-year-old to undertake – 600 kilometres to be negotiated on foot. He could not afford trains and buses that would have made the journey easier. He walked through the day in the desiccating heat of interior Karnataka and Tamil Nadu and rested at night in the *thinnais* (balconies) of strangers.

When he arrived, he encountered an old man seated under a tree and asked him where he could find Nammalvar's tamarind tree. The old man said nothing, but he indicated a direction with a movement of his head. Following this instruction, Krishnamacharya found himself in a mango grove, by the river Tamrapani. Exhausted from his journey, he went into a trance-like state. Three sages appeared before him and he begged them to reveal the *Yoga Rahasya* to him. They did, in voices mellifluous and musical. That is when he noticed that the sage in the centre was Nathamuni. When he came out of the trance, the sages had disappeared. There was no sign of a mango orchard, there was no old man and all that remained was the memory of the verses that had been revealed to him by Nathamuni himself.

Krishnamacharya's own students now feel that the *Yoga Rahasya* was a 'masterpiece' created by their own guru, based on the fact that he often changed it as he recited it, and possibly because of the implausible story associated with its inception.

Whether it was reality or a glorious dream, Krishnamacharya's purpose in life was now clear to him. He had to spread the knowledge he had received. He decided that to be taken seriously he would have to equip himself with immense knowledge.

Returning to Mysore, he studied the shastras and earned the title of Vidhwan (Professor) but he found that this only fuelled his desire to know more.

Varanasi, with its rich culture, bursting at the seams with spirituality and learning, beckoned him. In Varanasi, he met Siva Kumara Sastri. One evening, Siva Kumara called Krishnamacharya to him and channelled the entire reservoir of his learning of the Sanskrit language to the young adept. The next day, the master stopped speaking altogether.

Krishnamacharya spent years in Varanasi, immersing himself in the learning of the Vedas, yoga and Samkhya. He earned the most advanced qualifications in all these subjects.

He was told that if he wanted to truly understand the *Yoga Sutras* of Patanjali, he should meet Rama Mohana Brahmachari in Tibet. Refusing a lucrative job offer from the Maharaja of Kashi, he set his sights on Tibet.

Divine intervention led him to Srinivas Iyengar, an officer in the East India Railway Company, who was so impressed with the young man and his incredible store of knowledge that he offered him a lifetime pass to travel on the railways, wherever or whenever his heart desired. Armed with this railway pass, Krishnamacharya travelled to Simla and waited for an audience with Lord Curzon, then the viceroy, who was the only one who could grant him the papers with which he could travel to Tibet. Lord Curzon was laid up with diabetes but fortunately, his attending physician was the son of Krishnamacharya's teacher. This made it easy for him to get an audience with his Excellency. The young man impressed the viceroy enough for him to start taking yoga lessons from Krishnamacharya to control his diabetes. In six months the diabetes was under control and Krishnamacharya not only had the papers to enable him to travel to Tibet, but also two aides provided by the viceroy to ease the discomfort of the journey. The only proviso was that Krishnamacharya had to return to Simla. The viceroy wanted to stay in touch with the yoga he had just learned.

Even in these days of highly priced and specialized mountaineering equipment and porters, the trek to Mansarovar is classified as a risky one. The trek entails walking in treacherous conditions through cold and rugged terrain at altitudes of 19,500 feet, demanding extreme levels of physical and mental fitness. And this is today, when every modern convenience is at hand. When Pattabhi Jois, one of Krishnamacharya's students, was asked about this expedition, he reportedly burst into tears, saying, 'No one will be able to do that journey today.' To think Krishnamacharya embarked on this arduous journey armed with just his faith! No pre-made packets of food, no thermal underwear, no down parkas and not even an appropriate pair of walking shoes. After twenty-two days and 340 kilometres of walking, they reached Mansarovar and found the teacher for whom Krishnamacharya had made this dangerous trip.

For the next eight years, Krishnamacharya engaged himself in absorbing all he could from his guru. At the end of it, the guru commanded him to pay his guru *dakshina*. He ordered him to return to his homeland, live the life of a householder and spread the message of yoga. Krishnamacharya returned from his life-changing trip with only his master's wooden sandals and sketches of asanas hand-drawn by his teacher's daughter.

After his return from Tibet, he travelled to many princely states at the invitation of their rulers. He was asked by the Maharaja of

Jaipur to take over as Principal of the College of Education. He refused, as he did not want to be tied down.

His reputation as a scholar had reached his native state and he was being invited back to the Parkala Math to be the pontiff. Refusing the offer would be unbecoming. But Krishnamacharya had to keep his promise to his teacher. He had to repay his guru dakshina, which was to marry and spread the word of yoga, neither of which would be possible if he took up the position of pontiff. As pontiff, he would have to remain unmarried and only concentrate on the Sri Vaisnava tradition, which precluded the teaching of yoga.

He declined the offer to be pontiff, and embarked on fresh peregrinations instead – to Gangotri, Yamnotri and yet another arduous trip to Tibet. He visited several princely states and was wooed by royalty who wanted this man of immense learning to grace their courts and educational institutions.

In August 1924, he returned to Varanasi. After almost two decades of wandering and accumulating a deep and comprehensive understanding of all the subjects he had wanted to master, Krishnamacharya decided suddenly and abruptly that his education was over.

It was time to head home to Mysore.

The Iyengar home was abuzz. In the kitchen, Seshamma was roasting kadale mavu, fragrant split-pea flour, with ghee in a thick iron pan while her daughter, Rukkamma, stirred the sugar syrup with a ladle. The perennially-hungry Sundara, who had been hanging around in the kitchen, had been sent out to sweep the yard. Seetamma, Seshamma's other daughter, had been put in charge of bringing in the marigolds from the neighbour's garden. She was now arranging them in a pattern between the kolam that she had already created with rice paste on the floor at the entrance of the home. The fragrance of Mysoor pak wafted out from the little windows of the house, prompting the nosier neighbours to come around asking whether the Iyengars were expecting special guests.

Upstairs, little Namagiriamma, who had just turned twelve that year, was trying to drape a bright red silk Kanjeevaram saree around her waist. It was the same saree that her sister Rukamma had worn at her wedding. The fragrance of Mysoor pak was distracting Namagiriamma so she kept getting the drape wrong.

It was only after she had got her period that she had switched from the pavade (skirt and blouse) that she had been wearing all her life to the nine-yard saree. She was very confused about many things. Till just a few months ago, she had been allowed to play with her friends every evening, and now, she had to stay home and help her mother with the cooking and cleaning. All of a sudden, she had to stop going to school. During the days of her period, she was made to sit in a corner of the house and not touch anyone or anything. And to make matters worse, there was the awfully perplexing saree she was forced to wear. She felt she could never get used to so much fabric.

Today, the man from Kashi was coming to see her. He was fair and beautiful, they told her. Namagiriamma had applied an extra layer of turmeric on her face so he would think she was good enough for him. Her siblings teased her, calling him 'Kashi pandit'. She looked down at her pleats. Frustrated, she called out to her sister, 'Seetamma...inge vaango'. Seetamma came up with a small sample of Mysoor pak in her palm. If the marriage were to be fixed today, little Namagiriamma would not be enjoying her mother's Mysoor pak for very long.

As Seetamma was arranging the last pleats of the saree, they heard their father return with the visitors. Namagiriamma ran to the window before Seetamma could stop her. From the window, she caught the first glimpse of the man who was going to be her husband. She wasn't sure whether to be afraid or excited. Her stomach churned with all sorts of emotions she had never encountered before.

When Sundara met his brother-in-law for the first time, he had no idea of the wealth and depth of Krishnamacharya's knowledge and how far he had gone to acquire it. After all, at that time, the farthest Sundara had travelled was two hours on the bus from his native village Bellur to Bangalore.

All Sundara saw in Krishnamacharya was an older man with distinguished features, a shaved head, horn-rimmed glasses, with the u-shaped Iyengar caste mark on his forehead. Not much to impress a nine year old. According to the conventions of the time, child marriage was the norm. Krishnamacharya was thirty-seven and Namagiriamma was twelve. By the nine-year-old Sundara's standards, Krishnamacharya was far too old to be interesting.

The need to have a secure income and to look after his young wife created a dilemma in Krishnamacharya's life. In the early days of their marriage, the couple were so poor that Krishnamacharya wore a dhoti made of fabric torn from Namagiriamma's sari. Finally, despite his immense learning, he was forced to don the garb of a westerner – shorts and solar topee, and work at a coffee estate in Hassan. He did not want to subject his twelve-year-old wife to any difficulty so he took up the first employment that offered him a secure salary and a roof over their heads.

YOGA IN MYSORE

In 1931, Krishnamacharya was invited to teach at the Sanskrit College in Mysore. He could finally do what he really loved to do, and earn a livelihood too. The appointment at the Sanskrit College proved to be short-lived, as Krishnamacharya's volatile temper and his highly disciplined attitude did not go down too well with the students. However, a lecture on the Upanishads that Krishnamacharya delivered at the Mysore Town Hall attracted the attention of the Maharaja, who was quick to adopt and promote him.

Indian maharajas were a law unto themselves. The stories are legion. It was de rigueur for the Nizam of Hyderabad, who already had a crowded harem of forty-two wives, to marry a fresh wife on a Thursday and divorce her on Friday. The Maharaja of Patiala, offended by a salesman's high-handed treatment at a Rolls Royce showroom, bought every available car from the showroom, eviscerated each one of them and repurposed them as garbage trucks! The Maharaja of Mysore, who was then considered the second richest man in the world, used to buy Rolls Royces in multiples of seven, once even buying twenty-eight at one go. This went down in popular parlance as 'doing a Mysore'.

But the Maharaja's money was not frittered away only on personal indulgences; the royals of Mysore were long-time patrons of indigenous arts, actively supporting the revitalization of Indian culture. Their support and propagation of hatha yoga had already been on for more than a century. They were constantly looking for scholars and practitioners who would enhance the prestige of their court. In Krishnamacharya, the Mysore court had found a new jewel.

Maharaja Sri Sir Nalwadi Krishnaraja Wadiyar IV was a philosopher-king. Compared by scholars to the ideal ruler expressed in Plato's *Republic* and called 'Rajarishi' by Mahatma Gandhi, he was revered by his own subjects and the world. He was passionate about Mysore and wanted to make it the most glorious city in the country. To this end, he funded forward-thinking projects, making Mysore the first Asian state to have hydroelectricity and streetlights. He concentrated equally on economic development as he did on culture and the fine arts. When he saw a good thing, he lost no time in adopting it.

The Maharaja, who was diabetic, was very keen on re-establishing a connection between yoga and healing, which had been strongly discountenanced in the British Raj. Completely enamoured of Krishnamacharya and the wealth of wisdom he represented, the Maharaja offered him the use of the Mysore Palace's gymnastics hall as his own Yogashaala, or yoga school. Having benefitted greatly from yoga himself, he became one of Krishnamacharya's chief patrons and tried his best to propagate yoga whenever he could.

Krishnamacharya's wisdom and competence earned him the trust and friendship of the Maharaja, who began to depend on him for everything, from important matters of state, down to the buying of his horses.

The Yogashaala in the Mysore Palace was first established for the Maharaja and his family and was like a very exclusive club. At that time, outsiders would only be permitted at the special request of the Maharaja.

Though being employed by the Maharaja gave Krishnamacharya a sense of security, his detractors averred that it had other implications. The hitherto free-spirited and independent practitioner was now forced to compromise on some of his ideals. This came in part because of the impetus given by the Maharaja to change the traditional concept of yoga and to repackage it as a subject with popular appeal. India in the 1930s was still extremely enthused by western standards of beauty and body culture. It fell upon Krishnamacharya to create the same allure around yoga.

The lithe, stern-faced Krishnamacharya, with a Brahmin tuft of hair on an otherwise bald head was an unlikely icon of Indian physical perfection. This short Brahmin man with his long, lean muscles was going to be pitted against the shining stars of the body beautiful brigade in the West, the most famous of them being Eugen Sandow.

Sandow[5] was a bodybuilder and an international sex symbol with a huge Indian fan following. It was reported that 'he was capable of stirring up an erotic frenzy akin to the impact of the Beatles on their female audiences three quarters of a century later'. Given the sobriquet 'Sandow pahalwan', he was welcomed by royalty as well as the common Indian with equal fervour. It is reported that on his visit to Bombay in 1904, he gave a private audience to a group of Parsi women who were still in purdah. After he had taught them his form of exercise, the ladies were forward enough to want to feel his biceps from behind the beaded curtain.

---

5   Waller, David, *The Perfect Man: The Muscular Life and Times of Eugen Sandow, Victorian Strongman*, United Kingdom: Victorian Secrets Limited, 2011

By the time Sandow was ready to leave, he had captured the imagination of India with a ferocity that was unprecedented. Nationalist leaders took up the call for physical fitness as being the first step in asserting our independence. Though Sandow only visited India once, the subsequent frenzy that ensued lasted for decades. His system gained such popularity that he had a multitude of Indians signing up for his correspondence programme in fitness till the 1950s, almost half a century after his visit. Sandow was a powerful influencing factor, causing an upsurge of interest in physical culture, but similar enthusiasts were springing up across the world.

Henrik Ling, the Swedish Romantic poet, seemed an unlikely influence on physical culture in Mysore. This Renaissance man had taken it upon himself to resurrect the flagging physical culture of the Nordic citizenry, particularly after their resounding defeat in a war with Russia in 1809. He created a series of apparatus gymnastics, free standing exercises, standing and lunging movements, to create a holistic exercise regimen. In fact, his work with medical gymnastics and therapeutics is said to be the precursor to modern physiotherapy. The simplicity and economical nature of his regimen made it popular the world over, but nowhere was it taken up with such enthusiasm as in India.

Niels Bukh was a Danish gymnast who had created six sequences that were a progressive series of stretching and strengthening exercises (very similar to the jumping style Ashtanga sequences).

Bernarr Macfadden was a controversial figure in the world of health. From changing his name from Bernard to making it more closely resemble a lion's roar, to advocating sex for pleasure and not procreation, he created ripples in the world of health, which had always been associated with discipline and abstinence and not unrestrained pleasure seeking. Bernarr was a strong believer in the benefits of raw food and fasting, and was responsible for creating 'healthatoriums', which offered physical training programmes for the youth across the USA.

Bodybuilding and weight training were gaining more and more adherents the world over, and the 1930s were considered the golden years of bodybuilding. In India, too, gyms abounded and bodybuilding competitions increased in popularity. Most of them followed the systems created by Ling and Bukh, and they were invariably inspired by Macfadden and Sandow.

To an India that was trying to reach beyond itself and grasp at modernity and independence, the yoga class, in comparison, seemed like a vitiated village cousin and lacked colourful celebrity appeal. Yoga, with its association with asceticism and other-worldliness, seemed completely inappropriate for a resurgent nation that was reclaiming its destiny and its place in the world.

A stone's throw from Krishnamacharya's asana class was the K.V. Iyer Gymnasium[6]. The young and virile would flock there in quest of the perfect physique.

The primary aim of the Yogashaala of Mysore soon became to change the perception of yoga. Krishnamacharya had the daunting task of repackaging yoga for a new India. What had till now been considered an effete and antiquated system had now to be viewed as a vibrant, indigenous system, backed by the wisdom of ages, that was capable of ushering the youth into the modern era. The numerous demonstrations held at the Mysore University, many of which Sundara later took part in, were aimed at luring back a populace which had succumbed to the glamour of western systems. The demonstrations were often conducted with a view to providing entertainment and being spectacular enough to entice the audience back into what they may have, till then, considered a dying tradition.

6   Singleton, Mark, *Yoga Body: The Origins of Modern Posture Practice Mark*, United Kingdom: Oxford University Press, 2010

Accusations have been hurled at Krishnamacharya of popularizing his yoga by incorporating elements of bodybuilding and gymnastics, to make his yoga more appealing. Some of his erstwhile students later denigrated his system, comparing it to 'circus tricks'. For someone who had attained a great deal of proficiency in yogic philosophy and who had accumulated the highest degrees in Indian spiritual thought, the classes at the Yogashaala did not seem to reflect this depth. Some of Krishnamacharya's earliest students, Rangachar and T.R.S. Sharma, felt that the concentration was entirely on the physical aspect of angalaghava (lightness of body), with precious little attention given to the yogic aspects of dharana, dhyana and samadhi. This was an accusation that would later be levelled against Sundara as well.

4

SUNDARA AND HIS GURU

As a teacher Krishnamacharya was unpredictable, impetuous and had mercurial mood swings. He followed the old school in terms of discipline. His temper flared up often, and in unexpected ways. The young Sundara felt like he was treading on roasted papad. He was constantly on edge around the great man, afraid to spend any time in his presence in case he became the target of his bursts of ill temper.

Though Sundara started out enjoying school, it soon became drudgery, as none of his newly acquired friends were allowed to visit the home. He was not allowed to go anywhere after school either. Unable to bond with his schoolmates, he fell off the radar, and became lonely and friendless.

Though Krishnamacharya asked the young boy to practise yoga asanas, he did not provide him with the tools. Not being taught any asanas formally, Sundara tried to contort his unfit body into positions he had observed. His body was completely uncooperative. Months and years of illness had left him weak and inflexible; according to his own reports, he was unable to even touch his middle finger to his knees when he bent forward with his legs extended! Krishnamacharya lost interest in him quickly.

Sundara was not invited to the Yogashaala. For months after he shifted to Mysore, he did not even know where the Yogashaala was located. Understandably, he felt slighted and ignored.

It was a hard life for Sundara, much more arduous than the life that Krishnamacharya had experienced with his father. Sundara was woken up early to do household chores, draw water from the well, water the garden and wash the clothes. He would go off to school and then return home to finish more chores. If any of these things were not done to Krishnamacharya's exacting standards, then the much-feared blows would rain down on Sundara's back.

At night, when Sundara was ready to drop off to sleep, he would have to spend long hours massaging his guru's feet. If his nails ever scraped his guru's soft skin, he would feel a stinging blow. If his eyes, heavy with sleep, closed for an instant, he would feel a vicious wake-up call from his guru – a stinging slap across the face.

And then there was the persistent gnawing hunger that seemed to colour his world a dreary grey. Despite this, he sometimes could not get himself to eat the food that was served to him at his guru's home, as it was often smelly and rotten. When he refused to eat it or wanted to throw it away, he would invite the ire of Krishnamacharya. Sundara invented a new routine when he was served food that was inedible. He would slip into the bathroom and fling it outside the window, which opened out onto a barren space behind the home. It must have hurt to throw food away when pangs of hunger were tearing at his insides.

Sundara lived in the outhouse with the other students. When Krishnamacharya was not at home, Sundara's sister would sometimes summon Sundara into the kitchen and feed him leftovers. She was too afraid of her husband's wrath to do this openly. Consumed by hunger, he would, in the dead of night, tiptoe into the main house where his sister and Krishnamacharya lived. There, he would sneak into the kitchen and steal scraps of food. Desperation would sometimes drive him to steal money from his sister to buy himself food. His conscience would prick at having to steal from his sister. As he said later, 'A hungry man will commit any sin.'[7]

When Sundara's mother came to visit her son, Krishnamacharya, possibly irate at having yet another mouth to feed, temporarily threw both mother and son out of the house. What made the guru so irascible is a matter of conjecture. It is possible that he found Sundara's presence such a financial burden that he showed his disapproval of him in diverse ways. It was possible that he felt irritable with Sundara's stiff and weak body. It is possible that some particular trait in Sundara's character was rubbing his guru up the wrong way. On the other hand, it is not difficult to imagine that Sundara as a sensitive child was magnifying the slights that he was experiencing. But Sundara was not the only one being subjected to these continual assaults on his dignity and his person. One of his Brahmin students remembered Krishnamacharya's frequent beatings – 'After he hit you, you would have the impression of each of his five fingers on your face.'[8]

Jayalakshmi, Sundara's sister who stayed at the Mysore house for a while, also suffered Krishnamacharya's wrath.[9] In many Tamilian households, the preparation and drinking of their morning coffee is akin to a religious ritual. There are special filters, special coffee

---

7   Iyengar, B.K.S., *Iyengar, His Life and Work*, New Delhi: Timeless Books, 1988

8   Kadetsky, Elizabeth, *First There is a Mountain: A Yoga Romance*, United Kingdom: Little, Brown and Company, 2004

9   ibid

beans, special tumblers and just the perfect time and temperature for milk, decoction and sugar. All these have to be decanted from the little tumbler to the accompanying little vessel to get a nice head of froth on the coffee, whilst still ensuring the coffee remains steaming hot. Krishnamacharya spent a lot of time teaching Jayalakshmi how to brew coffee perfectly. It was one of those skills he felt would come very handy, as she was soon to be married. Jayalakshmi placed the freshly prepared cup of coffee for Krishnamacharya on the table, after decanting it from one container to the other to get the perfect amount of froth. As she placed it on the table, a drop of coffee insolently dripped off the rim and fell onto the table.

Krishnamacharya started off reasonably, but soon flew into an uncontrollable rage. 'You are getting married now. What will happen if you do this at your husband's house?' he ranted. He picked up the stainless-steel tumbler and flung it at the young girl. The edge of the tumbler cut her scalp and left a scar that was visible decades later. 'Guruji had a strong wrist,' Jayalakshmi said drily.

Early one morning, Krishnamacharya came up to Sundara and gave him a resounding slap. Sundara was as surprised as he was hurt.

'Why?' he asked his guru, as he blinked away the tears glinting in his eyes.

His voice quivering with anger, Krishnamacharya said, 'You are questioning me?' and slapped him again. [10]

'The question "why" we were not supposed to ask,' explained an old-time student of Krishnamacharya.

Unsure of what the next moment with his guru would bring, Sundara lived on tenterhooks. 'My Guru is a man of unpredictable knowledge with unpredictable moods. It was not easy to read his mind. If he said one thing at one time, he used to contradict the same

---

10   Kadetsky, Elizabeth, *First There is a Mountain: A Yoga Romance*, United Kingdom: Little, Brown and Company, 2004

at other time [sic]. We were made to accept and obey him without questioning. If I sit in the ordinary cross legs with the left leg first, he would say, take the right first. If the right is placed first, he would say, take the left first. If I stand, he would say, "Is that the way to stand?" If I changed, he would say, "Who asked you to change?"... Life became perplexing to me. Difference in age set fear in my heart and his presence was like a frightful nightmare.' Sundara writes in a compilation of memories on his seventieth birthday.[11]

When Sundara evinced interest in the *Yoga Sutras*, Krishnamacharya supposedly said, 'Do not utter those words with your impure mouth.' When Krishnamacharya taught yogic philosophy to the other students, he instructed Sundara to stand at the bottom of the garden. He used to often remind Sundara that he was a burden, eating and drinking what should have been rightfully reserved for Krishnamacharya's family.

One day, driven to desperation, Sundara walked 16 kilometres to the riverside. He had had enough. He had decided to end his life. The guru, whose intuitive powers were quite strong, sensed something was wrong. He borrowed the official car of the Maharaja and drove around the city trying to find his young brother-in-law. Just before the precious life was snuffed out, the guru drove up in the royal vehicle and prevented the worst from happening. He pushed him back into the car and drove him home. It would have reflected badly on him if this boy in his care had managed to drown himself in the river.

In 1934, Krishnamacharya brought an orphan boy, Keshavamurthy, into the house.[12] He performed a thread ceremony to initiate him into the fold of Brahmins and began

---

11   *70 Glorious Years of Yogacharya B.K.S. Iyengar*, Kirloskar Press, 1990
12   B.K.S. Iyengar and others, *Body the Shrine, Yoga thy Light*, India: Tata Press, 1978

to teach him yoga. The boy was immensely capable and could perform the asanas required of him with grace and strength, neither of which Sundara possessed. Instead of being jealous and petulant, Sundara embraced the young man into his life. He became Sundara's companion in misery and his first friend. Sundara felt the young orphan was destined for greatness. But Keshavamurthy, though the blue-eyed boy of Krishnamacharya, was not spared the chores that Sundara had been subjected to. The two adolescents would be dragged out of bed to water the garden even before the sun came up. The luxury of piped water was a convenience of the future. They had to physically haul up endless buckets of water to make sure that all the plants were watered. Often, the boys would be so sleepy that they would shut the front door, go out into the garden and take a nap, nestled under the canopy set out for the gourds. Krishnamacharya, the avid gardener, must have been surprised at how, with two boys now looking after it, his garden was still languishing.

His students were not the only ones who were terrified of Krishnamacharya. Tales of his temper were legendary, so the townsfolk would sensibly cross the road and walk on the opposite footpath when they saw Krishnamacharya walking towards them.

In May 1935, when Sundara visited Bangalore for his father's death anniversary, it felt like a reprieve. He exulted in the feeling of freedom, being away from the oppressive atmosphere of his sister's home. He borrowed a bicycle from a lawyer who was his brother Raja Iyengar's tenant. Driving at breakneck speed, as was his wont, he had an accident. Though he was not injured, the bike was wrecked and would need the staggering sum of four rupees and eight annas for its repair – a fortune for a struggling student with no means of livelihood. Thankfully, his favourite sister, Seetamma, came to his rescue and provided the bulk of it and he did household chores to earn the rest.

When he returned, Keshavamurthy had left. The orphan boy, who had arrived in a blaze of glory and light, disappeared suddenly and secretly, like a mist that had been subjected to an intense burst of sunshine. The heat of Krishnamacharya's expectations had proved too intense for Keshavamurthy to handle. [13]

Krishnamacharya had a yoga performance scheduled at the Mysore Palace in September 1935 and his prize student had escaped. His attention fell on the young Sundara. Krishnamacharya performed the thread ceremony for Sundara and began to teach him the Gayatri Mantra. Sundara was not half as flexible as Keshavamurthy and he was not half as amenable, but he would have to do. And so, reluctantly, Krishnamacharya adopted Sundara as his disciple.

In three months, Sundara was transformed from being the awkward, weak, inflexible boy to the star student. Sundara had to work hard to overcome his stiffness and the repercussions of a lifetime of ill health. It was years before Sundara began to enjoy his practise. The first few years were too arduous, painful and mechanical for his heart to be in it.

For the performance at the palace, Sundara received appreciation from the then Maharaja of Mysore and ₹ 50, which constituted his first earnings. At the time this was the equivalent of a government employee's average salary for a month. It must have been a strong incentive to continue.

Krishnamacharya asked Sundara to put the money away in a post office account, where it would be locked away for a number of years. Sundara put it into a bank instead. Now, when he was particularly hungry, he could buy himself food.

---

13   B.K.S. Iyengar and others, *Body the Shrine, Yoga thy Light*, India: Tata Press, 1978

Sundara's elevation to disciple status added new duties to his already full day. Not only did he still have to wake up at 4.30 to water the plants, he then had to study till 7 a.m. At 7.30 a.m., some of Krishnamacharya's students would come to the guru's home to master some difficult asanas, which Sundara had to teach them. At 8.30 a.m., he had just enough time for his bath, after which he went to the Yogashaala to learn and assist.

In what seems like irrational cruelty to Sundara, he was not allowed to go directly from school to the Yogashaala, which was barely ten minutes away. On the unreasonable insistence of his guru, Sundara was forced to walk home 5 kilometres, deposit his school books and loop back to the Yogashaala.[14] None of Krishnamacharya's pupils dared question even the most unreasonable order from their guru.

Small wonder then that Sundara's relationship with his guru was conflicted. He seemed to be continuously struggling with the dichotomy of the step-fatherly treatment meted out by Krishnamacharya to him and the traditional non-judgmental worshipfulness one is expected to feel for the guru.

In Sundara's reminiscences about his early life he says, 'My brother-in-law, though a very kind-hearted man, was hot-tempered.' Sundara, in the later accounts of his life, does not recount a single instance of the guru's kind-heartedness. Maybe the recollections of Krishnamacharya's kind-heartedness were erased by the more painful memories.

In 1935, V.V. Srinivas Iyengar, the legal luminary from Madras, was invited to the Yogashaala.[15] Krishnamacharya called upon each of his students to perform some asanas. Knowing that the other students could not perform Hanumanasana, the guru called

---

14   B.K.S. Iyengar and others, *Body the Shrine, Yoga thy Light*, India: Tata Press, 1978

15   *70 Glorious Years of Yogacharya B.K.S. Iyengar*, Kirloskar Press, 1990

Sundara to demonstrate this asana. Sundara tried to escape his fate
by claiming he did not know the asana. 'Stretch one leg in front of
you, one behind you and sit erect', was the guru's instruction. The
sound of the guru's voice and the look on his face brooked no excuse.
Feeling his heartbeat race and his pulse quicken, Sundara quietly
told his guru that his 'Hanuman chaddi', the tight-fitted shorts
he was wearing, would not allow him to stretch.[16] These 'chaddis'
were generally stitched so tight that they did not allow a finger to
slip in between the thigh and the fabric. The tightness of the fabric
would often leave permanent discolorations on the thighs. Sundara
hoped this excuse would save the day for him. Enraged at being
thwarted, Krishnamacharya ordered C.M. Bhat, one of his pupils,
to bring him a pair of scissors. Then Krishnamacharya proceeded
to snip the offending pair of shorts on either side, enough to enable
movement, leaving Sundara with no excuse. Sundara forced himself
into the complete pose. As he did so, he felt the tell-tale rip in his
hamstrings and a bright orange flame searing down his thigh. It
would take years to heal. As would his spirit, abraded by his master's
callousness.

Sundara's rigorous schedule left him sleep-deprived and
disinterested in his studies. He could barely find the energy to
get through the day. The Secondary School Leaving Certificate
Examination loomed large on the horizon. With so little time to
devote to his academic pursuits, he was very unsure of his ability to
get through the big exam. But he couldn't give up without trying.
He scrounged around again and with great difficulty managed to
raise the money required for exam fees. Summoning every ounce
of courage he could muster, he appeared for the big school final
in May. He had one month of vacation till the results came out in

16 *Astadala Yogamala Vol.1: The Collected Works of B.K.S. Iyengar*, New
    Delhi: Allied Publishers, 2000

June, but even when he was pleasantly occupied, the nagging storm cloud of failure loomed over his head.

When the results were declared he found, to his disappointment, that he had failed in English by a mere three marks. He had passed in every other subject. The way the system was designed, failing in English left him ineligible to join any college.

It seems unfair that this young man, hailing from a little village in Karnataka, with little exposure to English, and with teachers who could barely speak the language themselves, was denied further education and the prospects of a job because of a shortfall of three marks in a foreign tongue.

As if to compensate for his failure in the school-leaving exam, he appeared for the Yogashaala Certificate exam, in which he managed to get 98 per cent in all the disciplines. It seemed like destiny's finger was tracing out the future course of the young boy's life.

In December 1935, the World YMCA conference was going to be held in Mysore.[17] Now that Keshavamurthy had deserted him so unceremoniously, Krishnamacharya had to concentrate on Sundara to make him the shining attraction. A week before the demonstration, Sundara was summoned by his teacher. He was tutored for three days in the most difficult poses that no one else could master. His body exploded with pain, every muscle hurt, but he persisted. Then without further supervision or aid, he was expected to perfect the asanas till they were show worthy. This was the first time his guru had trusted him with something this huge. He could not disappoint him. He could not disappoint himself. And he did not.

The yoga demonstration was a huge success, earning Sundara another fifty rupees and accolades from the audience. More

---

17   *B.K.S. Iyengar and others, Body the Shrine, Yoga thy Light*, India: Tata Press, 1978

importantly, his guru congratulated him, telling him he never
thought Sundara would be capable of such a performance, especially
after just three days of instruction. The effort involved in getting
his body to relent to these complicated asanas left him racked with
pain and his muscles sore for months after. On the other hand, he
was developing another muscle that would stand him in good stead
in the years to come – an indomitable will.

According to Krishnamacharya's thinking, students should be
ready for a performance anytime, anywhere, without question. If
they refused they were punished: no water, no food, no sleep, till
the perfect asana was presented, with the additional privilege of
massaging the guru's legs till he asked them to stop. In case their
fingers tired or they were sleepy and they slowed down, they would
be rewarded with slaps that left burn marks across their cheeks.

Sundara developed a renewed interest in asana. Though he had
performed well in the yoga exams, he was personally dissatisfied
with his performance of some of the asanas. Anyway, his academic
career had ground to a standstill. It was then, when all other options
seemed to have closed before him, that he began applying himself
to perfecting his asana practise.

The Mysore Palace was continuously hosting dignitaries from
all over the world. That same year, Swami Yogananda had come
to Mysore as a guest of the Maharaja. The Swami went on to write
Autobiography of a Yogi, acclaimed on many book lists across the
world as being amongst the 100 most important spiritual books of
the twentieth century and also called 'the book that has changed
a million lives'. When Swami Yogananda came to Mysore, it was
part of his yearlong tour of India. He had already lived in the USA
for fifteen years and established the International Center for Self-
Realization Fellowship in Los Angeles, California.

At the Mysore Yogashaala, Yogananda was so impressed with the
techniques of Krishnamacharya that he praised him lavishly and

openly. Then spotting the flexible young boy who had now gained the position of star student, Yogananda asked Krishnamacharya if he could take the boy back to America with him. [18]

In an instant, a thought bubble transported Sundara to America. He saw himself going to school, living a comfortable life in a comfortable home, away from the daily oppressions and continuous hunger that Mysore represented.

But love suddenly sprouted in Krishnamacharya's heart. 'No,' he protested, 'this is my young brother-in-law. We are responsible for him. I can't let him go so far away.' Maybe, with Keshavamurthy gone, Krishnamacharya felt like he was now dependent on his ugly duckling-turned-swan brother-in-law. For whatever reason, Krishnamacharya refused, adding that Sundara could possibly accompany the swami when he returned on his next visit to India. However, that was never to be.

Sundara was not, as his father had predicted, destined for the instant fame that would have come from being Yogananda's protégé. He had years of struggle before him.

In the meanwhile, the fact that his guru was not teaching him all he knew was worrying Sundara. He recounts a time when two French doctors, Dr Therese Brosse and Dr Charles Laubry, came to Mysore. Being heart specialists and yoga aficionados, they stayed in Mysore for almost three weeks, observing the practice both of Krishnamacharya and Sundara, and other students. They used an array of modern equipment to measure the effects of different types of pranayama. [19]

---

18   B.K.S. Iyengar and others, *Body the Shrine, Yoga thy Light*, India: Tata Press, 1978

19   Kadetsky, Elizabeth, *First There is a Mountain: A Yoga Romance*, United Kingdom: Little, Brown and Company, 2004

On the last day, they hooked Krishnamacharya up to a cardiogram machine to measure his heartbeats and pulse. Everything was progressing normally till, suddenly and dramatically, the oscillations on the machine stopped. The consistent rhythmic beat faded away. All the flashing lights went out. There was no activity on the machine for a while. In panic, the doctors declared that Krishnamacharya's heart had stopped beating. In a few minutes however, the machine resumed its regular, rhythmic beat, with no indication of the drama that had just occurred.

Krishnamacharya had just demonstrated, in a manner that the West could not contradict, the fact that he could stop his heartbeat at will. The young Sundara, a witness to this spectacle, was amazed at the control his guru had over his involuntary organs. To him, it was also irrefutable evidence that his guru was not sharing his most spectacular learning with his pupils.

Though the times in Mysore were the most painful memories of his youth, they were also the times that helped shape his character. His invincible will, his ability to keep believing in himself though the situation seemed endlessly bleak and grey, his capacity to rebuild a body that had been battered with disease and malnourishment, his ability to learn, experiment and discover; all these were the positive attributes that helped mould him into the person he was going to be.

In modern yogic circles, the Krishnamacharya legacy is like an ancient river; it runs deep and wide and has scores of distributaries. In some ways he is the 'dada guru' (grandfather guru) of a large percentage of yoga practitioners the world over. Besides Bellur Krishnamachar Sundararaja Iyengar, there were several other prominent students who have shaped the world of yoga as we know it today.

Indra Devi, considered the mother of western yoga, was the progeny of a Swedish banker and a Russian actress. Born in Latvia,

Indra Devi's birth name was Zhenia Labunskaia. She came to India financed by her banker fiancé in what was meant to be her last bachelorette trip and lost her heart to the country. Returning her fiancé's ring, she returned to India to came back Krishnamacharya's first female student.[20]

Pattabhi Jois became Krishnamacharya's student at the age of twelve after attending one of his lectures in Hassan. Three years later he ran away from home to Mysore and became one of Krishnamacharya's most devoted followers.

Desikachar, Krishnamacharya's son, came to yoga through a longer and more circuitous route than the rest, with the first part of his life steeped in the world of civil engineering.

Krishnamacharya was the source from which many streams of yoga originated.

'You may have never heard of him, but Tirumalai Krishnamacharya influenced or perhaps even invented your yoga. Whether you practise the dynamic series of Pattabhi Jois, the refined alignments of B.K.S. Iyengar, the classical postures of Indra Devi, or the customized vinyasa [of Desikachar], your practise stems from one source: a five-foot, two-inch Brahmin born more than one hundred years ago in a small south Indian village,' said Fernando Pages Ruiz in the *Yoga Journal* of May 2001.

In 1936, the Maharaja requested Krishnamacharya and his team to embark on a tour of northern Karnataka. Being the youngest of the retinue, Sundara was forced to serve the elders in the group, which, for him, meant everyone. He would have to wake up early to draw water for their baths. The water table being low in central Karnataka, he would have to draw the water from a depth of 50-60 feet for each bucket and since he had to draw dozens

---

20 http://www.yogajournal.com/article/philosophy/krishnamacharya-s-
    legacy/

of buckets of water, this left the skin on his palms chafed and
peeling. He went to the older students and informed them that
he would not be able to draw water for anyone but his guru. The
rest would have to handle their own requirements, he told them.
This caused a buzz of hostility and the complaints about Sundara's
defiance of Krishnamacharya's orders reached the guru's ears. The
guru summoned him and said that Sundara was the one who had
been designated to fetch the water for everyone and he should
continue to do it. Sundara showed his guru his calloused hands.
He told him that he was not willing to perform menial tasks for
the entourage anymore. Even the iciness of his guru's disapproval
and silent treatment that he meted out for the next few days did
not make Sundara reconsider. But somehow this protest helped
him reclaim his dignity. Though Krishnamacharya taunted him,
calling him 'Commissioner', implying he was getting too big for
his boots, he did allow Sundara to demonstrate in public with the
other students.[21] Sundara had won this round.

Touring the towns of Harihar, Dharwar and Hubli with his guru
was Sundara's first exposure to a larger world. On this trip, the boy
who had failed his school-leaving exam found himself hobnobbing
with professors, students, doctors and their families. The yoga
classes generated a strong interest among this academic community.

In the 1930s, Indian women were still finding their feet in
society. The purdah system was being shed all over the country.
Inspired by Mahatma Gandhi, more women emerged into the
social sphere and took active part in the political process. There
was still, however, a restriction on women's activities, one of the
repercussions of patriarchy that would take decades to shed. This
turned out to be a factor that worked to the benefit of young
Sundara.

---

21   *70 Glorious Years of Yogacharya B.K.S. Iyengar*, Kirloskar Press, 1990

The women of Dharwar, largely the family members of the doctors and professors whom Krishnamacharya had been teaching, demanded a separate class, devoted exclusively to them. Though keen to learn yoga, they were not happy to be part of a class that included men. And seventeen-year-old Sundara, still underdeveloped and not quite as threatening a specimen of full-blown masculinity as the rest, was adjudged to be the most innocuous teacher for this group of young, adolescent women. When Sundara protested that he didn't know the first thing about teaching, Krishnamacharya said, 'Do whatever you can, but go teach.' Not sure if he should interpret this as a blessing or an order, Sundara began his first teaching assignment. Instructing this bunch of effervescent adolescent women, who considered him so safe that they discussed their intimate personal issues in his presence, Sundara cut his yogic teeth.

This marked the modest beginning of what was to be one of the most meteoric careers in yoga.

When it was time for Krishnamacharya's team to depart, the professors of Dharwar College wanted someone to stay behind and continue with the yoga classes. Krishnamacharya recommended a student called Panduranga Bhatt. The professors declined. Sundara had already made his mark on the intelligentsia. They insisted they would have Sundara and no one else. Even Krishnamacharya's protests about his student being too young to teach were summarily rejected.

Sundara stayed in Dharwar for a month and a half, teaching, sharing and learning. At the end of the stipulated period, the professors and their families plied him with gifts – clothes, silver tumblers, a train ticket to Mysore and a shawl for his teacher, Krishnamacharya. Enriched and fulfilled by the experience, Sundara returned to Mysore, his misgivings about the future slightly allayed.

THE ROAD ONCE TRAVELLED

After the positive experience in Dharwar, in February 1937 Sundara was chosen to do a tour of several places in Mysore state. He embarked on it enthusiastically but soon realized that yoga was not yet a viable source of income. He found that he often had to spend his own money travelling to these places, with scant hope of recompense.

His next assignment was to treat a Mr Narasingarao of Koratagere, Karnataka, who was suffering from hydrocele. Hydrocele is one of those uncomfortable diseases, which causes the testicles to swell up with water. Narasingarao unfortunately turned out to be one of those opportunistic people who, once cured, did not think it fit to compensate his teacher. Impoverished and dejected, Sundara returned to Mysore.

When Krishnamacharya and his team had earlier performed in Belgaum, they had attracted the attention of Dr V.B. Gokhale, the civil surgeon there. Dr Gokhale was quite a luminary in the world of medicine and had been instrumental in providing care to Gandhiji when the great leader suddenly took ill in jail with appendicitis.

The doctor was very impressed by the proficiency and flexibility of Krishnamacharya's team. This was multiplied manifold when Krishnamacharya demonstrated to Dr Gokhale his impressive trick of voluntarily stopping his pulse and heartbeat.

The yoga he had witnessed stayed with the doctor, so when three months later he retired from his post as civil surgeon of Belgaum and shifted to Pune, he wrote to Krishnamacharya inviting him to send one of the members of his team to train the students in Pune's colleges.

Though Sundara had failed in the school-leaving examination, he was the chosen one – the only one who could speak enough English to venture into this unfamiliar place. In Pune, Sundara would no longer have the ease of slipping into Kannada. He would have to depend on his sketchy and sparse English, which he had never used outside the portals of his government school. And even that had been two years ago!

For Sundara, Pune was to be an assignment that lasted six months, earning him the sum of sixty rupees per month. Sundara had just withdrawn his lifetime's savings from the bank for his trip. It amounted to all of twenty-eight rupees.

At the time, Krishnamacharya was travelling to Bezwada (now called Vijayawada, in Andhra Pradesh) on the instruction of the Maharaja. He invited one of his students to travel with him on the condition that the student would pay his own fare.

Sundara's fellow student, very keen on accompanying Krishnamacharya to Bezwada, asked Sundara for a loan of fifteen rupees. Sundara, displaying the generosity that was to later become his hallmark, immediately gave him more than half of all he possessed, leaving himself with thirteen rupees to travel the 902 kilometres from Mysore to Pune and to begin his new life there.[22]

---

22 Iyengar, B.K.S., *Iyengar, His Life and Work*, New Delhi: Timeless Books, 1988

He left Mysore in July 1937. He was to start class in Pune only in August. In an effort to raise some more money, he decided to break his journey at Hubli. Having had such positive experiences in Dharwar the previous year, he hoped that Hubli, her sister city, would be as kind to him.

He had one solitary connection in the city, a Mr Ramaswamy, who had been a student of the Yogashaala in Mysore. Sundara wrote to Mr Ramaswamy, informing him that he would stay in Hubli for a month. Ramaswamy went out of his way to arrange for the young man to stay at a friend's home. Sundara taught his hosts and five or six of their friends and this helped him cover his expenses. His new students had also kindly agreed to pay his train fare to Pune.

Hoping to replicate his success in Dharwar the previous year, he decided to try his luck there again. At six every morning, he would walk three miles to take the train to Dharwar. Each time he made the trip, he spent two annas (twelve paise) of his precious savings. The previous year, with the backing of Krishnamacharya and the Maharaja, he had taught a class of thirty people. This time, he could barely round up one solitary pupil. And this pupil did not pay him in money, but bought him lunch. After lunch, he would walk back the 24 kilometres to Hubli. This would take about five hours of non-stop walking. Reaching Hubli at 4 p.m., he would teach yoga to his host family and their friends. By the end of the day, he would have walked almost 30 kilometres. And he did this for six weeks without a break! He also did two lecture demonstrations, one each in Hubli and Dharwar. For all his efforts he earned a railway ticket to Pune and five rupees for his expenses there.

His pupils were from middle-class families, with very little money to spare, but they wished him well. He left for Pune on 29 August 1937. Mr Ramaswamy and his students, who had become quite fond of him, were there to say goodbye.

By the time he reached Pune a day later, his cache had already been whittled down to four rupees and fifty paise.

ANOTHER CITY, ANOTHER LIFE

30 August 1937
Poona, Maharashtra

The train choked and coughed into the station. The sky was like a giant vat of cement slurry being stirred around by an unseen hand. The southwest monsoon exhaled a fine mist into the air. Persistent and steady rain punctuated by slivers of intermittent sunshine made the shops and carts glow with a strange luminescence.

Iyengar waited and watched as the passengers oozed out of the narrow compartment doors onto the platform. As they argued in strange accents with porters uniformed in red, Iyengar allowed himself to inhale the first breath of freedom in a new city. It was a heady amalgam of urine and wood fires. Despite the bleakness of the weather, he felt an explosive fizz of happiness in his heart. The light that filled the compartment seemed exceptional, soft and buttery yellow like a champa flower. The rain, to everyone else an inconvenience, filled him with the promise of new beginnings.

He stood up and shook the weariness out of his limbs from having spent many hours cramped between strangers. His thighs held the imprint of the unforgiving wooden slats that masqueraded as seats in the third-class compartment.

A short, bright-eyed porter came up to him and sized him up. He shot off some quick words in Marathi and gauged from the befuddled look in Iyengar's eyes that this was a fortuitous find – a stranger to the land of the Marathas.

Using sign language and an outrageous fee of four annas (twenty-five paise), Iyengar hired the porter to take him to Deccan

Gymkhana, the centre of Pune. Once he was there, he looked for the cheapest accommodation he could find, one rupee twelve annas for boarding and lodging at Café Unique.[23]

The next day he met Dr Gokhale, who introduced him to the Deccan Gymkhana Club – from where they hoped that many of Iyengar's prospective students would come.

The Deccan Gymkhana, like all gymkhanas of the day, was a snooty place with a prodigious reputation for sports. It was established in 1916 by the freedom fighter Bal Gangadhar Tilak who, with a disciplined regimen of sports and exercise, turned his health around so he could serve his nation better. His belief in the power of a solid physical culture for the youth was part of his dream of independent India. The club started as a cricket club and then diversified into other sports as well. It was a member of the Deccan Gymkhana who had first proposed the idea of having an Indian Olympic team. The selections of the athletics and wrestling teams for the 1920 Antwerp Olympics had been held at the Deccan Gymkhana. Besides outdoor sports, they had facilities for bridge and billiards. Understandably, they had a reputation they were proud of and the only reason Iyengar was entertained was because he was in the exalted company of Dr Gokhale.

Having paid the daily rate at Café Unique for two days, Iyengar was down to his last twelve annas. The connection with Dr Gokhale was beneficial for him in many ways. To start with, it helped him buy some time from the owner of Café Unique to whom he owed forty rupees as advance payment for a stay of a month. Not able to ask for any more favours from Dr Gokhale, he steeled himself to survive on twelve annas for the rest of the month. His worldly possessions at the time consisted of two shirts,

---

23   Iyengar, B.K.S., *Iyengar, His Life and Work*, New Delhi: Timeless Books, 1988

two dhotis and a roll of bedding. One of the dhotis doubled up as his towel. He could not afford a bar of soap. To keep up the appearance of respectability, he had to shave every day and so he invested one paisa in a razor blade and perfected the art of using it without a razor or soap. Now, even the economical Café Unique seemed too expensive. He had to shift to cheaper accommodation in the second month.

Iyengar was an anomaly in the Maharashtrian city. He stood out because of his strong Dravidian features, his South-Indian style *veshti* (dhoti) and his *kudumi*, the long lock of hair that signifies the Brahmin's one-pointed focus on God. The front of his head was clean-shaven, with the kudumi like a long ponytail hanging behind him. This ponytail, which the Maharashtrians disparagingly called a *shendi*, was the object of much mirth, particularly amongst the youngsters of Pune. Iyengar took to covering his head with a cap to prevent people from taunting him. To add to this ignominy, people would call him a lunatic when he told them that he was a yoga practitioner. But all these were minor difficulties when weighed against the prospect of returning to Mysore and the claustrophobic life he had been leading there. Pune allowed him a chance at a new kind of life.

When he first came to Pune, he was often asked whether a couple would conceive if they did yoga. Barely eighteen and, by his own admission, a complete innocent in matters pertaining to sex, he would confidently say, 'Yes. Yoga will help if you practise regularly for three years.'

From 1937-40 he stayed at a hotel at Raasta Peth close to the racecourse; it was populated by regular race-goers. The race-goers in the hotel, wanting to cash in on his power of intuition, routinely asked him for a number between eight and fourteen. Iyengar had no idea why they did this and he was far too absorbed in earning his livelihood to pay much attention to the strange quirks of city folk. He had no idea that they were betting on the horse with the number that he chose that day. Seemingly he had a high enough success rate to keep them coming back.

Soon he started getting even more suspicious calls from people who wanted him to choose any two numbers between 1 and 100. The race-goers had apparently publicized his prowess with picking the winning horse and now he had people who were speculating on the opening and closing prices of American Cotton stock calling him every day. As soon as Iyengar realized that he had been used as a pawn to make some quick bucks, he stopped obliging these people. He would find many more productive uses for his intuition in his teaching.

Dr Gokhale had made an arrangement with six colleges and the Deccan Gymkhana, that each of these institutions could, on the payment of eight rupees fifty paise a month, send ten selected students for lessons with Iyengar, which would earn him sixty rupees a month. The classes were held at the Deccan Gymkhana Club and there were ten students in all. Not one of those who enrolled was from the Deccan Gymkhana Club. After six months, the colleges, feeling that there was not enough interest among the students, rescinded the contract with Iyengar. Though his students wanted to continue, Iyengar was faced with the prospect of shutting down his fledgling class.

Thankfully, some friends of Dr Gokhale chipped in to help fund the class for another six months.

Dr Gokhale also arranged for lecture demonstrations in the Club. With their antagonistic attitude towards yoga and towards Iyengar, the demonstrations were squeezed into the last ten minutes of the lecture. Dr Gokhale was clear about the distribution of labour. 'The body is known to me,' Dr Gokhale said to Iyengar. 'You leave it to me. I will explain very accurately. You just do the poses.'[24] The doctor's profound knowledge of anatomy and physiology added much interest to the demonstrations, but more importantly, it provided Iyengar his first acquaintance with a precise scientific understanding of the systems of the body. The reputation for anatomical precision that Iyengar later acquired was probably sparked off by his early association with Dr Gokhale.

After one of his demonstrations, Dr Gokhale asked him why despite his great prowess with the asanas, his body was so under-developed and lacking in muscle. Iyengar told him about the diverse illnesses that had plagued him and the extreme privations of his childhood. Dr Gokhale remarked that in all his life as a surgeon, he had not seen anything as remarkable as Iyengar's performances.

All Iyengar's students were taller, better built, better educated and more articulate than he was. He was still struggling to master both Marathi and English. He taught himself English by preserving shredded newspaper pieces in which bhel-puri was served and reading these in his spare time. But about his physique, there was not much he could do.

Iyengar was so skinny in comparison to even the average man that he became the butt of ridicule. This was an India that was obsessed with the ideal of the 'body beautiful'. Why would they want to pay to do yoga if this is what they would end up looking like?

Despite his emaciated appearance, in strength, flexibility and endurance, Iyengar was infinitely superior to any of his well-fed pupils. They would often see him practise for ten hours without a break, and they began to look beyond the thinness and the broken English to the passion that was driving him. In their hearts they felt a stirring of admiration.

---

24   http://www.kofibusia.com/iyengarbiography/iyengarbio16.php

The Deccan Gymkhana often held wrestling matches that were widely attended. Pune was bubbling over with excitement about an upcoming match between Imam Baksh, brother of the famous Gama, and a hefty Punjabi wrestler called Puran Singh. Imam Baksh had, a decade ago, already fought and defeated world legends like the Swiss wrestler John Lemm. After that historical win, the press fawningly declared that Lemm looked 'quite commonplace' in comparison with Baksh, who was 'really like a great cat, wonderfully nimble and lissome, able to turn and twist with lightning-like dexterity,' writes Graham Noble in his book, *The Lion of Punjab.*

The year was 1937. The Deccan Gymkhana wrestling arena seethed with people waiting with great expectations for the big fight. There were hordes more waiting at the ticket stands to buy a ticket to enter. Excitement sparked through the air as the tall, loose-limbed Imam Baksh wrestled Puran Singh to the ground in a few deft manoeuvres. The umpire counted to ten and declared the fight over. Imam Baksh was the winner. The audience felt cheated. The match had hardly lasted minutes and was over before many of them had even entered the wrestling area. In the manner of displeased crowds in India, they vented their aggression by vandalizing the Gymkhana. The police found it impossible to control the mob.

Some members of the Deccan Gymkhana called Iyengar and asked him to do a demonstration of his yoga asanas.[25]

---

25   Iyengar, B.K.S., *Astadala Yogamala: Collected works Volume 1*, New Delhi: Allied Publishers, 2000

It was like walking into a live minefield. No one had any idea how his demonstration would be received. Would the crowds laugh and jeer at this scrawny lad with his bald head and Brahmin ponytail who was daring to replace their heroes? Would the crowds, unhappy at being denied a glimpse of the heroes they had come to watch, throw their footwear at him? Or would they, inspired by his appearance, choose a more violent option?

Iyengar, however, didn't seem to sense the danger in the situation. Instead, all he smelt was the alluring aroma of opportunity. He could see a potential audience, the largest he had ever had. He could see the most famous wrestlers of India, Gama and Imam Baksh, amongst them. This, he felt, was a great time to display his prowess. Brimming with confidence, not a thought of possible failure in his head, he approached the wrestling ring.

One can imagine the collective titter of amusement that rippled through the crowd when this frail young man came on in his skimpy Hanuman chaddis. It looked distinctly like three of him would fit into one wrestler's clothes. Iyengar went on to do a breath-taking forty-minute demonstration of his most advanced asanas. By the end of it, the audience was eating out of his hand.

As a result of this spectacle, Iyengar became extremely friendly with the wrestlers who lived next door to him in a cheap room provided by the Gymkhana to its employees. He puzzled over the fact that every time they entered or left their rooms they would knock on his door and ask Iyengar, who was much shorter than they were, to lock or unlock the latches on the top of their doors for them. Iyengar, polite as always, obliged, but could not help wondering at the strangeness of this request. When he got to know them better, he understood that their exercise routine left their shoulders so muscle-bound that it was impossible for them to raise their arms above their heads.

These were the same wrestlers who in England in 1910 had issued a challenge to anyone in the world to come forth and fight them.

'NO ONE BARRED!!
ALL CHAMPIONS CORDIALLY INVITED!!
THE BIGGER THE BETTER!!'

For four months no one dared take up the challenge. After four months, Doc Roller, a full foot taller than Gama, rose to the challenge. In the first round, Gama had brought Roller down in one minute and forty seconds. And this powerful wrestler could not open the door for himself!

Iyengar, who had been working on his flexibility for many years now, was aghast that their exercise regimen had actually left them incapable, rather than more capable. He later found out, when he got to know them much better, that they had difficulty sitting on the Indian-style squatting toilets. This made it impossible for them to evacuate their bowels completely, and was the cause of many other attendant ills. Iyengar's encounter with the wrestlers left Iyengar more convinced than ever of the importance of a holistic regimen like yoga.

Loneliness also led him to befriend characters whom he may not ordinarily have chosen. Some of the people he met at the Gymkhana were regular drinkers, and would spend many of their evenings going out into the town. These people invited him along on their riotous evenings. Though he did not drink, his longing for companionship in this city of strangers made him accompany them on their escapades. After the boys had had a reasonable amount to drink, they would inexplicably disappear into the by-lanes nearby, asking him to wait till they returned. Within half an hour, they would generally be back, always much more genial and cheerful than when they left.

On one of these days, as he stood waiting for his friends to return, another of his acquaintances spotted him. The man stopped and asked what he was doing there. Iyengar told him he was waiting for his friends to return. The man told the young Iyengar that this was not a savoury place for a decent young man like him to be hanging around and advised him to go home immediately. It was only when he was slightly older that the innocent Iyengar found out that he had been standing under the street lamps of Pune's infamous red light district. Finally, he understood the reason for his friends' exuberance when they returned from their excursions into those by-lanes.

HIS FIRST STUDENTS

Cricket, like wrestling, was another national obsession. Indians followed cricket with an urgency that seemed as if their lives depended on the outcome of these matches. In 1938, Professor Dinkar Deodhar, the captain of the Maharashtra Team, developed a knee injury for which doctors advised surgery. As luck would have it, he approached Dr Gokhale, who recommended Iyengar instead of surgery. If Iyengar failed, they could always fall back on surgery, said Dr Gokhale. To start with, Deodhar could not even stand for any length of time. After many setbacks and much experimentation, Deodhar first began to flex his knees without pain and then, to his own great surprise, was able to play cricket again. With Deodhar's astounding return to cricket came Iyengar's belief in his own ability to be able to look beyond the skin, deep into the workings of the human body. With continuous investigation and experiments on himself, he was able to better understand the mechanics of the human body and help people with innovative solutions that were the result of his own personal journey.

Iyengar began experimenting with props in 1938 when Professor Rajawade, the ex-principal of Fergusson College, came to him at the age of eighty-five. His body was so enfeebled from dysentery that he could barely stand. That was when Iyengar began to experiment with the traditional positions to help him get the benefit of the asanas without the exertion. He made the elderly gentleman do many of the standing poses in a supine position and used supports like chairs, wooden blocks and rods to rejuvenate his abdominal organs and the inflamed peritoneum.

Continuing his role as Iyengar's benefactor, Dr Gokhale arranged more lecture demonstrations in schools and colleges. The colleges, now realizing how Iyengar yoga was benefitting the students, made the monetary contributions necessary to enable the classes to run for another year.

As his students were becoming more serious about their yoga practise, Iyengar felt it was time for his guru, Krishnamacharya, to pay a visit to Pune.

During this visit in 1938, Krishnamacharya was invited to speak and demonstrate at Agnihotri Rajwade's home. At this demonstration, Krishnamacharya asked Iyengar to demonstrate Kandasana. When Iyengar feigned ignorance, Krishnamacharya told him in clipped tones, 'Bring both feet towards the chest like doing namaskar with the feet.' Being away from Krishnamacharya for a few months emboldened Iyengar. He told his guru he could not do it. All hell broke loose. In full view of the audience, Krishnamacharya lost his temper and began chiding him in Tamil. Even those in the audience who could not understand the language could understand the import of what was being said. Embarrassed, Iyengar had to give in once again to the ferociousness of his guru's personality. He did the extremely challenging asana as best he could.

Though Iyengar's early experiences with his guru were hardly conducive to faith, after he came to Pune some strange dreams and occurrences had strengthened his belief in his guru.

The first was a dream in which he had gone to visit the Ananta Padmanabha Swami Temple in Trivandrum. At the temple, the idol could be approached through three doors. The first door led to the head, the next to the torso and the last to the feet. After looking through the first two doors Iyengar went to the third door, and since it was his last chance, tried to have a peek at the entire idol.

As he shut his eyes to pray, flames emanated from the forehead of the idol towards him. They seemed to be intent on devouring him. He prayed to the Lord for forgiveness, but the flames did not abate. Then he turned towards his guru and asked for his forgiveness and blessings. As soon as he did this, the flames died down and disappeared.

Some of his students had taken Iyengar to a temple in Shivaji Nagar, where a spiritual adept called Phadke Maharaj resided. Phadke Maharaj told him that though he had been practising yoga for a while, he had not yet developed a spiritual practise and that with the right training he would eventually turn towards spirituality. When Phadke Maharaj later came into Iyengar's room and saw a photograph of his guru, he stopped in his tracks and stared. Then he asked for writing implements. He wrote that Krishnamacharya was a great soul and that Iyengar should never forget or neglect him as that would bring about his downfall. He also said that Iyengar would be able to get anything he wanted with the blessings of his guru as Krishnamacharya was immensely fond of Iyengar. Though experience might have had him believe otherwise, Iyengar decided to take the holy man's words for the truth.

When Krishnamacharya visited, the more adept of the students were awarded certificates from the Mysore Yogashaala. Iyengar was a relative non-entity in Pune society. He realized that neither his presence, nor the presence of his guru, an even more obscure teacher from Mysore, would induce the average Puneite to sacrifice his evening of theatre or classical music. So Iyengar invited high-profile celebrities, who he was sure would draw in the crowds.

Iyengar also arranged lecture demonstrations, which were presided over by these people of great standing. The two people he invited to grace the occasion were each celebrities in their own right. Ganesh Mavalankar, the speaker of the Bombay Legislative Assembly, had the reputation of being a great intellectual, a man of immense moral rectitude and a humane soul. He was an author, a lawyer and a champion of democracy.

Sarojini Naidu was one of the most famous activists for Indian independence. Outspoken, witty, and a commanding speaker, she was a magnetic draw at any function she attended. Naidu, who at the time was serving as the governor of Uttar Pradesh, was definitely one of India's darlings.

At a time when companies have large budgets allocated for public relations and have professionals managing events to garner public visibility, one can only be amazed that as far back as 1938, this twenty-year-old who had not finished high school, who could scarcely speak the local language, and had barely spent a year in the big city, was pulling off events of this magnitude, making the sleepy city of Pune sit up and notice him.

As a result of these demonstrations, the Sir Parashurambhau College offered him a space, students and a salary. He was also asked to start an exclusive class for women at the Deccan Gymkhana. He had many people requesting him for individual classes. As the number of students at the Gymkhana began to burgeon, so did the number of enemies he began to accumulate.

Some rulers of the Deccan states, including the Raja Sahib of Aundh, who claimed he had founded the Surya Namsakar system,

visited Iyengar's class at the Deccan Gymkhana. Pleased with what
he saw, the Raja offered him a gift of money. Iyengar was livid
because the officials at the Deccan Gymkhana misappropriated
the gift. Their logic was that so long as he was teaching at the
gymkhana, he could not accept gifts.

Soon the collective strength of the classes rose to 200. That made
no difference to his income. However many people he taught,
Iyengar's remuneration from the club remained the same.

Iyengar got an extension of a year to carry on teaching there. Just
when things were beginning to look comfortable, some unknown
vandals broke into the space where the yoga equipment was stored
and burned it all. Iyengar believed it was an inside job. Fortunately,
the class was generating enough to afford new equipment, but the
incident left Iyengar smarting and feeling unwelcome.

The Deccan Gymkhana was benefitting from Iyengar's
presence in more ways than one. They had garnered a large grant
that year from the Government of Bombay for being the first
to introduce an Indian physical exercise regimen. Iyengar had
performed a demonstration for the chairman of the Physical
Board of India and got a renewal of the grant for the next year as
well. But their step-motherly attitude towards Iyengar continued
unabated.

Dr Gokhale continued to arrange lecture demonstrations, not
only in Pune, but also around the country. As a consequence of
these, Iyengar was constantly getting the opportunity to meet
and be in touch with people from the higher echelons, whom he
otherwise might only have encountered on the front page of his
newspaper.

The Prabhat Film Company, started by V. Shantaram in
Kolhapur, shifted to Pune in 1933. In the next ten years they made
some very remarkable films, the most famous of which was Sant
Tukaram. Cinema became the new obsession. Anyone with a story

to tell, and the resources to buy astronomically priced celluloid film, had the capacity to make a movie.

In September 1939, Dr Gokhale was bitten by the film bug. Funded by the Maharaja of Mysore, he decided to make a film of 2,000 feet featuring his new protégé. At the time that Dr Gokhale started filming, Krishnamacharya came down to Pune for a visit. Iyengar requested him to be part of the film too. Unfortunately, this black-and-white film was never finished because of some misunderstandings that arose between Dr Gokhale and Iyengar.

This roughly edited film has since become part of the Iyengar archives and is now available on YouTube. It features a twenty-year-old Iyengar, lithe and lean, still sporting his Brahmin kudumi, moving through vinyasas like his muscles are lubricated with butter. Though he looks sombre and serious through most of it, at one point he bursts into an involuntary smile which lights up the screen. The film also features the fifty-year-old Krishnamacharya displaying his prowess. [26]

Iyengar and Dr Gokhale seemed to have had mild disagreements about minor issues in the past. This unspecified 'misunderstanding' between the two, that Iyengar later wrote about, seemed to have been the death knell of a very special friendship. After this point, there is just a passing mention of Dr Gokhale's involvement in Iyengar's life. Iyengar, however, retained his sense of gratitude and indebtedness to Dr Gokhale throughout his life.

Dr Gokhale had been responsible for kick-starting Iyengar's yoga career by dipping into his deep pool of contacts to recommend him, finding students for him, partnering with him, and standing up for him even in the face of much opposition, particularly from the Deccan Gymkhana Club.

---

26 https://www.youtube.com/watch?v=lmOUZQi_6Tw

But while that relationship seemed to have run into trouble, his relationship with his guru was steadily improving. He accompanied his guru to Bombay, where Krishnamacharya was demonstrating at the Bombay University and at the Cawasji Jehangir Hall. There he encountered Sarojini Naidu yet again. At the venue, they received news that the Maharaja of Mysore was dead. Krishnamacharya had to rush back to Mysore, cancelling the rest of his engagements.

In the meanwhile, Sundara had received a letter from his sister, Jayamma. She lived with their mother at the home of one of their older brothers. She wrote that their mother had been wearing the same saree for so long that it had become threadbare with use. Mother had tied knots all over the saree to conceal the holes, said Jayamma's letter. Being a widow, the mother was not allowed to eat in the normal metal plates that most people used, but by convention was required to eat on leaf plates. But the monetary situation was so bad that the older brother had not been able to buy leaf plates for their mother and she was forced to eat her meals off the floor.

Iyengar was distraught. Despite his own financial difficulties, he wanted his mother to come and live with him in Pune. But that was impossible, considering the religious restrictions that governed her life. So the son, heavy at heart about not being able to look after his mother adequately, sent a substantial part of his meagre earnings so she could buy herself a new saree and leaf plates for her food.

In August 1940, Iyengar's contract with the Deccan Gymkhana would end. Just five months before this he had taken a loan of a hundred rupees to help finance the wedding of his sister, Jayamma. He was driven by the Indian sense of duty which says that when the father is no more, the brothers are responsible for getting their sisters married.

By July 1940, he had paid off half the amount he owed to the gymkhana. In August, when it was time to leave their services, they deducted the amount that was due, adding interest to it and leaving him with four rupees to call his own. His rent for the month was yet to be paid.

With no mentor, no students, no place to teach and soon, no roof over his head, Iyengar felt more alone than he had felt when he first came to Pune. His sense of disillusionment was so keen that he felt he should leave the city and try to build a life somewhere else. He was dissuaded by the fact that he had already invested three years of his life in the city. However depressing this situation seemed, he did not want to start afresh in another city.

The Industrial Exhibition in September 1940 seemed an unlikely setting for a yoga demonstration, but it did make business sense. Rich industrialists leading unhealthy lifestyles, with cash to spare. That was a perfect mix for a struggling yoga teacher. However, without the validating voice of Dr Gokhale accompanying his demonstration, there was only one taker. But one student was enough for a struggling yoga teacher to get by on for a while.

Laxman Manchharam Motee came from the family which made race cards, which were touted to be the 'most informative and reliable race cards in existence'. Going by the name 'Motee' or 'Cole', these cards were used at horse races by betting enthusiasts. The race card contained the horses' names, their weights and tips. The distinctive blue and white race cards were such a ubiquitous feature of a day at the races that a reporter once said, 'You can go to the race course without sporting a terry wool tuxedo, a strapless satin gown, an imported top hat, Rayban sunglasses or even your cuddly Pomeranian, but you cannot possibly be seen without your favourite "Cole" race card in your hand!!'[27]

27   http://www.coleracecard.com/about_us.html

Starting off as a one-room establishment in Bombay, the Motee family had worked its way up to monopolize the racing card trade. In 1919, Laxman shifted to Pune and set up shop there.

Pune, which used to be a ten-bicycle town, perfect for retirees, was converted by its proximity to Bombay and by the establishment of the Pune Race Course in 1830, from a sleepy town to a swarming city. The Deccan Queen was started in 1930 as a weekend train to ferry horseracing fans from Bombay to Poona. The Motee family had made their millions on these horse races.

Mr Motee requested Iyengar to teach him and his family, offering him forty rupees a month. This was like offering a rope to a drowning man.

Iyengar started teaching the family immediately, but simultaneously began looking for a place where he could hold general classes. He thought he was in luck when he found a large hall in the cantonment area. Called 'Camp' by the locals, it was the place to be. Whether you wanted to eat biryani at the spanking new 'George' restaurant, or bun maskaa at Dorabjee's, or catch a movie at the West End Cinema, you could do it all on Main Street. A bustling thoroughfare, it seemed like the ideal location for a yoga class in a sleepy city. When Iyengar found out that the rent was an affordable ten rupees a month, he jumped at it.

But after he had taken up the offer, he found his students were refusing to sign up. When he probed, he found that the place had a reputation for being haunted. The first night he stayed there, he woke up to find a crowd of inquisitive locals peering in through his window. They were all curious to know whether he would emerge alive. Though he lived there, the haunted house reputation scared off many of his prospective pupils. Some of his students who lived in the cantonment area came for a short while and then stopped coming. The distance from the old city daunted many of his previous students.

Mr Motee ended up being his new benefactor, buying blankets and supplies for the class, paying the ten-rupee rent and sending him a bottle of milk every day. Despite these efforts, the new class could not sustain itself and had to be shut down.

He was now left with two sets of students, Mr Motee and his family and a Mr Dinshaw, who owned a restaurant in Pune.

When Dinshaw started with Iyengar in September 1940, he was a sick man. His approach to health was pretty counterintuitive. He did not have an appetite, so he drank to create an appetite. He felt nauseous after he ate, so he smoked and ate betel leaves laced with tobacco to digest his food. Barely able to walk when he started with Iyengar, he rapidly took control of his life, and within a year he had turned vegetarian, teetotaller and devoted yoga practitioner.

In the summer of 1941, another cycling accident left Iyengar with pain and a swelling that lasted three years. When he consulted a doctor, it was diagnosed as an inguinal hernia and he was advised rest. Iyengar could not afford to rest. If he had to live, he had to work.

Even though he had only two classes a day, he still woke up at four to do his personal practise. The intensity of his physical practise was exhausting but it was made worse by the gnawing hunger. A plate of rice, which cost twelve paise, was not something he could afford every day. It would sometimes be two or three days before he could buy himself a plate of rice, and the rest of the time he would try to quell the rumblings in his stomach with water and tea.

Iyengar always loved jalebis. All he could afford at the time was to stand by the jalebi-seller and inhale the fragrance. The syrupy sweetness combined with the heady fragrance of ghee would fill his senses till he could imagine he was biting into one and feeling the crunchiness and the sweet sugar syrup exploding on his tongue.

He reached a point where he would offer to perform on any plain surface available, to any audience available, showcasing his art for a paltry contribution of twenty-five paise. Though the constant struggle was wearing his nerves down, something in the core of his being was telling him to persist.

Iyengar calls this time the 'darkest period' of his life. His faith in yoga as a means of sustenance was being put severely to the test. So, in a fit of desperation, he wrote to Uday Shankar, the internationally renowned dancer, who was recruiting people for his dance troupe. Iyengar offered to teach the troupe yoga in exchange for dance lessons, so long as his boarding and lodging were covered. His offer was refused. Iyengar never learned to dance.

Even at this point, the lowest ebb of his independent life, Iyengar was still making efforts to reach out to both Indian and international magazines, publications and film companies, to ask them to cover his yoga. If there was anyone who understood the power of the press and public relations, it was Iyengar.

In 1941 he had, on a visit to Mysore, asked his guru to teach him pranayama. Krishnamacharya refused, saying Iyengar with his meagre lung capacity and underdeveloped chest was still unfit for pranayama. In 1942–43, when Iyengar went back to Mysore, he decided that he was going to silently observe his guru's practise and imbibe the essentials; the rise and fall of the chest, the stillness of the eyelids, the dropping of the eyeballs, the relaxation of the internal organs and the facial muscles, and the sound of the breath.

After days of observation, Iyengar finally worked up the courage to ask his guru to teach him again. He approached Krishnamacharya with all the confidence he could muster. Once again it was not just a refusal. It was humiliation. Krishnamacharya told Iyengar that he would never be able to do pranayama in his present life.

This was just the encouragement Iyengar needed. He began a daily pranayama practise. This was fraught with as many difficulties as his early asana practise. The much-touted peace and equanimity, which is normally the offshoot of a pranayama practise, was a long time coming. It was almost two decades before he could establish a rhythm and sit down to do a continuous hour of pranayama.

This reluctance of Krishnamacharya to teach him probably made Iyengar the generous teacher he was. Every moment in class he would share, precisely and poetically, each sensation his students should be feeling in the asana or pranayama. 'Body is the bow, asana is the arrow and the soul is the target,' he would say, as he exhorted students to push themselves to the limits of their physical endurance. He would combine anatomical precision with metaphorical allusions to create an unforgettable experience for his students. 'Asana does not just pertain to this physical body, but it moulds our intelligence and our thoughts. It changes the texture of our *chitta*, cultures our intelligence and sharpens our sensitivity. Let eyes of sensitivity sprout forth from your skin. With their assistance, can you gauge your position in time and space?' His keenness for his students to take in and absorb what he was giving was so strong that he became impatient when he felt that they were not completely locked into the experience. He was intolerant of inattention, of insubordination and of ingratitude, but not of incapacity. When someone was coping with something beyond their means to handle, he became the soul of consideration: gentle, compassionate, giving and supportive. But one of his pupils had only to move the skin of their toe in the wrong direction, and in an instant the lion would be back with a fearsome roar, brandishing his bright white teeth, his eyebrows quivering, his eyes flashing like split granite.

In the early 1940s, India began to feel the impact of World War II. There were food shortages and rationing, making life difficult for everyone. People began to skimp on expenses, and yoga classes became a luxury few could afford. As often happens in trying times, Iyengar's mind began to turn inward, his connection to God grew stronger, and his faith in yoga became more resolute. He found an inner store of resources that he did not know he possessed. He resolved that this was his journey and he would live it without compromise.

With this acceptance, the world began to brighten up slightly. A friend from Mysore, Prahlad, who now worked at Prabhat Film Company, introduced him to several of his colleagues in the film industry. Prahlad was such a personable young man that Iyengar was very fond of him. His passing in 1943 left a void in Iyengar's life. He had lost his first real friend.

Another friend he made at the time was Bhal Pendharkar, director of many of Prabhat Film Company's silent films like *Bajirao Mastani* and *Vande Mataram Ashram*. Based on strongly nationalistic themes, these films created ripples, eventually earning him the most prestigious Dadasaheb Phalke Lifetime Achievement Award at the age of ninety-four in 1991. At the time he met Iyengar, he was forty-three years old.

In August 1941, Pendharkar helped Iyengar take part in a charity show for flood relief in Gujarat and Rajasthan. The organizers, having probably accepted him into the show at Pendharkar's request, were all but trying to squeeze him out of the show. Finally, Iyengar bargained and got ten minutes at the end, though the organizers were uncertain he would be able to hold the crowd's attention for that long.

It was a star-studded event held in Bombay. In attendance were two famous female matinee stars Snehprabha and Vasanti, Gaurishankar the dancer, and Sarojini Naidu. Sarojini was scheduled to inaugurate the affair and leave. She recognized Iyengar from the last performance she had watched and asked the organizers to shift Iyengar to the first slot so she and some foreign dignitaries could watch the demonstration before they left. The organizers were left with no choice but to agree.

Thanks to Mrs Naidu, Iyengar got pride of place. Later, much to the embarrassment of the organizers, dignitaries from the crowd came up to congratulate Iyengar for being the star of the show.

Pendharkar learned yoga from Iyengar. He was quite appalled at the way Iyengar was running his classes and his finances. He suggested that Iyengar stop teaching everyone besides the Motee family and Dinshaw. He wanted Iyengar to systematize the arrangements for fees and even offered to be his manager. Pendharkar's own film company was running at a loss. In 1941, his financial situation deteriorated so badly that he was forced to shut down his establishment and leave for Kolhapur.

Some divine force had ensured this debacle before he could start rearranging Iyengar's finances. It seemed like God had not completely deserted Iyengar yet!

AND THEN THERE WERE TWO

In 1943, Iyengar went back to Bangalore to attend his father's death anniversary. It turned out to be a much more eventful trip than he had envisaged. To start with, he was commandeered by his guru and made to perform at a lecture demonstration at an Ayurvedic seminar in a little river town in Andhra Pradesh called Narsapuram. As guru and pupil stood talking at the beautiful confluence of the River Godavari and the Bay of Bengal, Krishnamacharya asked Iyengar why he was not thinking of getting married. Iyengar told him of his travails in the city and that he was finding it difficult enough to maintain himself. His guru had a different theory. 'You teach a lot of girls,' he said. 'You must have fallen in love, so you are not keen to marry.'

Iyengar went to visit his brother Vedantachar in Malur, a village barely an hour's drive from Bangalore. Krishnamacharya told Vedantachar that it was now time for Iyengar to be married. His guru's fears had also been relayed to the family. The strength of Krishnamacharya's personality had them all imagining Iyengar gaily cavorting with the young pretties of Pune.

Iyengar, however, saw flashes of the hard life he had been leading. He thought marrying an unsuspecting girl and expecting her to share his hardships would be unfair and unnecessary. He refused outright.

His family was suspicious. Their heads were now filled with fanciful imaginings of what a twenty-one-year-old boy could get up to when left alone in a big city. They felt he would do well with a settling influence. His brother had been furiously writing to friends and relatives, in search of a prospective bride. The next stage in the proceedings was to have the girl come to Bangalore, so the families could meet. Iyengar's refusal did not seem to be a deterrent to the matrimonial process. The family juggernaut had swung into action.

His cousin Shamachar had suggested a girl called Ramamani. Ramamani's mother, Shrungariamma was the sister of Shamachar's son-in-law. Her father, Anekal Ramachandrar was, like Iyengar's father, a schoolteacher. Rama was born on 2 November 1927 at Anekal, 75 kilometre from Bellur, where Iyengar was born. She was one of the eight surviving children of the couple.

Rama had lived all through her childhood with her sister and brother-in-law and had spent her life in and around Bangalore. She had made many friends over the years, but every time they moved, she lost touch with them. One of her closest friends, a girl called Almelu, had shifted away after marriage and was now just a warm, fuzzy memory in Rama's head.

When Iyengar reached Malur, he found out that his brother, Vedantachar, had just been transferred from Malur to Bangalore. The family was packing up their home and possessions in Malur, and making their way back to Bangalore, where Vedantachar had a new job waiting. Iyengar arrived in time to help with the packing and left with them to go to Bangalore.

When Vedantachar and the family left Malur, they had been given no indication that a prospective bride was coming to

Bangalore to meet Iyengar and the family. Their topmost priority was to move the family and their possessions without incident to their new residence.

When Ramamani made her way to Bangalore for the first meeting with her prospective groom, she reached his brother's home during the day. There was no sign of the prospective groom. Instead of her groom-to-be, Rama discovered her long-lost childhood friend, Almelu. Almelu had married Iyengar's brother and now lived in this home. The two friends were excited, because if this alliance worked out, then they would become sisters-in-law.

The hours passed in a blur, with Almelu filling Ramamani in on all the news, and telling her about her new life in Bangalore. Rama, tranquil and reserved, listened patiently as she waited for her potential groom to turn up. The sun went down and still there was no sign of him.

It was finally 10 p.m. when Iyengar came in, bedraggled and travel-worn. In the last twenty-four hours, he had been engaged in packing up a home and had then been through a journey on the Indian railways. He hadn't shaved in days. He had no intention of acquiring a wife, and had not been warned that he had to make himself presentable.

The two were introduced to each other. Rama had a quiet compelling presence, but Iyengar wanted some time to think. His family wanted Iyengar to give the girl's family an answer immediately. Iyengar thought of the poor girl who had been waiting in a strange home without a word of complaint. He felt he owed her something. He said yes, so long as she accepted him of her own accord. She did.

Then Iyengar thought he would buy some time so he could make life at least slightly more comfortable for his new wife.

Let's fix the wedding for December, he said.

No, said the bride's party, we want it early.

So the wedding was fixed for 9 July 1943.

It seemed like nothing was going Iyengar's way. However, it was like one of God's perennial jokes. From this point on, things were only going to get better.

Rama was a soft-spoken, soft-eyed girl, with a sweet heart and an equanimity that surrounded her like a cloud.

Iyengar and Rama were distantly related to each other, as Rama's father, Ramachandrar, and Iyengar's mother, Seshamma, were cousins. Rather than functioning as a disqualification, this gave the alliance an additional layer of legitimacy.

Rama's father, Ramachandrar, had passed away years before her marriage. He had been a scholar in many languages, including Urdu and English. He had translated many books from English to the vernacular. This was besides his day job as village schoolteacher.

Ramamani's mother, Shrungari, had elevated the telling of stories into an art form. Many of them were the stories translated by Ramachandrar. Shrungari also had the skill of being able to cure illnesses through the power of mantra, whether it was making infected sores dry up or making catches and cramps disappear.

With Ramachandrar's early passing, Shrungari was forced to handle many things that were traditionally outside the sphere of a woman's activities in India. She looked after everything – from disputes over land, to visits to courts and gram panchayats, with complete aplomb.

Rama, on being told that Iyengar was a yoga teacher, was befuddled. She had no idea what that meant. 'But what exactly does he do?' she asked her brother. Her brother, slightly more knowledgeable about the world at that point, got into Paschimottanasana to give her a physical demonstration of her future husband's profession.

Iyengar had come to Bangalore to attend his father's death ceremony. He had less than a hundred rupees, which would have sufficed if this new development had not occurred. Though he did not ask for a dowry, the bride's family gifted him 150 rupees to be used on clothes and tickets to Tumkur where the marriage was to be held.

In July 1943, Iyengar's students in Pune got a letter from Iyengar requesting them to send him some money, which he would later repay. Motee and Dinshaw sent him 100 rupees each. With that and some outstanding payments trickling in from other Pune students, he took the figure up to about 500 rupees and spent it on the marriage. All his brothers and sisters came to attend the wedding, as did their families and children.

He was delighted to have all his family there, but paying for their tickets devoured about half of the money he had for expenses. After making the calculations for all the other wedding expenditure, including the invitation cards, the venue, the priests and the pooja, he had neither enough money for the *thaali*, the gold pendant Tamilian Brahmins wear to signify that they are married, nor for a new dhoti for himself. They made the perfect couple. Iyengar got married in his old dhoti. Rama was wearing a borrowed saree and jewellery that belonged to someone else!

Weddings in the Tamilian Iyengar community are elaborate ceremonies, which go on for hours. There is a charming ritual called the *Kashi yatra* (pilgrimage to Kashi), where the groom embarks on a mock pilgrimage just before the main wedding ceremony, dressed as a pilgrim wearing a simple veshti (white dhoti), slippers, and carrying an umbrella and walking stick. He makes an attempt to retire to Kashi to take up sanyas and lead an austere, celibate life. The bride's relatives prevail upon him to give up this ill-timed thought and to come in and marry their lovely girl instead. After much cajoling the groom relents and returns to the *mantapam*, a temporary structure erected under which marriage takes place, to get married.

After the *kanyadanam*, when the bride is given away, the *saptapadi* or seven steps around the ritual fire and the tying of the sacred thaali around her neck, Ramamani and Sundara Iyengar were officially married. Though most Tamilian brides wear two thaalis, one from the mother, the other from the husband, Rama wore only one thaali – from her mother's house. Smiling faces of their closest relatives surrounded them. They showered the couple with coloured rice and blessings for a wonderful future together.

After the wedding, when the party returned to Bangalore, Iyengar had to host a lunch for his relatives. His finances were now precariously at the brink and he still had to make his way back to Pune. He could not afford to take his wife back home with him yet. And he could not afford to stay back in Tumkur with her either. Waving to her at the Tumkur station as he carried on to Pune, Iyengar was already devising ways that they could be together again.

When he returned to Pune in August 1943, instead of acquiring more pupils, his old student Mr Motee, who had been a support and a father figure to the young Iyengar, informed him that the family would not be taking classes from him anymore. The news left Iyengar leaden-hearted. This had been his one dependable source of income. But how could he argue?

Mr Motee had come to him because he had three daughters. Like so many in India, he longed for a son. Iyengar had promised the couple that if they did yoga with him religiously, this would happen. Now it had. The Motees felt that with the original purpose achieved, they had no reason to continue learning yoga.

But Mr Motee had always been generous with Iyengar. He told him that the money sent to him for the wedding was a gift not a loan and he gave him an additional 100 rupees as a gift when he saw him in person. But this one-time gesture of generosity, though helpful, was not what Iyengar needed. He needed students. He needed a sustainable means of livelihood. He needed to have a comfortable home for his new wife.

Iyengar's old Parsi student, Dinshaw, now living a more sattvic life, continued to come to him for lessons. But that earning was scarcely enough for Iyengar's own needs.

In October 1943, the superintendent of the Maharashtra Education Society (MES) approached Iyengar to train the girls from his school. This meant a stable monthly income.

The time had come for Ramamani to be brought to Pune.

A WELCOME FOR A WIFE

Ramamani came to Pune in November 1943. She had few possessions, only a couple of sarees and the single golden thaali from her maternal home that her husband had tied around her neck on their wedding day. It was an auspicious day for Iyengar. 'Lakshmi' had stepped into the house.

For the rest of India though, things were not looking so good. The Indian army was in the throes of World War II. It was the year of the Bengal Famine. No one could put a finger on the cause of it, probably because there were so many reasons. The Indians blamed their colonisers. The British administrators blamed the failure of the rice crop in Burma (India, at the time, imported 15,00,000 tons of rice from Burma), a cyclone in Bengal that destroyed the winter crop, a failed monsoon in Tamil Nadu, and large amounts of grain being bought up for the army. All this, they claimed, had caused the price of rice to go up 950 per cent above pre-war prices. In Calcutta, particularly, people were dying of starvation every day. All over India, people were struggling to survive.

Ramamani's small bunch of keys jingled at her waist as she walked. The Iyengars had just paid the landlord in crisp one rupee notes and the rest of their life savings were tied in a neat knot at the end of Ramamani's saree. A wooden plaque at the entrance read 'Subhash Nagar' in Marathi.

Before they entered the home, Iyengar set a small steel pot of rice on the floor. Ramamani stepped in, touching the steel pot of rice with her foot. The rice grains dusted with kumkum powder scattered on the floor and Ramamani took her first steps into her new home. Her footprints left red imprints as she walked across the house. This makeshift ceremony was all the couple could afford to mark their entry into their first marital home.

Iyengar with Rama

Iyengar looked around at the modest home. In comparison to the rich houses he visited everyday to teach, this was miniscule. Barely 150 square-feet in all, there were two rooms on the ground floor and a small space upstairs. Downstairs was a kitchen and a space that doubled as living space, bedroom and yoga room. The home looked larger than it was because of the paucity of possessions in it. In the kitchen was a solitary aluminium vessel and two plates and a stove. Everything in the kitchen had been lent to them by Iyengar's students.

Iyengar watched Rama as she slipped the few annas that they had left for the rest of the month under a small deity. Deprivation had been a way of life for both of them. But for the first time, Iyengar felt complete. He was passionately in love with this new entrant in his life. Ramamani, with her quiet adoration of her husband, would wake up before 4 a.m. By the time he was awake, the aromatic flavour of freshly ground coffee would curl around the two little rooms, tempting Iyengar out of bed.

Rama and Iyengar would share their morning cup of strong, sweet, filter coffee. She would then sit by and watch him as he did his asana and pranayama practice. As they grew closer, in mind, body and spirit, he would use her as a mirror, he would use her as a prop, he would use her as a student, he would use her as a teacher and she would, willingly, always put his needs before her own. Often, when he had finished his classes, he would sit by her and watch her cook, absorbing the poise in her movements and the aroma of coconut oil mingling with the flavour of the spices in the food.

Though Iyengar was still struggling to feed two mouths with his meagre income, Ramamani's entry into the home seemed to make it easier, not more difficult, as he had earlier expected. With a few annas, Rama would spin an endless variety of simple, home-cooked meals every day. To Iyengar, the fragrance of Rama's sambhar and rice became the fragrance of home.

One day Iyengar came home to find Rama poring over a sheet where she had made a detailed account of their family finances. As they examined the sheet together, Iyengar was amazed to find that he was spending the same amount as he was before his wife had come into his life. He looked at Rama's calm and possessed demeanour. Life was still difficult, but much more beautiful than he had imagined it would be.

Most importantly, Iyengar finally felt he had someone he could talk to and confide in, someone who would share the burden of his day, someone who would give him sage and empathetic advice. Any of the natural urges, temptations and attractions that Iyengar might have felt as a youth to the women he met, were all sublimated in his wife. Often, after a long day at work, he would watch her as she slept. He was flooded with all sorts of feelings – respect, gratitude, contentment, and a deep love.[28]

SURVIVING ON LOVE AND HOPE

In December 1943, Iyengar acquired another patron, F.P. Pocha, who owned a seed company in Pune. When a searing pain down his leg from sciatica became debilitating, he decided to consult Iyengar. Lessons with Iyengar cured his pain, and he became a convert to yoga. This well-connected Parsi gentleman was, in the next few years, to direct many more students to Iyengar.

In March 1944, Ramamani found out that she was pregnant. Iyengar was elated, but he realized a baby would tip their delicately poised financial situation over the edge. He began thinking of schemes to attract more pupils.

Iyengar had a photographer friend, Ram, who worked with the Royal Western India Turf Club. Iyengar requested Ram to take some photographs of him in yoga poses. Photography was the preserve of the wealthy. Film was outrageously expensive. But it had to be done. After consultation with Ramamani, a portion of the household budget that month was set aside for acquiring film.

In two days, Iyengar did 150 poses for the camera. At the end of the two days, he was laid up in bed with a high fever. Because

---

28 B.K.S. Iyengar and others, *Body the Shrine, Yoga thy Light*, India: Tata Press, 1978

Ramamani was already seven months pregnant, his photographer friend was called to nurse Iyengar. Ram arrived to nurse Iyengar, and in no time at all, he was ill too. Now Ramamani had two patients on her hands.

Relatives were summoned from Bangalore to help nurse the duo. The ailing men had to both be admitted to hospital. Iyengar was discharged after a few days, while Ram, who had acute malaria was made to stay on longer. Iyengar's brother convinced Rama and Iyengar that they should both travel back to Bangalore with him for a while, so that they could rest and be taken care of. Iyengar cycled or walked to each of his pupil's homes to tell each of them, individually, that he was going to Bangalore to rest for a few days and would not be able to take class for a while. This uncalled-for exertion ensured that he was burning with temperature by the time he reached Bangalore. He had contracted malaria too. Lying in bed for twenty days to recover, he had to resort to borrowing money from Motee and Pocha to cover his expenses.

After he recovered from malaria, both Ramamani and he decided it was time to visit Krishnamacharya, as the guru had not been able to attend their wedding.

Every year there was a celebration at the Yogashaala, and in October that year the Iyengars reached in time to attend it. But Krishnamacharya, as in the past, had rubbed some of his students up the wrong way. They refused to participate in the function. Iyengar, feeling that this public occasion was not a good time to air private grievances, tried to convince them to relent. When he failed, he ended up being the sole participant in the yoga demonstration. He had barely recovered from malaria, but he did his duty by his teacher and gave a fantastic demonstration.

Indian tradition dictates that the wife go back to her maternal home for the birth of her children. It was now time to drop Rama at Tumkur and get back to Pune. It would be a full five months before he saw his wife again. And when he did, she would be accompanied by their baby daughter, Geeta, born on 7 December 1944.

Mr Pocha was still zealously recommending Iyengar. He sent him to some patients of Dr Dinshaw Mehta, a naturopath closely associated with Mahatma Gandhi. Dr Mehta ran a naturopathic hospital in which he treated patients without allopathic medication. Gandhiji himself had stayed there often. When yoga brought marked improvements in the patients' health, Mr Pocha suggested that Dr Mehta employ Iyengar at his centre. Dr Mehta made him a desultory offer of a paltry salary, and went on to place further restrictions upon Iyengar. Iyengar, he said, would not be allowed to work anywhere else and Dr Mehta would personally choose a few appropriate asanas, which the patient would be allowed to do.

It was an offer that Iyengar found easy to refuse.

When Mr Pocha, who was then the governor of the Rotary Club, went abroad for a Rotary meeting in 1946, he did not stop paying Iyengar his fees. Realizing that the loss of income would affect Iyengar's fledgling family adversely, he transferred his classes to Mrs Vasudhara Gharpure, the wife of a very successful surgeon in Pune. Dr Gharpure had watched one of Iyengar's early demonstrations in 1937, and though impressed, he dismissed this kind of yoga as out of bounds for normal people. When he saw his wife doing yoga with Iyengar, he was inspired. He began taking classes as well.

When Mr Pocha returned from USA, he arranged for Iyengar to have a demonstration at the Rotary Club. Dr Gharpure, who was the president of the Club, spoke to the audience and convinced them that yoga did not strain the heart and that even people with debility and low energy could practise yoga and feel better. Now Iyengar had two patrons. Dr Gharpure also started recommending patients to Iyengar.

FREEDOM AND FULFILLMENT

The war had ended. There was optimism in the air. Clement Atlee asked Jawarharlal Nehru to form an interim government in August 1946. It seemed like it might not be long before the people of India, after almost 300 years of an exploitative British rule, would be masters of their own fate.

As if in consonance with India's destiny, life for the Iyengar family was also about to change.

In October 1946, both husband and wife had strange and fortuitous dreams.

In Iyengar's dream Lord Venkateshwara of Tirupathi blessed him with one hand, and offered him a sheaf of paddy (which traditionally indicates prosperity) with the other. The Lord assured him that his difficult days were over and that he should devote all his time to practising and teaching yoga.

In Ramamani's dream, a glorious goddess-like figure appeared dressed in a yellow saree, with long hair and her forehead adorned with red kumkum. In her dream, the deity handed Rama a golden coin. Rama was told that the Goddess and her husband owed the Iyengars a debt that they wanted to repay. From that day on, the Iyengars were sure that their financial troubles were over.

Pune was, in many ways, one of the hotbeds of the Indian independence struggle. It was home to the Yerawada Central Jail, where many Indian nationalist leaders were incarcerated. The Aga Khan Palace, where Gandhiji, his wife Kasturba, and Sarojini Naidu were placed under house arrest, was also in the city. It was also the headquarters of V.D. Savarkar, the fundamentalist Hindu leader, and many of his acolytes. The fiery anti-British newspapers

Kesari and *Mahratta* edited by Bal Gangadhar Tilak emerged from Pune. Over the years, many people associated with the freedom struggle were visitors to the Iyengar home.

Fathema Ismail was a nationalist leader who was later nominated to the Rajya Sabha. She was a feisty woman who had actively worked with Gandhiji through the independence struggle. Fathema's daughter, Usha, had been afflicted with polio and they had travelled near and far in hope of a cure. They tried spine specialists, masseurs, physiotherapists and quacks. After Dr Kini, the most famous orthopaedic surgeon of the time had treated her, there was a general improvement but her spine remained in the same state as before. This was when Dr Gharpure introduced them to Iyengar. Within a few weeks of doing yoga with Iyengar, Usha's spine showed improvement.

Iyengar was not sure what he was being tested for, but every time he came to work with Usha, Fathema Ismail would pretend to not be home, but would secretly watch the class from some hidden spot. Iyengar was not really concerned with the vagaries of the mother's mind. He had found a patient who needed his help and he got to work single-mindedly. Finally, when Ismail was convinced of Iyengar's legitimacy, she confessed to him that she had been watching him all the while. 'You are an ustad,' she conceded. To Iyengar, it did not matter at all. His treatment of Usha proceeded in exactly the same way whether her mother was watching or not. Iyengar had his God watching him all the time.

Ms Ismail later came to trust him so implicitly that when she founded the Fellowship for the Physically Handicapped in Bombay, she wanted Iyengar to work with the children personally. While Iyengar was happy to help, he realized that she expected him to work single-handedly as she didn't trust anyone else with the children. That would have been physically impossible and Iyengar had to refuse.

Pune was crammed with patriots who were part of India's freedom struggle. Achyut Patwardhan, the socialist, had been one of the moving forces of the Quit India Movement, in which Gandhiji, leading a mass protest, demanded the withdrawal of the British from India. Achyut and his brother often came to attend Iyengar's classes. Geeta Iyengar remembers being carried around the garden by him as they examined which guava fruit was ripe for picking. Patwardhan was the one who taught Geeta how to climb trees.

Iyengar's fame was spreading. Another friend of Ms Ismail, Mr Pakseema, had a daughter who had polio. Mr Pakseema was the owner of the Muratore restaurant in Pune. Having also gone through expensive courses of treatment with several eminent doctors to no avail, they finally approached Iyengar. After just a few months, the girl began showing much improvement. Her limp, which had been quite pronounced, almost disappeared.

Mr Pakseema shifted to Pakistan after independence but his daughter persisted with the yoga, which allowed her to lead a life that was close to normal. Eventually, she got married and had children.

In the course of teaching Pakseema's daughter, Iyengar spent a lot of time with him discussing religious philosophy and the Koran. Pakseema pointed out to him ways in which the Koran and Vedic texts are similar. He spoke to Iyengar about the universal oneness of the soul, regardless of the religion which one belonged to.

These conversations made Iyengar realize how far he had come from that teenager who had first stepped into Pune. At that time he was convinced of his ideas of Brahminical superiority and was very careful not to eat and drink with men of other communities and castes. Now two decades in the city had rubbed away all those distinctions. Here he was, enjoying the hospitality of a Muslim and actually absorbing the wisdom of his words. It helped Iyengar realize that it was a man's inner being that counts, not the clothes he wears. Underneath the veneer of religious, racial and class differences, he began to see and appreciate the commonalities that bind us as humans.

In 1947, when Mr Pakseema and his family left for Pakistan, it was a great financial loss to Iyengar. More importantly, he felt the loss of a friend.

Though rumbles of Partition and the violence it engendered were already reaching the people, there was nothing that could scotch the euphoria. The air rang with possibilities and hearts sang with hope, as India spilled out on the streets to celebrate her freedom. It was a giant festival, a huge celebration, devoted to the motherland and her infant democracy.

As midnight approached, one could hear the sound of trumpets, music, balloons and firecrackers on the streets. Iyengar, Ramamani (who was close to her full-term with another baby), and their little toddler Geeta, celebrated the formation of the new nation, their hearts bursting with pride.

Every year after this, even years after his grandchildren were born, the Iyengars celebrated Independence Day with fervour. There were miniature flags that festooned the home, special sweets to celebrate the day and even a family flag hoisting.

'At the stroke of the midnight hour, when the world sleeps, India will awake to life and freedom. A moment comes, which comes but rarely in history, when we step out from the old to the new, when an age ends, and when the soul of a nation, long suppressed, finds utterance.' Nehru's gravelly voice said over the public-address system to the nation on Independence Day.

The only people who did not share the country's optimism after India got her freedom were the 555 kings and princes, whom Sardar Patel, with his persuasive power, had convinced to become part of the Indian Union. For the ex-royals, this stepping out from the old to the new brought many hardships. They were now restricted to a 'privy purse' which amounted to about 8.5 per cent of their state's annual revenue. The Maharaja of Mysore, being one of these rulers, was also subject to the same treatment. As a result of this agreement, most of these rulers had their wings clipped. They were suddenly incapable of living the lives they had become accustomed to.

For the Maharaja of Mysore, it meant giving up a lot of his pet projects. One of the last to be axed was the Mysore Yogashaala, which he could no longer afford to finance and which the Indian government had no intention of funding.

In April 1951 his guru asked Iyengar to attend the annual Yogashaala event. Iyengar was unable to attend what would be the last celebration of the Yogashaala in Mysore. Soon after, he received a letter from his guru informing him of the closure of the Mysore Yogashaala.

Iyengar was understandably upset. This meant his guru was left completely in the lurch after a lifetime of service. For Iyengar, it was also the place where he himself had learned the art of yoga, which was now sustaining him. He still retained a strong emotional attachment to the school in Mysore. Feeling helpless, Iyengar wrote two articles in Bangalore newspapers and several imploring letters to the government authorities. They were appeals to a government that had no ears and no heart. The Yogashaala was never reopened.

On 29 August 1947, Ramamani and Iyengar had their second daughter, Vanita. The little home at Subash Nagar was now filled with the sounds of two little baby girls. Considered Lakshmi, the goddess of wealth, the birth of each daughter brought a corresponding increase in the family's prosperity.

All through his life Iyengar retained an honesty about his attainments that was charming and childlike. Of course, there was the other side of him, which sometimes came across as harsh, vain and arrogant.

He could make someone do a pose in the middle of a full class, then point at the hapless student disparagingly and even kick and slap him into the requisite position. When he had reduced the poor student into a quivering puddle of nervousness, Iyengar would do the pose himself and then puff up his chest and gloat, 'You people only know how to talk and give big lectures. No one can do it like me.' On another occasion, he told his pupils in his strongly inflected English, 'All these people went to the West, Mahesh (Maharishi Mahesh yogi) went, that Dhirendra (Dhirendra Brahmachari) went, but they did not make a dent. Who did it? No one else. Only I made yoga popular as you see today.'

Despite the bombast in his speech, there was a guilelessness and an inherent honesty. There was no attempt to dissimulate or hoodwink people into believing he was greater, more accomplished, more pious or even more modest than he believed he was. With him, what you saw was what you got. And if it was sometimes brash and aggressive, at least it was the truth. Even his spirituality, he had always claimed, emanated from his connection with his physical body.

Given his matter-of-factness about his own strengths and weaknesses, he was always a bit perplexed when he saw people trying to pull the wool over others' eyes.

In 1948 a Swami Ramanand was said to have arrived from the Himalayas and he was going to give a public demonstration of being buried underground for twenty-four hours. Fascinated by any extreme physical or mental skill, Iyengar went to watch him and found him having emerged from his underground confinement before the twenty-four hours were over. The swami claimed he was in Samadhi and was extremely tired. Though this did not correspond with his own understanding, Iyengar accepted the swami's explanation, only pointing out how his own experience of Samadhi differed from the swami's.

Despite several newspapers trying to discredit the swami's performance, Iyengar still tried to get an audience with him. He was told that besides the one hour that the swami spent with the press, he was in Samadhi the rest of the time. Finally, Iyengar managed to not only talk to him, but also have the swami watch his asana demonstration. The swami, thrilled with the performance, told him that he hadn't witnessed anything like this even in the Himalaya. He gave Iyengar permission to see him every day. This surprised Iyengar because he had expected the swami to be busy with his spiritual practices all day. Iyengar was even more surprised when he did walk in to visit him at different times of the day and found the swami engaged in thoroughly ordinary pursuits with not a whiff of spirituality in the air.

Two years later, the swami was planning a trip to the US and suggested that Iyengar accompany him. Iyengar felt that he did not have enough faith in the authenticity of the swami's yogic practices to join forces with him despite the lure of a trip abroad.

Iyengar now had enough happening in Pune to keep him rooted there. He had a wonderful wife at home with whom he was besotted. His two little girls were growing up and learning to speak. Their language was a curious amalgam of Tamil, Kannada and Marathi, but he loved the sound of their prattle. For the Iyengars, it was a halcyon time.

On 30 January 1948, Iyengar was just winding up his workday, when a crackly announcement over All India Radio told the nation that Mahatma Gandhi was dead. Gandhiji was the most beloved political leader India had ever had, and the country, barely over the carnage of Partition, was poised at the edge of another bloodbath in case the killer was a Muslim. The nation collectively held its breath waiting for more details. The killer, it was announced, was a Brahmin from Pune, Nathuram Godse, who had made a public proclamation that he felt no remorse about killing Gandhiji. Pune bore the brunt of the backlash.

The conspiracy had been hatched in Shaniwar Peth, not even a ten-minute drive from their home in Subhash Nagar, Shukrawar Peth. Barely 2 kilometres from the home of the Iyengars was the home and office of Nathuram Godse, the killer. As the Iyengars had been carrying on with the business of life, Godse and his accomplices had been planning the most heinous crime of the time, the killing of the Mahatma.

In the days that followed, Pune was filled with angry mobs burning, looting, rioting and pillaging Brahmin homes all over the city. The Iyengars were afraid. Geeta was four and Vanita had just turned one. However, not being part of the Chitpawan Brahmin community, which the alleged killers belonged to, the Iyengar family fortunately escaped the wrath of the mobs.

THE YOGI AND THE PHILOSOPHER

In 1948, J. Krishnamurthy the philosopher nurtured and created by the Theosophical Society as a world leader, came to Pune. His early life was strangely similar to Iyengar's, as he too was born to a Brahmin family in a place called Madanapalle in Madras Presidency (now Andhra Pradesh).

Brought up by a single parent, in his case his father, Krishnamurthy was a sickly child, weakened by recurrent bouts of malaria. His father got a job as a clerk at the Theosophical Society, Chennai, and they shifted there. This is when the pale and scrawny, but magnetically good-looking boy got noticed by Charles Webster Leadbeater. Leadbeater was a disillusioned Anglican priest who under the tutelage of Madame Blavatsky embraced the Theosophical movement and shifted from England to Madras (now Chennai) to eventually lead the society's activities in the city. Leadbeater claimed that Krishnamurthy had the potential to be the new world leader, as his aura was so free of blemish. Leadbeater, who later had several allegations of sexual molestation of underage youth pinned to him, may have just been attracted by Krishnamurthy's compelling looks. Krishnamurthy, was adopted by Madame Blavatsky and Leadbeater when he was barely thirteen. From that point on, the Theosophical Society lavished money and attention on him, giving him the best training available in preparation of his role as a 'World Messiah'. Despite this extensive training (or possibly because of it), the adult Krishnamurthy broke away from the expectations foisted on him by the Theosophical Society, and began his own spiritual journey. In 1929, Krishnamurthy gave a historical speech severing his connection with the Theosophical Society claiming his only concern was 'to set man absolutely, unconditionally free'. When Krishnamurthy came to Pune in 1948, Iyengar attended every one of his lectures. Mr Pocha, as usual, was the one to introduce Iyengar to the philosopher. Iyengar demonstrated his asanas and when Jiddu called his performance 'professional', Iyengar smarted. He considered his yogic prowess a God-given gift and not a professional exposition. Later, Krishnamurthy summoned him and asked him to cast an eye over the asanas he was practising. Though Krishnamurthy was able to do a large number of asanas, judged with Iyengar's eye for perfection and detail, none of them reached the mark. Also, the way Krishnamurthy was performing the asanas left him breathless and tired. Iyengar told Krishnamurthy that he could help him perfect his poses and correct his faulty breathing patterns.

Krishnamurthy insisted that the breathlessness was because he was repeating the practice, having done it once through already that morning. Iyengar, instead of arguing with him, said that he could make him do the asanas all over again, with no trace of breathlessness. And he did. By supporting him, with a leg here, a knee there, the flat of his palm somewhere else, Iyengar worked his magic; transferring the exertion and fatigue away from Krishnamurthy's muscles, relaxing his overwrought nervous system, calming his breath.

At the end of the session, Krishnamurthy said that he would love to learn with Iyengar, but that he could not afford to pay him, as he was a poor man. Iyengar found it hard to believe, but he was willing to accommodate and teach Krishnamurthy free of charge at a time when he did not have other classes. The only available time was at four in the morning. This, Krishnamurthy said, was too early. They reached an impasse, as Iyengar was not willing to accommodate him any further.

Iyengar spoke to Mr Pocha about this conversation with Krishnamurthy. Mr Pocha gave up his own 6 a.m. slot and requested Iyengar to go to Krishnamurthy at that time instead for two days. Mr Pocha was happy to bear the cost of the lessons. After two days of having experienced the class with Iyengar, Krishnamurthy felt that the benefits of doing yoga with Iyengar outweighed the fact that he would have to forego some sleep. By the third day, he was ready at 4 a.m. everyday, personally opening the door to Iyengar, as everyone else was asleep. Classes with Iyengar continued as long as Krishnamurthy was in Pune and for years after, in Gstaad, Switzerland.

Iyengar also attended some of his talks, and was not impressed by the dissonance between what he said and what he did. 'Do not criticize and do not justify' were Krishnamurthy's mantras in the early days and these words, Iyengar noted wryly, would be sandwiched between hearty critiques of all the religions and religious leaders of the world.

Though Krishnamurthy advised his followers to break away from their conditioning, he himself had not assimilated this fully. In his room, which had a glorious view of the Alps, he would want his blanket to be aligned in a particular direction so he could always face the wall and not the mountains in Shirshasana. Iyengar wanted him to do his Shirshasana facing the mountain and so changed the alignment of his blanket. Krishnamurthy immediately turned it back. Iyengar gently reminded him that regardless of the direction of the blanket, it was the direction of his head that would determine the final position of Shirshasana. There was really no need for Krishnamurthy to change the orientation of the blanket, except for his conditioning.

On the other hand, Krishnamurthy was open to learning and would deprecate himself if he felt he was wrong. When Iyengar explained to him how he should be stretching out his legs without any undulations in the muscles, he allegedly said, 'What a stupid man I am not to understand this much.'[29]

Krishnamurthy did not ever publicise his relationship with Iyengar, but to Iyengar, this was one of the relationships that leveraged him into the realm of the wealthy and well known. On an emotional level, however, he was left embittered by Krishnamurthy's treatment of him and would always smart a little when the philosopher's name came up in later conversations.

THE DAWNING OF CONFIDENCE

Mr Pocha of the Pocha Seed Company had suddenly taken very ill. The diagnosis was a strangulated spine, which had paralyzed his digestive system. He was advised by a well-known physician Dr M.S.H. Mody to have an emergency operation performed by Dr Ginde, a neurosurgeon of repute. If the operation was not performed, the prognosis was paralysis. The family rushed Mr Pocha to the Breach Candy Hospital in Bombay, where the operation was performed immediately.

A month after the operation, Mr Pocha was still not showing signs of recovery. The physiotherapist had been seeing him everyday since the operation, but his condition remained unchanged. Mr Pocha, who had been helped by Iyengar before the operation, summoned him from Pune. He was sure that yoga would help him

---

29   *70 Glorious Years of Yogacharya B.K.S. Iyengar*, Kirloskar Press, 1990

get back on his feet. Dr Ginde, however, was completely against yoga. He reluctantly agreed to call Iyengar, but Dr Ginde's first instruction to the yoga teacher was, 'No yoga!'

Dr Ginde wanted Iyengar to follow the protocol that he himself recommended for his patient. He had apparently carried a negative feeling for yoga because of the number of yoga practitioners who came to him after developing infections because of their practices of *neti* and *dhauti*, methods of detoxifying the body. Though Iyengar protested that he taught only asanas and pranayama, the doctor was not convinced. To start with, Iyengar made Mr Pocha practise the exercises that the doctor advised.

Every weekend, the doctor would drive to Pune and visit his patient, Mr Pocha. Though these weekend visits went on for three months, there was no improvement. Finally, out of desperation, the doctor allowed Iyengar to use his own methods, but insisted on seeing results within two weeks. This was despite the fact that the doctor's regimen had not brought any positive results despite a major spinal operation and three months of intensive post-operative care.

Iyengar began working with Mr Pocha's bladder incontinence. Within the stipulated two weeks, not only was there better bladder control, but Mr Pocha also began to sit and stand with support. The doctor was amazed at his progress. 'You labour, and I get the credit,' Dr Ginde said to Iyengar, frankly. From that time on, till his death years later, Dr Ginde sent many of his intractable cases to Iyengar. Iyengar had converted another diehard to the cause of yoga.

The Iyengars still lived in their small two-room home. The back room was now designated as the kitchen, nursery and playroom, while the front room was reserved for Iyengar's yoga classes. On 2 July 1949, Prashant, Iyengar's only son, was born. The two-room home was now getting pretty crowded.

As soon as he could afford it, Iyengar became an avid newspaper reader. Till the end of his life, he spent an average of an hour every day reading them. His nephew, Seshadri, who visited him every summer in Pune, remembers sitting perched on a stool, reading a diverse collection of newspapers to him for two or three hours, while Iyengar continued with his practise. It may have been Iyengar's avid consumption of the news that increased his faith in the power of the media.

During these visits to Iyengar, Seshadri remembers the long lists of books that Iyengar would recommend he read. This was not so much a passive recommendation as most of us are prone to make. The young Seshadri was expected to read these books when Iyengar was out teaching and write out a summary of each book. This was then submitted to Iyengar, who would discuss the book with him. Seshadri credits much of the learning he acquired outside of school to these sessions with his uncle, who mentored him so assiduously. From the works of Swami Vivekananda to Patanjali's works, they explored them all together.

Seshadri was one of Iyengar's favourite nephews. Seshadri believes that it was because he was more academically inclined than the rest that he received his uncle's benevolent attention. Actually, Iyengar treated him more like a younger brother, as there was barely a few years' difference between them. Besides, he was the son of one of Iyengar's favourite sisters, Seetamma.

It was while reading the papers in August 1949, that Iyengar came across an article announcing that Kaivalyadhama, a yoga institute run by Swami Kuvalayananda, had been given a government grant.

Iyengar had had enough experience and positive results and feedback to feel that his system of yoga could compete with any other system available. He was also determined that yoga should be introduced as part of the curriculum for schools all over India.

He not only made a representation himself, he also asked Krishnamacharya to make a representation requesting a grant. This started off a two-year correspondence, at the end of which the government grant was still a distant dream.

Then he came up with a new scheme. He wrote to the chief minister of Bombay, B.G. Kher, asking him to hold an all-India yoga programme, allowing people to showcase their work, and then giving grants to the ones who seemed most deserving. Kher promised to get back to Iyengar.

A month later, Iyengar received a dead letter in the mail. A dead letter is one that cannot be delivered to the addressee for some reason. It was Iyengar's letter, which he had sent to Kher. Kher had forwarded the letter to Swami Kuvalayananda, whom it had presumably not reached. The swami, at the time, was director of the Physical Education Board in Bombay. Iyengar sent the ragged letter back to Kher. He received an acknowledgement, but no reply.

Iyengar would not give up without a fight. When Kher shifted to Pune, Iyengar was still struggling for an audience with him. Iyengar's staunch supporter, Mr Pocha, was acquainted with Kher. One of Kher's sons had polio and Pocha recommended that Iyengar help him. He told him of the miraculous effects Iyengar's yoga had had on Usha Ismail and Pakseema's daughters. Mr Pocha's introduction worked its usual magic and after months of trying, Iyengar finally had an audience with Kher.

When he met Kher on 17 October 1949, Iyengar brought up his idea for yoga to be introduced in schools around the country. He also advised him that institutions should be assessed adequately before government funding was offered. Kher asked Iyengar to come back a few days later to give a demonstration at his residence.

After the demonstration, Kher was impressed enough to tell Iyengar that he would one day receive recognition from the government. Iyengar told him, in frustrated tones, that the government honour would probably come to him long after he was dead. One of the guests bemoaned the fact that the government had castrated the maharajas who were strong patrons of the arts, and was doing nothing in its turn to support artistes. Kher's bland answer was that the government had no funds.

Realising that Iyengar was truly an innocent in the way political funding worked, one of Kher's sons, probably feeling sorry for Iyengar, took him aside to another room. He gave him a calming glass of milk, and in the course of conversation, let it slip that Kuvalayananda who had procured government aid, was Kher's maternal uncle. Iyengar finally stopped asking Kher for aid. The veil had cleared.

In December 1949, Iyengar bumped into his old friend Dr Gokhale again. It was a decade since they had last met. Their misunderstanding minimized by the mist of time, they were happy to see each other again. Mr Gokhale asked Iyengar if he would perform at the All-India Physical conference, where General Cariappa would preside.

General Cariappa was also from Karnataka, but from the cool coffee-growing climes of Coorg. He had joined the army after World War I, and served with distinction in World War II. In 1949, after a career of excellence, he had been declared the first Commander-in-Chief of the Indian army. The general was pleased with the demonstration and, thinking it fit that his soldiers be exposed to Iyengar's masterly control over his body, requested another performance at the Army School of Physical Training.

After his demonstration, some of the poses Iyengar had shown them were added to the army training manual. The army also wanted Iyengar to do an anatomical, physiological and pathological analysis of each asana. Iyengar did not have the time for that just yet.

In October 1950, Iyengar heard from Mr Pocha that Sri Nithyananda would be visiting Pune. Sri Nithyananda, originally from Tamil Nadu, was said to have become enlightened at the age of twelve when his teacher's body merged into his own. He established an ashram in Bangalore and travelled around the country, giving lectures on spiritual subjects.

When they met in Pune, Iyengar requested the swami for some time for a demonstration. This was arranged at the home of Walchand Hirachand, the business magnate.

The swami watched the demonstration with rapt attention. At the end of it he pronounced that it was the most spectacular yoga performance he had ever witnessed, 'flowing like a perennial river'. Nithyananda called Iyengar a 'sidhha purusha' – a man who has attained special or supernatural powers. He told him not to be dejected by the dearth of money. 'Poverty,' he averred, was 'a garland for knowledge'. Later, when the swami was giving a public discourse, he spoke of Iyengar and his *tapas*, discipline, that had led him to become a master of his art.

On 3 July 1951, the Iyengar family was blessed with another baby daughter, Sunita.

In 1951, Iyengar was requested to teach a Jain saint, Badrankarji Maharaj in Bombay. He had heard of Iyengar from some of his Jain pupils in Pune who had shared stories of Iyengar's proficiency. The saint had been looking for a yoga teacher for a long time. When Iyengar went to meet him, he found that though the saint was receptive, his devotees were parochial in their attitude and not happy having a young boy who was not a Jain coming to teach their great guru. After watching Iyengar demonstrate his yoga and engaging in a spiritual discussion with him, the saint decided that he would have Iyengar teach him despite the protestations of his devotees.

Every Saturday morning, Iyengar would leave by the 11 a.m. train for Bombay and return to Pune in the evening. At the time he was travelling seven hours to teach this one solitary class, but it reaped rich dividends. Since other people in Bombay heard that he was coming in to Bombay to teach the Jain muni, they wanted lessons from him too.

THE SPREADING OF WINGS

When Khurshid Kapadia introduced Iyengar to Mehera Rustom Vakil in June 1948, it seemed like any other day. But this was a meeting that was destined to catapult the young man from Bellur into the limelight and turn him into a global phenomenon like the Beatles or Coca Cola.

Mehera had come to Pune for a month to learn yoga from Iyengar. Her husband and mother-in-law were understandably perturbed, as they felt Mehera was indulging in some esoteric religious rituals. They were relieved to find, instead of a half-dressed fakir on a bed of nails, a Mr Iyengar, his head clean-shaven but for his kudumi, riding his bicycle in his neatly ironed kurta and dhoti.

Mehera was born into wealth, and it showed. From the tips of her manicured nails to the perfectly coiffed hair, from her cultured version of the Bombay Parsi accent to the exquisite hand-embroidered gharaa sarees she wore, from her evenings at the Bombay Chamber Orchestra, to the delicate tea sandwiches she served (their crusts neatly trimmed off!), from her liveried house help to the antique Chinese vases that crowded her home, she belonged to a very different world.

Driving down arterial Pedder Road, full of traffic, clamour and people, reminds you continuously that you are in one of the noisiest cities in the world. When you veer off the busy thoroughfare and drive into Carmichael Road, you feel like you have reached an oasis in the frenetic city. Your heartbeat slows down. It feels like you are visiting a place untouched by time. The further down this tree-lined road you travel, the more you feel you have left Bombay behind. Even today, almost seventy years later, this road retains a magical serenity. Many of the bungalows have been replaced by monstrous high-rises, but the Vakil bungalow still remains as it was when Iyengar used to visit it. Tucked away in the corner of a street lined with gorgeous gulmohurs, there it stands – a two-storied bungalow emanating an air of understated, elegant luxury, the ancestral property of Mehera's husband's family. One can imagine Iyengar walking into this home and comparing it with his own two little rooms shared by his family and students. His two-room home would comfortably be accommodated in the smallest room of 'Shengrela', as the home was called.

Mehera didn't just start taking classes with Iyengar. She adopted him. Her family was amused beyond belief. Here was Mehera playing Professor Higgins to this little yogi who, dressed like a clerk, had a face like a thundercloud and could barely speak English.

Every weekend, after he had finished class with her, Mehera would leave instructions with her staff to feed him soft, buttery cucumber sandwiches and the other three-and-a-half vegetarian dishes her cook could make. And she would insist he eat with a fork and spoon.

For all her refinement, Mehera also had another side to her, a whacky, eccentric Parsi side. Maybe from centuries of inbreeding or from a slightly maladjusted social barometer, or possibly a lower need to conform to societal pressures that stemmed from being 'outsiders', Parsis have always been renowned for their quirkiness. They were known for things as innocuous as walking around with a scooped out watermelon on their heads during a bad summer, and rubbing sweetened rose syrup on the skin to treat diabetes, or things as gory as cutting off a mother-in-law's nose for interfering in the couple's marital bliss.

Mehera's nuttiness was of the harmless kind. She would, and no one knew why, make her domestic help walk in front of her with a mug of water and sprinkle the path as she walked. She was a great lover of animals and would go to any lengths to rescue them. She was awarded the 'Pranimitra', or 'Friend of Animals' award. She once saw an injured cow on the road and, to her husband's consternation, wanted to load the cow into their fancy car, so that they could take it home and care for it. It may have been the same irrepressible instinct to help the helpless that made her reach out to Iyengar.

Mehera was married to the man who was called the Father of Indian Cardiology, Dr Rustom Jal Vakil. At a time when the world had no drugs for hypertension, Dr Vakil's landmark research on rauwolfia (sarpagandha) and its effects on hypertension as well as psychiatric therapy earned him the Albert Lasker Prize and later a Padma Bhushan.

Mehera and Rustom Jal Vakil were, in today's parlance, a power couple.

In Bombay, their lives revolved around the 7 kilometres between Colaba and Carmichael Road, but the world was their oyster.

When Mehera and her husband travelled to England in 1950, she carried with her an album of photographs. This was the same set of 150 photographs that had been so painstakingly clicked over two days by Iyengar's friend, Ram, with extremely expensive film, just before Iyengar and he both came down with malaria. That album was just about to prove that the effort had actually been worthwhile.

THE MUSIC MAESTRO MEETS HIS YOGA MASTER

In 1952, the Indian Prime Minister Jawaharlal Nehru invited Yehudi Menuhin to play some concerts for famine relief in Madras. Yehudi and his wife, Diana, had arranged a tour of India, with Yehudi playing the violin in several cities and donating all profit that accrued from the performances to the Famine Relief Fund.

For Menuhin, the yoga bug bit him as he waited at an osteopath's clinic in New Zealand. He encountered a little book about yoga that shifted something in him. The life of a performer is fraught with pains in the muscles and nerves because of continuous imbalance and tension in particular positions. Menuhin was immediately interested in the esoteric art.

In the few days that Menuhin stayed with Nehru at 10 Janpath before embarking on his tour, Nehru discovered the maestro's predilection for yoga. Nehru immediately challenged Menuhin to a headstand competition. Just then, the butler walked in to announce dinner and was amazed to find these two distinguished men, both upside down, on their heads.

Menuhin welcomed to Mumbai with garlands

The media picked up the headstand story. It was widely publicized. And who should chance upon it but that avid reader of newspapers, Iyengar. At around the same time, Dr Meher Homji, a Pune dentist, had been asked by Mehli Mehta (father of Zubin Mehta of New York Philharmonic fame), if he knew someone who could teach yoga to Menuhin. Knowing Iyengar had taught Krishnamurthy, his was the first name that popped into the doctor's head. Dr Meher Homji asked if Iyengar would be willing to go to Bombay. Mr Iyengar said he would, if his trip to Bombay was paid for. In the meanwhile, the doctor found that some local yoga practitioners had already been lined up to teach Menuhin.

Iyengar, in his weekly correspondence with Mehera, mentioned his talk with Dr Meher Homji. Mehera could not stand to have her protégé disappointed. Mehera was delighted when she received an appointment to tea with the Menuhins. She gathered together every ounce of her considerable charm and was determined to secure an appointment with Menuhin for Mr Iyengar.

Amidst the clinking of silver teaspoons in translucent bone china teacups and waiters serving bite-sized hors d'oeuvres, Mehera sighted Menuhin, deep in conversation, in one corner of the room. In no time at all, she had cornered him and shown him the album of Mr Iyengar's photographs. Menuhin had already seen an endless array of potential yoga teachers and his patience was wearing thin. He had recently met Kuvalayananda and C.M. Bhat, a colleague of Iyengar from the Mysore days, and was not adequately impressed. On seeing Iyengar's photographs, Menuhin's interest was aroused.

To Menuhin's objections that Mr Iyengar was too young, Mehera assured him that the yogi was an adept and understood the intricacies of yoga better than people who were much older. She informed him that Mr Iyengar was very precise in his understanding of the physiology and anatomy of the body. Convinced by the earnest testimonial, Menuhin asked for a five-minute meeting with Mr Iyengar.

Iyengar was amused. He had never in his life had a five-minute meeting with anyone. He undertook a four-hour journey from Pune to Bombay for the five-minute meeting. Mehera drove him to the Governor's Bungalow, where Menuhin was staying. When he reached there, there was no sign of anyone. Not even the domestic staff. After waiting about an hour, he started looking around. He saw someone sleeping in a bedroom. The person woke up, upset to

find an intruder in his bedroom. Iyengar informed him that he was
looking for Menuhin and that he had travelled a long way and had
already waited an hour. When he heard that, the sleeping man –
who turned out to be Menuhin – was profusely apologetic. From
that moment on he was the epitome of the charming host.

When Iyengar said he would like to demonstrate for him,
however, he excused himself, saying he loved the album he had
seen, but he was too tired. Iyengar asked him if he would like to
be able to relax. The musician, with nerves as tightly strung as his
violin strings, could not resist the offer.

The guru placed his fingers on Menuhin's hot and fevered eyes
in *shanmukhi mudra*. In minutes, Menuhin was asleep. Iyengar
received word that Dr Homi Bhabha and other personages were
waiting to see Menuhin, but Menuhin was sleeping so soundly
that he could not get himself to shift his hands off Menuhin's eyes.
When Menuhin awoke, he claimed that the forty-five minutes
had been the most restful sleep he had had in years. He asked the
guru to come back to teach him the next morning. The forty-five-
minute class, in which his pupil did nothing but sleep, was going to
be the class that changed Iyengar's life.

When Mehera was escorting Mr Iyengar to the Governor's
Bungalow the next day, she told him that Menuhin had spoken
about him to all the other guests at dinner the day before. He had
mentioned to all the distinguished guests that he would like to take
Mr Iyengar abroad to train Menuhin and his family in yoga. The
other guests at dinner that evening were Prime Minister Jawaharlal
Nehru, his sister Vijaylakshmi Pandit and Eleanor Roosevelt.
Iyengar was flying in the rarefied social stratosphere. He would
now need to take deeper breaths.

Mr Iyengar's class the day after also comprised of Menuhin's wife
and his accompanist, Marcel Gazelle. The class went on for three-
and-a-half hours, after which Menuhin popped the question.

'Will you,' he asked his guru, 'visit my home for a year?' Iyengar reminded him that he had family in India. Menuhin told him that four months was the minimum he would like to have him in Europe, and he left it at that so Mr Iyengar could mull over it.

All through the trip, Iyengar gave Menuhin private lessons. Menuhin's performance in Bombay was an unqualified success. When Menuhin travelled to the other cities of India, he did not enjoy the benefit of the guru's teachings and found a substantial difference between his performance in Bombay and the other cities.

Though the trip to Menuhin's home in Europe did not materialize that year, Menuhin realized that Mr Iyengar was as special as Mehera had promised he would be.

Of his meeting with the yogi he later said, 'There were other gurus and other lessons, but not until I met Mr Iyengar did I take up the study regularly. My first meeting with him was like the casting of a spell. We made each other's acquaintance in Bombay. He appeared in my rooms one morning and straightaway made it clear that the "audition" to follow was mine as much as his. For all my celebrity, to him I was just another Western body knotted through and through.'

Menuhin came back to India in 1954. This time he didn't have to shop around for a yoga teacher. As soon as he arrived, he started classes with Iyengar. Soon, Menuhin had to leave for Delhi. Not wanting to miss out on his yoga, he requested his teacher to accompany him on this trip. When Iyengar went to Delhi, he had the opportunity of meeting Nehru. The yogi was very touched by the meeting and presented the prime minister with a copy of the album of his yoga poses. After the Delhi trip, Menuhin was addicted to the well-being engendered by his yoga practise. He convinced Iyengar to accompany him to Switzerland for six weeks.

SO MANY FAMILIES

In the meanwhile, on the home front, the family was growing. Rama had just had another baby girl, Suchita, on 21 July 1953. Geeta, the oldest, had just started going to school. Their father was getting busier with teaching. Dinnertime, when he came back home from teaching, was their special time with him.

In the early days in Pune, a group of people who spoke Kannada and Tamil would meet every Sunday. This later became an association called the Karnataka Sangha. They would have social gatherings at the homes of one of their fifteen or so members. When the meeting was at the Iyengar home, the members would look forward to the special upma made by Rama. Upma is a basic breakfast dish made of semolina, but Rama, with her special touch, managed to elevate it to a food for the gods. The Iyengars and their friends would sit around in the little house and share this warm upma, redolent with the flavour of ghee, and the even warmer feeling of camaraderie and conversation, washed down with hot delicious South Indian coffee.

It was in the year 1954 that Iyengar started classes in Bombay. Besides Mehera, who would have a private class in her bungalow, one of the earliest students in Bombay was Martha Wartenburger, a Jewish lady who lived in the city. Another pupil who would play an important role in the making of the Iyengar phenomenon was Barzo Taraporewala. Barzo was a tall, lanky Parsi gentleman who had hypnotic eyes and a voice like a subterranean stream. He was known to have told someone who once had the temerity to ask him to speak louder that she should 'listen beyond the words to the sound of his soul'.

Barzo was an early convert to Iyengar Yoga. Besides being a lawyer, Barzo was an intrepid photographer, a legal reporter for the *Indian Express* and a nature enthusiast. He grew to be one of Iyengar's closest friends and associates.

Barzo's children were not part of the class but would join their parents in class, and sit by the sidelines, watching the adults. Irach, Barzo's son, remembers that if they began to get too noisy, Iyengar would come to him and imitate an angry lion's roar. If this didn't squelch his exuberant spirits enough, Iyengar would threaten to knot Irach up in Padmasana. This just proved to be more a challenge than a threat to the little boy who would then begin to scamper around the class, daring Iyengar to catch him. Iyengar, despite his infamous temper, had a surprising amount of patience with younger children.

Dhan Palkhivala walked into the cavernous Bombay High Court Library without her characteristic smile. Her doctor had just told her that she would never conceive because of the terrible condition of her uterus. The faint ray of hope that he gave her was that yoga might help her condition. When Dhan confided in Barzo, he looked at her through his thick glasses and said in his measured fashion, 'If yoga, then who else but Iyengar?'

Dhan went on to have three boys under the eagle eye of Guruji, who supervised her yoga practise. Between the first and second boy, she conceived, but miscarried, because Iyengar was in Europe. She was not allowed to do her practise without his guidance.

After a disastrous first meeting at the age of four when Iyengar Uncle had whirled him in circles in the air, Jehangir, Dhan's second son, developed a mortal dread of him. Every Sunday, when Iyengar Uncle came for breakfast with the family, the four-year-old was not to be found, reappearing long after the yogi had left. By the time he turned seven, he had joined class too and got so fond of Iyengar Uncle that he would rush to be the first to open the door to him when he arrived at their home. One of those days, as he was rushing to the door, he tripped over his little velvet Parsi *sapaat* (traditional Parsi footwear) and landed on the floor contorted with pain. He remembers being picked up and cradled in his guru's arms for a long time, as Iyengar Uncle set the bone and held it in place. Jehangir had broken his radius and ulna. The pain is long gone, but Jehangir still remembers the warm feeling of comfort as Iyengar Uncle held him that day. Geeta says of this relationship, that with the three Palkhivala children, Anna (as the Iyengar children called their father) was 'like a child.'

Aadil, Jehangir and Phiroze, the Palkhivala children, remember the pranayama turns very well. They were, as children, not allowed to do pranayama. They would instead be given endless cycles of backbends and handstands and a great deal of flipping back and forth from one asana to the other.

This was their time with their Iyengar Uncle. They would show him their newly acquired toys and gizmos, which he seemed to enjoy as much as they did. There was a peashooter of which they were all enamoured. Jehangir remembers them stifling their giggles as Iyengar uncle shot peas with them at the back of the class, as all the older students were engaged in serious pranayama.

The regulars of the Bombay class in the early 1960s were Barzo Taraporewala, the Palkhivalas, the Motiwalas, Rati Unwala, Minoo Chhoi, Mary Sethna, Dolly and Villoo Pithawala. The majority of his early pupils were Parsis. This was perhaps because a section of them was always more open-minded about spirituality and about exploring a culture that was not their own. Maybe because they could see that his temper came from his desire for perfection, a trait that they themselves could identify with so closely. Maybe, despite his accented and Indianized English, there was an intrinsic honesty about Guruji that appealed to this community, which placed such a premium on this virtue.

When he was asked why there was such a predominance of Parsis in his class, Guruji was said to have responded with 'because they are a cultured race,' leaving the questioner befuddled about whether Iyengar was complimenting the Parsi community or congratulating himself.

Iyengar conducting Mumbai class in the 1970s

Later, Sam and Freny Motivala, Madhu Tijoriwala, the Bangera family and the Mehta family joined the class. Many of the young children who attended the class then, constitute the second generation of Iyengar yoga teachers.

Every Saturday, Guruji would board the newly introduced Deccan Queen from Pune to conduct classes in Bombay. Often, when it was a pranayama turn, Rama and the children would accompany Iyengar to Bombay as well.

In Bombay, he would teach Mehera and the Tarachand sisters individually and then go on to teach a group class. After the Saturday class at the Bhulabhai Desai Auditorium, Iyengar would spend the evening with his Saturday class students at one of the clubs in South Bombay or at Barzo's home. At night, he would retire to the Railway Hotel in the crowded innards of the city and spend the night there. Even when he was much friendlier with his

Bombay students and they implored him to stay over with them, he continued to patronise his modest lodgings. The next morning, he would teach the Sunday morning class. Then he would join the Palkhivala family for a light breakfast and Dhan would drop him to the Victoria Terminus railway station to catch the morning train back to Pune.

Firooza Munawar Ali, who joined the classes a decade later, says with great certainty, 'The older students from Bombay were Guruji's first friends. They became like extended family to him.' When one of his students in the later years suggested that Iyengar stop coming to the Bombay class, he said unequivocally, 'So long as I have life and energy in me, I shall never stop conducting my Bombay classes. I love my Bombay pupils. Many of them have been devoted to me for years and despite the trouble involved in travelling to and from Bombay, I love to meet my Bombay pupils.'

Mehera, who had adopted Iyengar, would sit with him after class in the family verandah with a cup of fragrant mint tea while he drank his coffee. They would have long conversations about life and yoga with raucous ravens outside the windows trying to drown out their voices.

This closeness also characterized his relationship with Barzo, with whom he spent more time than with any other student. Barzo was as serene as an impassive Himalayan glacier, the complete antithesis to Iyengar's fieriness. Barzo was the one person who attended both Saturday and Sunday classes. He was also the person from whom you had to extract words with a chisel. Despite their differences, the closeness between these two unlikely men was undeniable.

Dhan remembers talking to Guruji about everything under the sun, whether it was her period pains or a domestic problem within the family. Every time Guruji left for Europe, the entire

Iyengar family would accompany him to Bombay and stay with the Palkhivala family. The night before he left, the Palkhivalas would have a party for him at their Ness Baug home, or at the Motivala residence in Dadar, with all his Bombay pupils in attendance.

One on one, Guruji was the most delightful companion. Listening with complete, respectful attention, he would often break out into his signature laugh, which emerged volcano-like from deep within him. Like a spectacular eruption, it would spread light and sparkles into the space he was in and among the people he was with.

In class, he was a terror. As soon as his footsteps padded into the room, it would be filled with a frisson that was palpable. Everyone was in a heightened state of awareness; every muscle, nerve and sinew ready to follow his instructions. And if there were any preoccupations in their heads, which made them unable to follow his directions, they would feel it – the Iyengar kick or slap on their spine or chest or legs, or whichever part of them was being unresponsive. In class, Guruji demanded complete attention and complete dedication.

He was willing to give as much as he got. There were classes devoted to backbends, in which he spent a large part of the class supporting each person by the waist, helping them drop down into a backbend. Once they had created the ideal rainbow shape on the floor, he would hold them by the waist again and help them stand upright. And this would go on and on and on...for thirty students... for as many repetitions as he had asked them to do. So a backbend class would generally be much tougher on the guru than it was on his students.

Guruji would help every student go up into headstand himself. One over-enthusiastic pupil kicked up in the pose before Guruji was ready and knocked out two of Guruji's front teeth.

The Bombay students had already realized that their teacher was special, without testimonials from others. But this was confirmed by a psychic soul. Dhan and Behram once chanced upon a *chaaya shastri* who they felt was tremendously accurate with reading the past and very specific in his predictions for the future. A chaaya shastri is able to access this information by reading the shadow of a person. Impressed, they told Guruji about him. Barzo and Iyengar made their way to the chaaya shastri. The astrologer measured the yogi's shadow in three positions.

'This is a very special soul,' he told Iyengar and Barzo. Then he checked the guru's horoscope and said, 'This person will cure people, not with medicine, but with his hands. In his last life he was a doctor.'

The chaaya shastri was right. Guruji managed to cure people of myriad problems in different ways. When Dhan had a stone in her kidney, the pain was so excruciating that she had to have painkillers and be confined to bed. After missing her classes week after week, she finally decided to go in at least for the pranayama sessions. Her teacher knew she had been suffering for a while with the pain. He made the class do forty-five straight minutes of nadi shodhana. When Dhan went to the bathroom after, she heard the sharp sound of a stone tinkling down the edge of the ceramic pot. Looking down, she saw a black stone glittering in the water. There had been no pain, no blood and no discomfort.

When she informed Guruji about having passed the stone with her urine, he said, 'Now go home!' As soon as she reached home, she passed all the detritus – a terrifying amount of pus and blood – with her urine. Iyengar had done it yet again.

The Bombay students were now an inextricable part of Guruji's life. They were all excited that their teacher was finally being publicly recognized because of the Menuhin connection. They decided that they would collectively treat the Menuhins to dinner at a fancy restaurant. The day after this dinner, Menuhin (slightly uncharitably) expressed the fact that this kind of dinner was not a very special thing for them who spent so much of their lives socializing, and that he had had many better dinners.

That was like throwing down the gauntlet to Iyengar. After all, to him, his wife Rama was the best cook in the world. Iyengar immediately decided that Menuhin would now have a taste of real Indian food. He would have a meal homecooked by Rama.

The dinner was going to be held at Dhan and Behram's home in Ness Baug. Dhan had made sure that, as per Guruji's instructions, the hall was cleared of furniture. Mats were arranged on the floor near the walls. She had borrowed silverware to serve the great man, as their finances at the time did not allow for such luxuries.

On the morning of the dinner, Rama and Guruji were leaving to pick up the supplies required. Five minutes away was 'Bhaji galli', where they could get the freshest and largest selection of vegetables in the area. The Palkhivalas came out into the corridor outside their home to see the Iyengars off at the lift. An ill-timed breeze swung the door shut, locking them all out of the house.

What a day for this to happen! Everyone's nerves were already fraught with the effort to please the great violinist.

Guruji asked Dhan if he could go into the neighbour's home and have a look. The neighbour was happy to help. The yogi went to the neighbour's balcony, which adjoined the Palkhivala balcony, with just a thick cement wall separating the two. He looked down at the five-storey drop. He gauged the depth of the wall. And before anyone could begin to object, he had climbed up the balcony wall on the neighbour's side and, holding the wall, swung one leg over to the other side onto the Palkhivala side of the wall. And then with one Hanuman-like jump, he was on the other side. His spectators were standing there aghast, their mouths open, their hearts pounding and their pulses racing. They looked down thankfully at the ground so far below, at what would have been almost certain death if there had been a little slip.

In a moment, Guruji opened the Palkhivala home from the inside and, with his signature laugh, welcomed them back into their home as if nothing had happened.

Rama and Dhan at the Palkhivala home with Geeta and Vanita

Dhan was so upset that, teacher or not, she gave him an earful about his callous disregard for such a precious life. He must have felt the care behind it, because as she scolded, he laughed.

An hour later, the couple returned from the market laden with groceries for the eight or more delicacies that Rama was to prepare. If it were left to Dhan to plan this party, she would have started preparations three days earlier. By 3 p.m. on the day of the party, her dishes would have been steaming and ready to be dished out into the fancy crockery.

As Rama sat with her on the bed, talking to her in soft engaging tones about the newest exploits of Geeta, Vanita and Prashant, Dhan's attention began to wander. She felt the knot of anxiety in her tummy grow more and more intense. Her mind was furiously reviewing how much was left to do and the fact that nothing was done. What were they going to serve this international celebrity if they hadn't even started cooking yet?

At about 4 p.m., when Rama finally felt it was time, she started cooking. In her quiet, efficient way, she single-handedly cut, chopped, ground, mixed and pounded. By seven, she had the meal almost ready, but for the puris that needed to be fried once they were ready to eat. Not once did she need to taste anything to check for salt or seasoning. Dhan was amazed. This was another kind of yoga she had just imbibed from her guru's wife.

As they heard Guruji and Menuhin approach, the frying of the puris began. Instead of leading Menuhin directly to the hall, the yogi, eliminating any trace of formality, brought Menuhin directly into the kitchen to meet Rama and Dhan.

Menuhin watched with fascination as the flat brown discs of flour were inserted into the hot oil and the top and bottom magically separated, turning them into golden-brown puffs of delight. The music maestro asked, to the amusement of all those present, 'Pray, how do they part company?'

Guruji led him outside and made him sit on a mat on the floor. As the food was served, Menuhin realized he was supposed to eat with his hands. Most Tamilian Brahmins have a glorious way of eating, where only the tips of their fingers get soiled with food, except for the end of the meal, when they swoop up the liquid remains with a dextrous sweep of the hands and a flick of the wrist to the centre of their palms from where it is slurped up. It is as complicated as it sounds, requiring great proficiency and expertise.

Rama and Dhan in the Palkhivala home (with Aadil in between)

One of the guests was trying to persuade Menuhin to use this technique. Looking on was Nani Palkhivala, Behram's brother and India's top constitutional lawyer of the time. Feeling sorry for Menuhin, he said, 'There is an easier way,' and offered the musician a spoon. The spoon was summarily seized by Iyengar, who wanted Menuhin to have the complete Indian experience. He made Menuhin finish his meal Indian-style.

After the meal, in which Rama had surpassed herself, Dhan offered Menuhin some soap to wash his hands. No, he insisted, he wanted the fragrance of the delicate spices to linger on his fingers for as long as it would.

In the course of this visit, Menuhin had a bad bout of the flu. He was laid up in bed, unable to practise the violin or yoga, even though he had a concert at the Regal Theatre just days away. Iyengar decided to take over the situation. He forbade the staff of the governor from feeding Menuhin anything but fresh 'pepper water', a special dish made by Rama. Pepper water is a delicious, warming concoction made of a combination of mung dal, urad dal, coconut and pepper, roasted together in ghee till the flavours emerge. They are then ground into a thick soup-like consistency. This is what the Iyengars ate when they were trying to recuperate from an illness. This is what Menuhin was given too. The pepper water ensured that he was back on his feet in time to give a magnificent performance in Bombay.

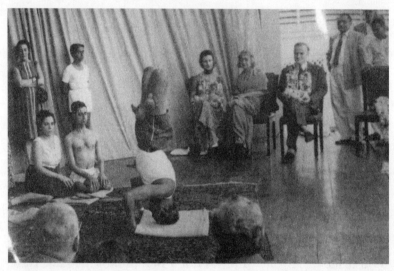

Iyengar demonstrating for the Menuhins. Dhan and Behram Palkhivala looking on

Menuhin's early trips to India had Iyengar written all over them. These interactions marked the beginning of a long-standing relationship between the two maestros.

THE FLIGHT OF THE YOGI

It was 1954. Sundara's first trip abroad. The concept of *Samudra Ullanghana* prevents a Brahmin from crossing the seas. There is a belief in Hindu mythology that the ocean is a resting place for gods and they should never be disturbed. The penalty for doing this was a loss of caste. Ever since he had arrived in Pune, the yogi had had to do many things that breached the strict rules that governed the caste system. Brahmins were proscribed from eating food made by anyone who was not a Brahmin of the same caste. Though many of these rules seemed like they had outlived their time, they were still followed religiously in the smaller towns and villages. Sundara was not very sure how his relatives in Bangalore were going to react to his proposed trip abroad.

Before he embarked on his trip, Sundara went to Bangalore to seek his mother's blessings. If she had some objections to his crossing the ocean, he had decided he would reconsider his plan. His mother was all encouragement. Her brothers were, however, extremely upset, and swore that Sundara would not be allowed to step into their homes when he returned from this trip. But Sundara had his mother's blessings. He decided to go.

Mehera Vakil was the one to mould him and prepare him so he did not feel like too much of an outsider when he socialized with westerners from the highest echelons of society. Before Mehera, Iyengar ate food with his hands, and licked his fingers, Indian-style, to show his appreciation.

From Mehera, he learned how to place his fork and spoon, hold a door open for a lady and take off his headgear when he visited someone's home.

In preparation for his trip to Europe to teach Menuhin, Mehera convinced Iyengar to have a haircut and get rid of his shendi. She also acted as his wardrobe consultant, advising him on the kinds of clothes he should take with him to counter the cold and to fit in with the kind of people he was going to be rubbing shoulders with.

Iyengar shed his long Brahmin lock and coaxed his newly shorn locks into a style reminiscent of Cary Grant. His fiery eyes sparkled under eyebrows that had not yet become unruly. Dressed in a western suit for the first time, he looked ready to conquer the world.

When he went to Bombay airport, his entire family and all his close students were there to see him off. There is a picture of Iyengar at the airport, wearing trousers and a full-sleeved shirt, his hair parted in the centre and slicked back with coconut oil, a garland around his neck, his daughter in his arms, looking decidedly grim.

Gstaad, called 'the Place' by *Time* magazine in 1960, was a village in southwestern Switzerland. It had a floating population of international jet setting vacationers, and a few people who lived there through the year for the mountain air. Though much smaller in area than his hometown Pune, Gstaad overpowered Pune on the celebrity factor; it boasted of residents like Roger Moore, Elizabeth Taylor, Grace Kelly and Roman Polanski.

Menuhin introduced Mr Iyengar to many of his musical friends. Among them was Witold Malcuzinsky, a Polish pianist. Having lived an adventurous life in France during World War II, Malcuzinsky and his newly wedded wife had to flee after France capitulated to Hitler. After much wandering, he had settled in Switzerland. Malcuzinsky was as enamoured of Mr Iyengar as Menuhin was and wanted the yogi to accompany him to England. Mr Iyengar went to England with him and taught him for a while. Then he joined Menuhin in Paris, teaching him for a few weeks, before returning to India. He had crossed several oceans, but to Iyengar it did not seem like the gods were particularly angry.

Mr Iyengar taught Menuhin and his children. He also worked with Menuhin on the best way to hold his violin. He felt that Menuhin's present way of grasping the violin and his posture were creating an unnecessary tension, which reflected in his performances.

At the end of the trip, Menuhin presented him with an Omega watch. Inscribed on the back were the words:

'To my best violin teacher, BKS Iyengar,

Yehudi Menuhin, Gstaad, September 1954.'

The watch remained one of Iyengar's most treasured possessions.

When Iyengar returned to India after this trip, he was so emaciated that he seemed just a shadow of his former self. His student Dhan, not one to keep her questions to herself, asked him outright how he had become so thin. Her guru said laconically, 'Boiled potato, boiled cauliflower, boiled cabbage. Every day.'

'But why didn't you eat chocolate, Guruji?' Dhan asked him. 'Because chocolate has egg in it,' said Iyengar matter-of-factly. Dhan sat him down and gave the great yogi a lesson on how to read labels to decipher a product's ingredients. Now, thanks to her, there was one more item on the sparse Iyengar menu.

He then told her of formal dinners where the crème de la crème of western music would be seated, dressed in their formal best. As the yogi sat in his assigned seat, a fat suckling pig stuffed and dripping with juices, with an apple stuck in its mouth, would be wheeled in by a liveried waiter. Iyengar, the staunch vegetarian Brahmin, who had never seen anything like it in his life, would try not to react. As everyone else began tucking into the roast pig with gusto, Iyengar would be desultorily shifting around his boiled potato, cauliflower and cabbage on his plate, longing for one of Rama's meals at home.

What he did not speak about was the fact that the hotel had initially refused to allow a 'coloured' man to occupy one of their rooms. Menuhin had specially requested that Mr Iyengar be allowed to stay at the hotel though he was 'coloured'. At the request of the influential violinist, the hotel made an exception for Mr Iyengar, and reluctantly agreed to host him. They laid down a proviso that he should not come down for breakfast. He would be served upstairs, in the privacy of his room, so that he did not disturb the sentiments of the white-skinned guests of the hotel. Iyengar wasn't coming to Europe to do a Rosa Parks act. He was trying to earn a livelihood for his family. He stayed in his room as requested.

Even though he now had the coveted 'foreign-returned' label, on the inside Iyengar was still the poor boy from Bellur. His first brush with the West left him disconcerted. These people were from an alien culture and a very different social stratum. His responses to the world had to be more measured than instinctive. Iyengar later told one of his pupils, 'There was the complex. I felt the inferiority. These people were the very cream of society. I had to overcome that; at first it was not easy.' In Pune, even though he was not wealthy, his students accorded him that special deference that India reserved for its gurus. Here, in the West, he had become a yoga teacher.

One of the early years that Iyengar came over to London, Menuhin had him live in a palatial house belonging to his friend, Lady Calwill. After he had lived there a few days, the lady informed the yogi that he would have to start paying rent. Taken aback, Mr Iyengar approached Menuhin and informed him that he would not be able to afford the astronomical rent. Menuhin then took him to an old man whom he knew, who had space to spare, and told him that he should offer the man yoga lessons and stay with him free of charge. When they approached the man with this scheme, the old man said that it was impossible. He had a girlfriend, he confided in Menuhin. When Iyengar was told this, he said 'So what? He has a girlfriend. I can be his boyfriend and we can all stay together.' Finding it impossible to spell out the details of the old man's living arrangements to his innocent yoga teacher, Menuhin just sighed. 'Oh Mr Iyengar, you are so naïve.' Finally, Menuhin found an old couple who lived in a tiny one-bedroom house. The first question Iyengar asked them was how much they would charge. 'If I came to your home in India, would you charge me?' asked the old man. This seemed like a place where Iyengar could stay. Both Mr Iyengar and Menuhin were happy with the arrangement. It was decided that the yogi would stay there and sleep on the sofa in the hall. Every morning after he woke up, Iyengar would, as quietly as he could, shift the sofa to one side of the room and practise yoga. In the room next door, he could hear the soft snoring of the old couple.

For all Menuhin's wealth, it seemed amazing that he would go to such lengths to avoid paying for a hotel room. That he would not have Mr Iyengar stay in his home was obvious, because his wife Diana was not very charitably disposed to his yoga obsession. Diana was a gorgeous but opinionated woman, who could not be easily thwarted.

'We do have the most wonderful arguments,' she revealed in 1984, adding, 'I've thrown two trays and a typewriter at Yehudi.'[30]

His entire family was pretty discomfited by his fondness for yoga. His daughter Zamirah said, 'The most embarrassing thing he ever did to me – I was only ten – was to appear on the front of *Life* magazine with his tongue hanging out to his navel, doing yoga. I didn't go to school for three days after that.'[31]

Iyengar recounted the time when he was doing Viparitachakrasana in his hotel room. Hotel guests kept hearing the sound of his feet repeatedly slapping the floor as he landed. They couldn't find a human explanation for the sound, so they ascribed it to a ghost on the premises. He had been practising the jumping pose for a few days when the hotel authorities came to his room and said, 'Sir, we truly hope you are not being disturbed. Many of the guests have been complaining about some strange sounds emanating from this floor.' Mr Iyengar tried to look innocent and concerned, but inwardly he chuckled over the spooky effect of his harmless asana.

THE WAY IT WAS

Over the years, Iyengar had taught many Indian political figures and leaders, but his fondest ties were with Jayaprakash Narayan and his wife, Prabhavati, whom he had met in 1952 at Dr Dinshaw Mehta's clinic in Pune. Jayaprakash had been suffering from

---

30   *Telegraph*, 6 February 2003, London
31   http://www.telegraph.co.uk/culture/4718903/So-much-love-for-man-so-little-for-us.html

diabetes for quite a few years. Since Gandhiji himself was such an advocate of naturopathy and fasting, many younger Congress leaders also adopted this as a way to health. Jayaprakash was in Pune for a twenty-one-day cleansing fast at Dr Dinshaw's clinic. Achyut Patwardhan, feeling that Jayaprakash would benefit from Iyengar's teachings, introduced him to the yogi.

Jayaprakash was almost fifty-nine years old when he started yoga. Iyengar was charmed by his simplicity and his modesty. He used to visit the Iyengars when they lived in Subhash Nagar. The miniscule house, though spotless through Rama's untiring labours, was spartan and bare. They did not even have a mat on the floor or a chair to accommodate the distinguished guest. When Iyengar suggested they could borrow a chair from the neighbours, Jayaprakash refused. 'No, no, no,' he insisted, 'I don't want it. I am accustomed to sitting like this.' And he sat cross-legged on the floor, flanked by the Iyengar children, sharing one of Rama's delicious meals with the family.

Iyengar helped Jayaprakash resolve his sciatica and abdominal problems and control diabetes. Jayaprakash was seemingly a keen learner who picked up the asanas and continued practising them for years after.

Jayaprakash was a Gandhian who would go on to become one of the greatest defenders of India's democracy. In 1976, Indira Gandhi declared the infamous Emergency, clamping down on the basic rights of every Indian citizen. Fundamental rights were suspended and severe censorship was imposed on the grounds of 'internal disturbance'. When the Allahabad High Court passed a verdict against Mrs Gandhi for electoral malpractices, Jayaprakash Narayan demanded her resignation and asked the nation to join him in a movement for 'sampoorna kranti', or total revolution. It was believed that if anyone could get Mrs Gandhi to see reason, it would be Jayaprakash. Instead, all the senior leaders of the opposition were incarcerated. Jayaprakash fell seriously ill, but even from hospital, he continued his protest.

Till Jayaprakash's death in 1979, Iyengar and he would exchange letters, packed full of news about their health and their families.

At Jayaprakash's death, it was not just Iyengar, but most intellectuals and idealists of that era, who mourned the passing of a great soul.

On 5 May 1955, Iyengar's youngest daughter, Savita was born. Savita, being the baby of the house, was always the one to enjoy special privileges. She was allowed to tag along whenever her parents went out and got whatever she asked for.

She remembers being beaten only once in her life by her father, whereas Prashant and the rest would get regularly whacked. It was when she wandered off to a friend's home to play with him instead of going to school. She was summoned back home and greeted with a resounding slap. Iyengar did not want his children to miss out on schooling as he had.

Geeta and Prashant remember their father's Humber bicycle, on which he used to traverse miles and miles across Pune. Geeta used to travel double seat with him when he went to teach Krishnamurthy. She remembers the delicious feeling of anticipation when her mother bundled her up in warm clothes, before placing her on the bicycle seat in front of her father on cool Pune mornings.

The Humber was Iyengar's pride and joy, and every weekend he would lavish attention on it, cleaning it and polishing it to a shine. Prashant remembers that his father even attached a little motor to it in the later days. It was many years later that it was retired from service honourably when a five-horse power scooterette made its appearance in their lives.

When the family wanted to travel together they would call for a Victoria (a horse-drawn cart) owned by one of Iyengar's friends.

They would make trips to Bund Garden or one of the picnic spots nearby, armed with Rama's crisp, homemade *murukku* and Mysoor pak in case hunger pangs struck one of the six children.

When Savita was little, she managed to get into all sorts of scrapes. She had just turned four and was generally the family favourite, but her siblings began to complain every time she went near them of a strange smell that was emanating from their little sister. Though she did not feel particularly unwell, the family scheduled an appointment with a doctor who pronounced that nothing was wrong. They took her home, but the siblings' complaints carried on unabated. The next day, when Anna (as the Iyengar children called their father) was doing his pranayama practice he suddenly called out to Savita. Anna intuitively made the four-year-old do the forceful exhalations of Bhastrika pranayama and out popped a watermelon seed, a little worse for wear for its long residence in her nostril, but still recognizable despite its rottenness. How Anna knew it was there, when the doctor could not diagnose it with his instruments, was something that Savita could not comprehend.

Called 'cycle city' in the 1940s and 1950s, the city the Iyengar children grew up in was very different from Pune today. It abounded with green spaces and had the unhurried pace of a town full of people who were not in a particular hurry about anything. When they were younger, the Iyengar children remember being swathed in winter wear and taken into the woods that surrounded their home in Subhash Nagar. There they would get their dose of nature, picking up leaves, fruit, seeds and stones, relishing the quiet companionship of the family.

One of the most cherished memories of the Iyengar children was a month-long trip they made to Bangalore when Iyengar constructed a family home in the city. At the time of the house warming, the newly-built home was transformed into a hostel for the extended family. Iyengar's immediate family, his siblings, their spouses and their children, all thirty of them, were packed into too few bedrooms, the young boys spilling over onto the terrace. The cooks in charge of feeding the battalion were Rama and her girls. This month spent with Anna, Aai, cousins, aunts and uncles remains one of the highlights of their youth.

Iyengar nurtured his old relationships and made sure that he gave them enough attention to keep them thriving. So with his family back in Bangalore, his brothers, sisters and their children, he made it a point to meet and share a masala dosa at their favourite restaurant, Vishranti Bhavan, at least once a week as long as his trip lasted. To the young boy, who had spent the earlier part of his life fighting starvation, sharing food with people he loved became a happy bonding exercise. It was a sign that better times had come.

Iyengar's tryst with the Indian army came through Major General Habibullah who had served in the war in Burma and was now afflicted with painful dysentery. When regular yoga with Iyengar made his symptoms abate, Habibullah, who was the Commandant of the National Defence Academy, Khadakvaasla, wanted his cadets to experience the benefits of yoga.

In 1954, to prove the effects of yoga scientifically, a group of fifty weak cadets was divided into an experimental group and a control group. The control group continued with their army exercises and the experimental group did yoga with Iyengar. At the end of four months, the yoga group showed much better levels of fitness on every parameter. As a result of this, yoga was offered to all cadets in the army. The training was stopped for a short period and restarted in 1976 under the supervision of Geeta and Prashant, Iyengar's daughter and son.

During this period, Iyengar also met luminaries like Sadhu Vaswani, Dr Rajendra Prasad, India's first president, and Nikita

Khrushchev of Russia. He had the opportunity to dazzle them with his mastery of the asanas.

THE ANNUAL EXCURSION TO EUROPE

In 1956, Iyengar went to Europe again, and he continued to do this almost every year till the 1970s. Krishnamurthy was also in Gstaad some months of the year because of an annual talk he gave there and Iyengar continued to teach him till 1965. The circle widened. More and more people, largely musicians – Sir Clifford Curzon, Lilli Kraus and the cellist Jacqueline du Pré – began learning with the yogi.

There were two women who were part of Krishnamurthy's retinue who refused to believe that a man as handsome as Iyengar was not having illicit affairs. They began spying on him at night, to try to find out where he was going and whom he was meeting at night and inadvertently stumbled on some covert nightly operations that one of the female students was engaged in with someone else. The yogi, they found, to their great disappointment, was always sound asleep in bed.

Vanda Scaravelli, one of Krishnamurthy's European disciples, used to host Krishnamurthy every year in her Chalet Tannegg in Gstaad and that is where she first met Iyengar. Having been born into aristocracy, she was often called 'La signora' but she preferred the more down to earth Vanda. She gave grand dinners, inviting an eclectic bunch of people. Celebrities like Fellini, Frederick Le Boyer and Aldous Huxley might be hobnobbing with the butcher who gave her a ride home from the market. An artistic lady with strange proclivities, she would often leave her esteemed guests and go off into a corner to read a book.

Whenever she was hurt, whether it was a sprain or a shattered hip, her first and only question was, 'How soon can I start exercising?' She was once hit by a car and bounced off its hood. She went home, lay down on her bed and did her breathing till she felt fine again.

This passion for yoga was what endeared her to Iyengar, whom she adored, and with whom she conducted an affectionate correspondence.

Vanda used to say that she wasn't always informed in advance when Iyengar had arrived from India, but she knew immediately, from the altered quality of Krishnamurthy's speech, that the yogi had arrived. According to Vanda, Krishnamurthy, after his yoga lessons, was an entirely different person. He became positive, realistic and energetic, completely contrary to his normal self.

Krishnamurthy never wanted to officially admit that he took lessons from Iyengar. A timeline of Krishnamurthy's life mentions that in 1966, Desikachar, a young yoga teacher, was invited to Gstaad to teach Krishnamurthy some yoga exercises. There is no mention at all of Iyengar, who had taught him for a decade prior to this, except by implication in the claim that before 1966 Krishnamurthy had been doing yoga asanas for the sake of his health and not as a spiritual practice.

This was presumably to ward off any claims that Iyengar might make about having helped him on his spiritual journey.

When Iyengar's publisher wrote later in *Light on Yoga* that Krishnamurthy had taken lessons with the yogi, the Krishnamurthy community was up in arms and ready to sue him. Iyengar had no means to corroborate that he had actually taught Krishnamurthy. In all Krishnamurthy's letters to Iyengar, he had always referred to himself as 'K', never spelling out his entire name. Only in one incriminatory letter, which was clearly from Krishnamurthy, there was a sentence in which he openly acknowledged his gratitude to Iyengar for the yoga he had been taught, and this was what helped the yogi escape from being sued.

The acrimonious split between the philosopher and his yoga teacher came in 1965. Hearing Krishnamurthy complain once too often that he found Iyengar too rough, one of his retinue, a Frenchman called Gerard Blitz, had a suggestion. Blitz, the founder of the European Union of Yoga, recommended that instead of bothering with Iyengar, Krishnamurthy could call Iyengar's teacher. Of course when they approached Krishnamacharya he said he was too old, but he sent his son, Desikachar instead.

When Krishnamurthy suddenly and inexplicably shifted to Desikachar, Iyengar had reason to feel hurt. Vanda Scaravelli, who had not even been notified by Krishnamurthy of the fact that Krishnamurthy had decided to shift to Desikachar, was left to clear up the resultant mess. Vanda's fondness for Iyengar must have made it that much harder on her. Krishnamurthy, in his blasé fashion, claimed he had nothing to do with Desikachar being appointed and that it was the doing of his followers.

Iyengar kept in touch with Vanda till her death. Faeq Biria, who runs an Iyengar Yoga Centre in Paris, visited her in Italy with Iyengar. In his strong accent, which is a quaint mélange harking back to his roots in Russia and Iran and his later life in Paris, Faeq recalls Vanda's vivacity and ebullience, even when she was much older.

They were with her when Krishnamurthy passed away in 1986. When he died, 'there was no hole in his body without a tube in it,' Vanda described graphically. Vanda's home was flooded with calls and telegrams of condolence. 'Everyone calls me and sends me telegrams as if I were his wife,' she complained.

Faeq recalls a conversation about Krishnamurthy that left Iyengar stunned. Vanda had been such a long-time admirer and associate of Krishnamurthy, Iyengar thought this was a good time to ask her a question that had long been on his mind.

'Vanda,' he said to her 'You knew him for so long. What did you learn from him?'

'I learned...' Vanda said, with complete seriousness, 'I learned how to lie.'

Towards the end, though, Vanda told Biria that Krishnamurthy thought of Iyengar fondly, often saying he missed him and that he was the 'most genuine one'. Whether this was true or not, the rift between Krishnamurthy and the yogi had become irreparable.

Faeq remembers that Vanda would insist that he and Iyengar eat and would refuse to take a plate herself. 'You eat,' she would say, 'I will watch you.' Then, as soon as Iyengar had picked up his plate, she would start nibbling from his plate. The guru, slightly embarrassed and apologetic about her behaviour and afraid that his young student, Faeq, might get some wrong ideas, would mumble softly to him, 'She is like this only.'

On other occasions, Vanda would demand, 'Mr Iyengar, show me your feet.' Iyengar's feet have had a devoted fan following amongst his students, for their elegance and for the dexterity with which he used them to correct student's poses. But there was no one as direct in her appreciation as Vanda. Her long association with Iyengar, long before he acquired the aura of 'world guru', made her comfortable to do and say things that might have been scandalous coming from someone else. Iyengar, embarrassed, and trying to deflect the attention off his feet, would tell Faeq to display his feet as well. Vanda would dismiss them flatly. 'Long way to go,' she would say to him, as she continued to admire Iyengar's feet.

In the 1960s, Iyengar was on his way back from one of his annual trips to Switzerland. He was taking the train back from Bombay to Pune. When he reached Pune, he discovered that all his earnings, which he had collected for months of work abroad, had been stolen from his pocket. To start with he was devastated, but from this incident Iyengar learned '*vairagya*' or detachment. It was his duty to work, what God gave or took away from him would not be his concern.

Many of Iyengar's pupils, particularly his old Bombay pupils, would receive a letter a week, whether they wrote or not. It would often contain a remonstration because he had not heard from them. Depending on which part of the world he was writing from, the blue inland letters or the aerogrammes festooned with his large, loopy writing became a ubiquitous part of their lives.

Clifford Curzon continued a warm correspondence with Iyengar for many years after they met. In one of his letters he writes charmingly about the arduousness of the yogi's classes – 'We are deeply grateful for your refusal to do less than "kill" us daily.'

One remarkable fact about Iyengar was that he would reply to any correspondence he received either immediately or, when it got too overwhelming, within three days of the receipt of the letter. If he did not reply, one could safely presume that he had not received the letter.

His correspondence with his pupil Dhan was chatty; telling her about recent happenings, discussing the state of his health, answering questions about her health and deliberating over functional oaspects of life and teaching in India; about the transfer of money to India, the procurement of cement and the printing of certificates.

He would chide her when she didn't reply with his exemplary degree of promptness. 'Dear Dhan,' he starts one letter peremptorily, 'No letter from you. I wrote you and was expecting a reply. All want me to write but they do not want to reply. That is another sort of greatness.'

In another letter to Dhan, he recommends some asanas for one of her pupils with angina. At the end of the letter, he says with his characteristic humour, brushed with a stroke of philosophy,

'If you do not know what to do, ask Dhan Palkhivala. She will guide you.'

He often sent postcards to the younger kids from Europe. Irach and Sunoo Taraporevala (Barzo's son and daughter), and Aadil Palkhivala, used to wait for the postman to arrive with the gorgeous postcards with exotic stamps on them, in which Iyengar urged them to study hard or practise yoga every day.

When he returned from his trips, he would bring back gifts for his family. Savita remembers the dolls, dresses and a box of gorgeous Caran d'ache colour pencils that made her the envy of everyone in her school. He would bring sarees, purses and jewellery for Rama. Many of the students remember the pride with which Rama used the little gifts her husband brought back for her.

For some of his older students like Mehera, the Taraporewala family or the Palkhivalas, he would bring back cuckoo clocks, hand-embroidered tablecloths, pens and wonderful little mementoes of his trip.

'When is Anna coming home?' little Savita asked for the fourteenth time that morning.

Ramamani picked her husband's favourite saree from her suitcase. To go with it she carried the purse he had bought her the last time he returned from Europe. Outside, Prashant was still dawdling over his dahi bhaat. The girls were all completely ready. Their hair was neatly plaited and Geeta was helping them all into their special clothes. They had not seen the man of the house for four months. The children missed their father. Ramamani missed her husband. His prompt and newsy letters, though they were eagerly anticipated, would never be a substitute for his presence.

At the Bombay airport, all the local pupils had gathered at the arrival lounge, despite the late hour. The lily garland, which Barzo carried, was a fragrance that the Iyengar children would always remember. It was the fragrance of Anna coming home. After a flurry of namastes, welcome hugs and touching feet, and much excited chatter, the family was ready to have their father to themselves.

This time, as they were returning to Pune on the Deccan Queen, Anna ushered all the kids out of the compartment. The kids were surprised and excited. They went outside and stood in the vestibule, speculating over why Anna might have sent them out.

In the compartment, Sundara fished out a box from his pocket. He looked lovingly at his wife of many years. Opening the box, he took out a beautiful pearl ring and slid it on his wife's finger. When they were married, he could not afford to buy her any jewellery. He wanted to make up for that as soon as he had money. He gave his wife a long, loving hug.

The kids were summoned back into the compartment. Anna asked them to guess what was different about their mother now. The only thing the kids noticed was the warm flush on her cheeks, the contentment in her eyes and the smile that played shyly on her lips. It was not so much the ring, as her husband's care, that had put the smile on her face. Slowly she raised her right hand and showed the children her new acquisition. The girls burst into paroxysms of appreciation and delight. Prashant looked at them all, amused and disinterested. Sundara tried to capture the image of his family in his heart. It would serve him well when he missed them on his next trip abroad.

RECRUITED BY ROYALTY

When Sundara's father had predicted before he died that his son would have a successful life, he may not have seen royalty and such exalted company as Iyengar was now keeping.

Elisabeth of Bavaria, Queen of Belgium, was the wife of King Albert. Having led a full and colourful life, Elisabeth, though of German origin, was the darling of her nation. She had established a nursing unit at the front lines in World War I and had personally served in it as nurse, tending to gory and mangled soldiers and providing them succour as they suffered.

Hardly the occupation of a queen of the land, it imprinted itself on the hearts of the people, who loved her ever after. Her husband, King Albert, died in a climbing accident, a few years after World War I.

In World War II, she rescued thousands of children from sure death by using her influence as queen to prevent them from being deported to Germany. A firm supporter of the Allies, she offered her palace to the British corps, who used it as their headquarters after World War II.

She was dissuaded strongly by her son from visiting Russia. She was a strong-minded woman. Never afraid of what people might say, she travelled to Poland, China and Russia in the 1950s, prompting some people to call her the Red Queen. It was the first time European royalty had visited the Kremlin.

A great aficionado of music and the arts, the queen had always been a patron of famous musicians. Prominent in the music circle at the time was Yehudi Menuhin. Being the yoga teacher of an international celebrity like Menuhin opened many doors for Iyengar. One of them was the door to the palace of the Queen Mother of Belgium.

When they first met, Iyengar told her, 'I can't be your teacher and call you your majesty...Please your majesty, do Trikonasana, and please your majesty, do Virabhadrasana.'

The Queen Mother said, 'Then call me Elisabeth.'

The yogi said, 'No, I will call you Madam.'

This was the amount of respect he accorded every woman, whether she was royalty or not.

At the first meeting, Mr Iyengar greeted her with the traditional folded hands namaskar, which she tentatively returned. When she asked him what was wrong with the Western handshake, he told her that it was an egoistic way of greeting someone, whereas the namaskar expressed humility – the divine in me salutes the divine in you.

Iyengar could hear her think. 'Ok,' she said, 'Let's do it both ways.' As a compromise between East and West, they greeted each other with both a namaste and a handshake. Great yoga guru or not, she was not about to let herself be bludgeoned by his beliefs.

It was probably the same determination that made her demand that Iyengar teach her Shirshasana in 1956. She was eighty-five!

Iyengar was not used to being told by his students what he should teach them. Understandably, he was a trifle nervous. Not only was this a 'royal head', but it was also one that had never done any yoga before. A little alarmed, he asked to see her health reports, to determine if she was healthy enough to do a headstand.

'Do you have faith in yoga?' she countered. Iyengar told her that it was his belief in yoga that had caused him to spend the last thirty years of his life teaching and practising.

'Sir, if you have faith in yoga, why do you want the medical reports? I may be suffering from any number of ailments. Will you teach me to stand on my head or not?' She asked testily. 'If you are afraid to teach me to stand on my head, you can take the first available train to Gstaad and go back to your friend Menuhin who recommended you.' She said all this with probably the same firmness with which she had dealt with her son when he asked her not to visit Russia. Iyengar realized that this doughty old lady was going to brook no resistance. Placing his feet in the classical triangle position to support her, he gave her slow and precise instructions. She placed her hands and head in position and then, gingerly, raised one leg at a time. The eighty-five-year-old was standing on her royal head in a perfect Shirshasana!

In a couple of seconds, however, Iyengar felt her whole body collapse as he continued to hold her up. Her Royal Highness was now unconscious and upside down. Iyengar continued to support her till she regained consciousness.

After the episode was over, he told her that she had lost consciousness because of her high blood pressure and he worked with her over the next few days to bring it back to normal. After she had mastered Shirshasana, Iyengar commissioned the royal palace gardener to help her up in the pose in his absence.

In two weeks the cardiologist was summoned. When he tested her pressure and pulse, he found both completely normal. He was delighted that his medicine was working so well on her. She burst his bubble when she told him she had not been taking his

medication for a week and had instead been taking treatment from
an Indian doctor. The doctor, intrigued, asked to meet Iyengar.
When the yogi was summoned, the doctor asked him what line of
treatment he was using. Iyengar said that he was a yoga practitioner,
at which the Queen Mother piped in with, 'He gave me yogic pills
which made me well.'

Over the years Iyengar had received zillions of plaques, silver
plates, shawls and medallions as gifts for his services. But the queen
gave him one of the most precious gifts he had ever received: a
bronze bust of the yogi, made personally by her Royal Highness.
This likeness of Iyengar stands in the courtyard of the Iyengar home,
as permanent sentinel and reminder of that meeting between the
Queen Mother and the yogi in 1956.

In 1965, when he was teaching in Gstaad, Iyengar received a call
from Queen Elisabeth. She had just had a stroke and needed his
help. He flew there immediately and did some remedial work with
her. In a few days, she was able to grasp a fork in her hand again and
feed herself. 'That's good, but clumsy,' she said drily.

When Iyengar was ready to leave, she raised her right cheek up
to him and ordered, 'Kiss me.' Then she held up the other cheek.
'The other side too,' she said. As the yogi kissed her he felt a tell-tale
wetness on her face. There were tears rolling down her cheeks. He
knew it was the last time he would see her. Queen Elisabeth had
just said a royal goodbye to her yoga guru. She died soon after, on
23 November 1965.

11 July 1959
Bombay

The first thing that strikes Noelle Perez as she enters Bombay is
the peculiar smell in the air. The base note fragrance of Bombay is
reminiscent of wet decomposing garbage, with dominant notes of a

long-neglected public toilet, mixed with top notes of the fishy ocean and acrid vehicle fumes.

Iyengar's Bombay yoga class is in progress. At the back of the room sits the attractive young French woman. She has just travelled all the way from France and is wilting from the combined effects of the smell, the heat, the monsoon and Iyengar's fire. Noelle Perez-Christiaens makes furious mental notes. 'His students are much brighter than the ones I have seen in Europe'. 'He does not tolerate the half way manner of teaching we have in Europe. Everything has to be done right, to the smallest detail'.

After class, she joins the pupils and their teacher at the intimate post-yoga party. From them she learns her first Sanskrit word, 'bhog'. Enjoyment. 'First yog, then bhog,' they tell her, as they persuade her to try yet another fried savoury that sets her mouth on fire.

Two days later, she finds herself on a train to Pune. She eyes the breakfast that she has just been handed on a tray suspiciously. It is an omelette with flecks of red and green in it. She decides that she will pass.

When they reach Pune four hours later, she finds Iyengar himself waiting on the platform for her. She is touched to see her Indian teacher in his kurta and dhoti waiting patiently as she gathers her voluminous luggage. No one else in his family speaks English, he explains to her. This is why he had to come personally. They fix a time for Noelle's class the next day and her new teacher leaves her in the safe custody of her friend, Mrs Homji.

On the second day, she gets lost on the way to the Iyengar home. The son, Prashant is sent out to rescue her. He does not speak a word. He escorts her silently to their home and deposits her with his father, her teacher. 'He is an odd child,' Iyengar says of his only son. 'He does not speak to any woman besides his mother and his sisters.' When his wife was carrying Prashant, he tells Noelle, Mahatma Gandhi appeared in Iyengar's dream and blessed him. The next day he told his wife Rama that they were going to be blessed with a boy. He would be a peaceful philosopher, he had predicted, and decided to call him Prashant. Iyengar tells Noelle about the time they thought they had lost the little boy. Iyengar carried the corpse of the young Prashant to the cremation field in his arms, praying all the while. By the time they reached the cremation ground, Prashant's eyes began to flutter. In minutes, he came back to life. Now, many years older, Prashant stands in the corner of the room, listening to the conversation with dark watchful eyes. He is an unusual child, Noelle thinks as her guru pushes her right knee to the floor in Parshva Pindasana.

Five days later Noelle writes to her parents in France, 'He is a fantastic teacher, but his style of teaching is very hard at first...He knows that you have just relaxed a tiny little muscle in the big toe of your left foot whilst he was adjusting your right knee...He is aware that he is asking too much of me...but he trains me to teach. He truly tries to give the best of himself in concentrated form, to help all the French (people), indirectly, through me. He is truly the most passionate teacher I have met till now.'

When Iyengar finds out where she has been staying, he recommends a change of hotel. 'You have come here to study,' he says, 'not to get sick.'

Noelle wears a striped two-piece bikini for her yoga practise. It is the rage in Paris that year. The Iyengars have never even seen the members of their own family in this state of advanced undress. Only young Savita, too young to bridle her curiosity, creeps in from behind Noelle as she practices and keeps touching her. Thinking that it is the hand of her guru correcting her, Noelle keeps trying to better the pose till she exclaims aloud that she cannot go any further. Iyengar chuckles. It was Savita touching her all the while to see if Noelle's skin felt any different from theirs.

Noelle feels herself ensconced in the warmth of a family. Every time she comes into the home, Savita announces her arrival with, 'That girl as big as a house is back.' Geeta, with her pliable youthful body, does her yoga practise with Noelle. Rama feeds her unforgettable meals. The girls tie her hair into neat plaits. Her tall, slim frame is draped in one of Rama's sarees. Iyengar's arduous yoga sessions are punctuated by talk. He talks to her about Hindu philosophy, Christian philosophy, his yoga and his early life. Her spirit brims over with the generosity of her guru.

'He does not act the perfect irreproachable teacher. This way he is near to us and can take us in his wake. He is the Lord incarnate.' Noelle writes to her mother in a spurt of enthusiastic devotion to her new guru.

Months later, Noelle is in Bombay ready to fly home to France. Iyengar stands at the entrance of his train back to Pune and waves goodbye to his Bombay pupils. Then he looks at Noelle and says a fond farewell. 'Tell your mother I sent you back whole and not in pieces.'[32]

32 Perez-Christiaens, Noelle, *Sparks of Divinity: The Teachings of B.K.S. Iyengar*, Berkeley: Rodmell Press, 1976

'THE BOOK' IS BORN

B arzo Taraporewala, with his thick glasses and his Groucho Marx moustache was a ubiquitous presence in Guruji's life. When the irrepressible Mehera burst into class one day, telling them that a leading Indian publisher was interested in a book on yoga, it fell to Barzo Taraporewala to take an appointment with Jal Taraporewala, the proprietor of Taraporewala Publishers. Maybe it was felt that the fact that they shared the same last name would work some magic charm. Iyengar was summoned with his album of photographs, which was still doing yeoman service. The publisher saw them and liked them, but everyone present agreed that the photographs lacked commentary. The lay public needed more specific instructions on how to reach the final pose. It was decided that Barzo would write about three selected standing poses, mentioning the name of the asana, the history or story associated with it, and finally a list of the benefits of doing the pose.

This was to be done in the simplest, most unostentatious language possible, and submitted for approval. Barzo's background in legal writing had already trained him for just such a task. His training with Guruji prepared him to understand what his teacher wanted to say. His taciturn nature and his command over the language helped him reach the essence of what needed to be said in the fewest and simplest words.

In the meanwhile, Guruji approached the Weling Studio in Pune and took a series of black-and-white photographs to indicate each step in the progression of the asana. It was backbreaking work, entailing several retakes and much patience and attention to detail. Often, the Iyengar children would accompany their father to these interminable shooting sessions, and sit watching the shoot, telling him when there were shadows appearing in the camera frame.

Besides this, Guruji would now spend his three-hour train journey between Bombay and Pune penning notes on each asana, which could then be used as guidelines by Barzo who would reword them in more grammatical English. The other old student, Martha Wartenberger, proved invaluable too. A Jewish émigré from Hungary during World War II, she had made Bombay her home. She too, like Barzo, helped with the editing.

But even as they were working hard on this book, the Bombay publisher, feeling he did not want a book so heavy with illustrations, backed out. The trio decided that too much work had gone into it. They would persist and finish the work, regardless.

Guruji had brought several books from his personal library as reference material, including the *Hatha Yoga Pradipika*, the *Gherunda Samhita* and *Siva Samhita*, and classics like the *Bhagawad Geeta*, the Upanishads and the *Yoga Sutras* of Patanjali. To which Barzo added his own collection, the most precious being Apte's Sanskrit English dictionary and Barzo's hand-written notes from the discourses of an unknown pandit on the *Yoga Sutras*.

Armed with all these, they created what went on to become the top-selling yoga book the world over, for decades.

The trio would meet every Saturday evening after class in Barzo's flat at Kemps Corner. Over endless cups of coffee, and plied with snacks by Barzo's wife, Sheru, they ploughed through every pose in the book.

Undisturbed by the shrieks and screams of Barzo's three children playing around them, they would carry on their work, occasionally fortified by Guruji's favourite steaming-hot Punjabi samosa from a nondescript shop around the corner. They would stop for a break to read and review Barzo's immaculately typed manuscript for the day. Often they would be at loggerheads over the usage of a particular word or phrase, and Barzo, a stickler for language, would not want to settle for any word that he felt was even slightly inaccurate. Martha would pour out a cup of hot coffee and try to assuage everyone's feelings, generally convincing Barzo to allow Guruji to have the last word, as it was, after all, his book.

The last chapter of the book, on Pranayama, was written in Pune, with Rama providing the sustenance by way of all the wonderful South Indian delicacies she was so good at rustling up. This time they were working towards a deadline, so Barzo had to spend fifteen days asking his guru relentless questions, before he started any writing. Barzo compares the writing of this chapter to Ved Vyaasa and Ganapathi. Brahma the creator approached Ved Vyaasa to write down the *Mahabharata*. Ved Vyaasa realized that it was too daunting a task to undertake on his own and asked for help. Ganesha, the elephant-headed God was sent to him. Ganesha agreed to undertake the task, but laying down the condition that he would write non-stop. If Ved Vyaasa stopped the narration, Ganesha would leave. Ved Vyaasa was disconcerted. He wondered if he could keep up with Ganesha's writing. He came up with his own proviso; he said that Ganesha was to take nothing down if he did not understand it. And every time he felt Ganesha was catching up, Ved Vyaasa would throw an incomprehensible stanza at him, and force him to slow down. In Barzo's modern analogy it was the scribe who insisted on comprehending everything before he wrote it down.

When Iyengar went to Europe that year to teach, he took with him the manuscript that they had been labouring over. Angela Marris and Beatrice Harthan were musicians who played with Menuhin and took classes with Iyengar in Switzerland when he was teaching there. The two women were best friends and lived together all their lives in a little flat in London.

Iyengar gave Angela and Beatrice a copy of the manuscript so meticulously prepared in India and told them the story of its rejection. Since publishers in the UK accept manuscripts only formatted in a particular way, Angela and Beatrice undertook to retype the original manuscript. In the course of this exercise, they found that the continental typewriter was configured differently and that it had left the newly-typed manuscript peppered with errors. So the two decided to take it back home to England and type it out on a typewriter which they were used to.

The two women were not only busy musicians but were also avidly involved with Oriental spirituality, which was evidenced by their enjoyment of Iyengar's classes. Beatrice was making her way to the Buddhist Society Conference straight from the airport with the manuscript still in her bag. Fate directed her to sit beside Gerald Yorke, her old friend and then editor at the publishing company George Allen & Unwin. When Beatrice mentioned that she was just returning from the continent after a fulfilling session with her yoga teacher, Yorke told her that his company had been looking for a new yoga book that could replace a rival publisher, Rider & Company's very popular *Hatha Yoga* by Theos Barnard.

Coincidence layered upon coincidence. When Beatrice pulled out Iyengar's manuscript replete with black-and-white photographs and terse writing on each asana, Yorke leafed through it excitedly.

'This is the book I have been waiting for,' he said loudly, attracting several disapproving glances from the other participants.

This sounds like a corny sequence that has been written for a feel-good film, with a scant eye to reality, but that is how it happened. That is the way the most popular yoga book in modern history, *Light on Yoga*, came to see the light of day.

When Iyengar met Yorke in 1963, he apparently told the yogi, 'You are a very good teacher, but a very bad writer.' He warned him that the book would need considerable editing. Iyengar was impressed with his honesty and professionalism. From then on, he considered Yorke his 'literary guru', and was open to whatever suggestions Yorke had to make.

Barzo writes of Yorke that 'his ability to condense and clarify was uncanny, and with a few excisions and corrections...the writer's work improved immeasurably.'

Of course Yorke had a keen eye for what would work in the market. He demanded that the abstruse commentary on traditional texts be omitted. He wanted a fresh approach that did not weigh the book down with pedantry. If people wanted the classics, they would read translations. There was no need to regurgitate that information here.

Then he demanded a rewriting of the introduction, paring down the unnecessary and condensing the necessary. The trio in Bombay got to work again. It was re-sent to Yorke. He was still not happy. Iyengar, Barzo and Martha got to work again and many cups of coffee, sandwiches and samosas later, were able to finally come up with an introduction that Yorke approved of.

After the photos for the book were complete, Iyengar showed them to Krishnamacharya. The guru cast a critical eye over them and said, 'All the poses are wrong.'

Iyengar said, 'Please tell me what is wrong. I will correct them.'

'Everything is wrong.' His dealings with the world had given Iyengar enough confidence to feel he should go ahead despite his guru's disapproval.

In 1965, when *Light on Yoga* was complete, Iyengar asked his guru to write a foreword for the book. But Krishnamacharya, in his usual fashion, refused outright.

When Iyengar was writing *Light on Pranayama*, his guru had warned him that he could speak on pranayama if he liked, but that he should not write a word on this esoteric practise. But Iyengar had already committed himself to his publisher.

The process of writing was the same. On the Deccan Queen to and from Bombay, Iyengar would spend time formulating his thoughts and putting them down on paper. The next week, in sessions with Barzo and now a new collaborator, Madhu Tijoriwala, these would be crystallized into prose. When Iyengar began work on *Light on Pranayama*, there were more hands and minds to help put it together. Just like in the old days, this group of teachers would sit together and brainstorm on what should be added, what should be left out and how it could all be better expressed. By now Martha Wartenberger had passed away, so it was Tijoriwala who would convince Barzo to give up *le mot juste* and concede to Iyengar's wishes.

When it was ready, Sundara took it to Krishnamacharya. His guru took the book and asked Sundara to return at four the next evening. Sundara did not dare ask him for a foreword this time. When Iyengar returned, he asked his guru if he had looked through the book. 'Yes. I have read it. You can take it back.' Sundara, hungry for some acknowledgement from his guru, said, 'What did you think of it?'

'I have written inside,' said the guru. Sundara was happy to accept that as his guru's blessing. It became the foreword to his second book.

PUNE EMBRACES IYENGAR

It was much later in the 1960s that Iyengar's hometown, Pune, woke up to the jewel they had in their midst. They embraced Iyengar much after Bombay city and the world had claimed him as their own.

Jimmy Dastoor was a Parsi from Pune, endowed with the wonderful and whacky sense of humour that many of his community are blessed with. He owned a photography shop on East Street called the Vaman and Dastoor Photo Store. Iyengar often went to the store to pick up his supply of photographic film, but Jimmy did not know him by name.

Jimmy had a back problem that was getting worse every day. The best physicians in Pune had thrown up their hands in despair. Finally, Dr Modi, one of the most respected doctors in Pune, told him there was only one person who could help him with his back, an Iyengar, who taught yoga somewhere in Pune. After this, they got recommendations from several friends that Jimmy should see Iyengar. They kept trying to find out his address or phone number, but with no success. They had no idea how to find this elusive Iyengar.

Jimmy's pain was becoming so intense that he would complain if his kids played on the floor beside his bed. Even this mild vibration would send shooting pains up his spine. He was confined to bed, and had to be sponged and fed there.

Collie, Jimmy's wife, discovered that their friends the Pudumjees were learning yoga from Iyengar. She finally learnt that while they had been hunting all over Pune for him, he had actually been frequenting their shop for years.

When Collie approached Iyengar, she did it gingerly. She had heard he had a fearsome temper and she did not want to be at the receiving end of it. Iyengar set all her fears at rest in the first encounter. He was the epitome of sweetness. No, he told her, he had no general class in Pune yet. He was perfectly willing to start one though, if she managed to rope in eight students. The fee would be twenty-five rupees each month, as compared to sixty rupees for a private class.

Collie managed to persuade six people to join the class. They found a hall in a school called the Gujarathi Kalyan Shaala on Convent Street. Half an hour before the class, Iyengar would ride up to the class on his Lambretta scooter, with Rama and Savita riding pillion. A few minutes later, the older Iyengar children would whiz in on their bicycles, and join their parents. To make some extra money the school would often rent the hall out for wedding functions and parties. Then the class would summarily be shifted to another space at very short notice. On those days, Iyengar would ride towards his pupils' homes so as to catch them midway and inform them of the changed venue as they walked to class.

Guruji helped Jimmy get back on his feet. As soon as he got better, though, Jimmy left the class, as did the other four of the first pupils. Collie Dastoor was the only one left of the early students. What seemed an unfortunate situation turned out to be a blessing! It was a precious period for Collie. She still counts it amongst the most memorable times of her life. Guruji, Rama and all the children would come into class with her and they would all practise together.

Attendance to the Pune class remained desultory till Guruji got back home from his trip to Europe one year. The Pune newspapers featured an article on the Queen Mother of Belgium and Yehudi Menuhin taking yoga classes from Iyengar. When Guruji returned to Pune that year, there was no space to stand in his class.

The students went to class with their cotton blankets under their arms. Collie used to take a rope along that she would tie to the ventilator, so Guruji could have some pupils use the rope in class. There were no chairs, no wooden benches, no stools and no bolsters. Guruji would make the students use even the raised stage as a prop. Pupils hanging off the edge of the stage or dangling off the window ledge in a supported backbend was a common sight.

Geeta Iyengar was then an exquisite looking eighteen-year-old, dressed in a white saree, devoid of any jewellery, except for a slim watch on her wrist. Geeta had by now begun helping her father in class. When Geeta was a child, the Iyengars had taken her to an astrologer. He had told her astounded parents that this child would either become a scoundrel or a saint. Geeta seemed to have made the choice.

The young girls in the Pune class were looked after by Vanita, Guruji's second child. Guruji playfully called them all Gaja Lakshmis (Elephant Goddesses) or 'hippies' because many of them were overweight and had large hips. Like all children in Iyengar classes, they did endless backbends and Viparitachakrasanas. Guruji did not believe that meditation and pranayama should ever be taught to young children. When asked what kind of yoga and meditation children should be taught at a young age, he would often say, 'They should be taught to play.'

Collie's daughter, Navaz, and her younger sister went to the classes to start with but the sister walked out after a pranayama class and never came back. Both the children always breathed through their mouths because of their constant colds and sinuses. This was forbidden in a pranayama practise. When Guruji once caught the young girl doing pranayama through her mouth, he hit her across the mouth. Hurt both physically and emotionally, she never came back to class.

Navaz, for some reason, was not deterred by anything her guru said or did. Her dedication to yoga and her gratitude to her guru remain unabated even today.

Navaz remembers going to yoga class directly after school. She used to happily go off into a corner and fall asleep in Shirshasana. When Guruji noticed what she was doing, he decided he would teach her a Shirshasana she would never forget. He made her do her asana against a window with a wooden column in the centre. To make it worse, the top half of the wooden beam had some rusty wooden nails battered into it. Navaz's comfortable-enough-to-sleep-in asana had just been converted by a slight shift of position into one that demanded complete awareness and attention. One wrong move would have her either dangling outside the window or impaled on the rusty nails of her own personal cross.

The floor of the school was made of uneven mosaic chips. These would leave painful patterns on their limbs as they practised, making blankets an absolute necessity. Shirshasana was normally done along the sides of the room, in two rows facing each other. Guruji would nonchalantly walk between the two rows of students trying to keep their balance, and then playfully, quick as a flash, give someone a swift push so the poor student teetered over. The sound that emanated from the crashing body on the floor was proportionate to the size of the person who had just been pushed. Guruji would then grin and tell them that he was teaching them to have control over their bodies and the way they fell. The students were not sure how much control it created in them. What it definitely did was make them all very wary of Guruji when he passed by them as they did the asana.

Some years later, the pranayama class was started on Thursdays in the Vidya Bhavan hall. Father Antony Lobo, a Catholic priest from Pune, was also part of this class. For his old pupils this class was a long way from their homes. It entailed two changes of buses and for many of them the distance they had to travel made it feel like a picnic out of town.

The pranayama classes were intense, serious and demanding. After class, on moonlit nights, the Desai family, another Parsi family that attended the classes en masse, would make a giant cauldron of vegetable biryani, which the students would share by the pallid moonlight. The students and their teacher shared a warm camaraderie. With Guruji around, there was always a lot of gentle ribbing too, which everyone felt the brunt of at one time or other.

Guruji had an atavistic matchmaking gene that sometimes came to the fore, especially when he encountered single pupils who he felt were of marriageable age. At these biryani sessions, he would try his best to pair off one of his Parsi bachelor students called Pesi Pocha with a daughter of the Desai family. Though this particular attempt didn't bear fruit, there were many students who later became couples with Guruji playing Cupid. Later, in the 1980s and 1990s, his students Pandu, Birjoo and Faeq, all got married to the girls that Guruji picked for them.

SPREADING HIS WINGS

Like most Indians, Iyengar too had a fascination for pilgrimages. He had made multiple trips to Tirupathi and to other sacred spots in India. Now that he was travelling to Europe every year, his Western students suggested that he meet the Pope. Iyengar was excited by the thought, but procuring the permission was a protracted affair.

Iyengar had a preliminary meeting with the Bishop of Pune, who teased him about how he did not look like a yogi at all, considering he did not have matted hair, a beard, orange robes, beads and a kamandalu. His preconceptions about yogis were even more deeply shattered when he found out that Iyengar rode a scooter. He was a warm and friendly man and was happy to give Iyengar a letter, which was a personal introduction from him. 'Make sure you wear a false wig and beard,' he joshed, as he handed the letter to Iyengar.

The letter from the Bishop began,

'I am hereby introducing you to perhaps the greatest artiste of our time, an Indian Yogi...'

It went on to request an interview with the Pope who would be 'most interested in him and his art'.

Iyengar was given a date for his meeting with the Pope. By one of those strange miscommunications, he got the date wrong and had to request another date. On 18 July 1966, he got a cable confirming either 20 or 27 July for an interview.

27 July was fixed. Picked up by Alberto Scaravelli in a car that was none too dependable, they set off for the Vatican. Aghast at the disorganization of Roman traffic, they finally reached Castle Gandalfo, the Pope's summer residence. Negotiating intense security, they were shunted around from one place to the other. They finally made their way to the parking and had a quick coffee before they walked to the gates. When they got there, they found the invitation was for only one person and Alberto had to cool his heels in the cafeteria, as they refused to let him in.

Iyengar walked in alone into an ostentatiously decorated hall where 200 other people waited. Iyengar gasped. He thought it was going to be a private audience. Though there were people from all over the world, he was the only Indian there, looking rather regal in his dhoti, kurta and shawl.

People were summoned in a few at a time, and when his turn came, he felt a shiver of excitement to see the Pope, dressed in flowing yellow robes, with a white cap on his head. Though he was surrounded by the panoply of the Roman Catholic Church, there was simplicity in his demeanour that reached out to Iyengar. The Pope held Iyengar's hands firmly in his own and blessed him. When Iyengar asked if he could demonstrate for him, he begged off, saying there was no time, though he had seen the book and enjoyed it. Iyengar then gave him the gifts he had brought him, some spiritual literature by Sadhu Vaswani and a sandalwood walking stick. The Pope, in return, gave him a bronze medal with the Pope's profile on it and his dates. He gave this to Iyengar, held his hand and blessed his work yet again. Again Iyengar asked if he could demonstrate for him and the Pope refused. Iyengar was led out of the Vatican with the volunteers performing the guard of honour, which is reserved for heads of state and special guests of the Pope.

Iyengar was very touched to meet 'God's chosen representative on Earth' and receive his blessing. He counted it among the most special moments of his life.

Iyengar did not cringe when, after being refused once, he asked the Pope again whether he could demonstrate for him. This was vintage Iyengar. He had never been afraid of rejection. To him his ego had nothing to do with it. For a man who was famed for being egoistic, he displayed, on occasion, a childlike egolessness. He was doing this to further the cause of yoga and he never allowed it to degenerate into a personal slight. It was the attitude of a child at play. A few scrapes and bruises were not going to stop him. He was concentrating on the game. He would wipe his bloody elbow or knee with a muddied fist and get right back into it.

IMPRESSIONS OF AMERICA

Iyengar's welcome to America was not entirely wholesome. America was in the throes of the Civil Rights Movement when he visited. In his usual brisk and confident manner, Iyengar began to stride out of the aircraft. The officials held him back. 'Please wait for the white passengers to disembark,' they told him firmly. Iyengar had entered an unequal world.

In 1956, *Life* magazine had sandwiched between advertisements for Kodak slides and Durkee's homogenized margarine, an article entitled 'A New Twist for Society'. It featured Iyengar on his first visit to the USA. The high-profile reportage happened because he was teaching the heiress of the Standard Oil Company, Rebekah Harkness. A friend of Yehudi Menuhin, who fancied herself a music buff and a composer of value, she now wanted to discover the benefits of the yoga programme that had benefitted Menuhin.

The photograph that accompanies the article is a breath-taking one of Iyengar in Vrishchikasana. He is poised on a wall of barely one-and-a-half foot width with a sheer drop into the beach and ocean on one side and a serene stone Cupid overlooking the feat.

There are other photographs of Iyengar and the Harkness family doing a collective Paschimottanasana and another of Iyengar looking suspiciously like he is about to smack the son who has just collapsed in a shoulder stand variation, and a third photo of a free class that Harkness had, out of the generosity of her heart, arranged for her neighbours. Iyengar felt that these ladies clad in their skimpy shorts were not prompted by any true interest in yoga. He was sure they were lured there by the prospect of being captured, for posterity, by *Life* magazine. Still, he attempted to shepherd them into asanas.

The article speaks of how Rebekah and the children were feeling more relaxed and happy after their yoga practise and how she, personally, had plans to go to India for a year to study in Pune with Iyengar.

Despite the picture-perfect family poses and the high-wattage publicity, all was not well with the family. Besides her marriage into wealth, Rebekah had attained fame for some very dubious activities. When the rest of America was reeling under the effects of the Great Depression, Rebekah was known to have cleaned out her pool with Dom Perignon. She had once added mineral oil into the punch at her sister's debutante ball. Another time she had been escorted off an ocean liner for the collective sins of shouting obscenities at the general populace, throwing dinner plates at an orchestra of Filipinos who were innocuously playing the American national anthem, and for offending the sensibilities of her fellow passengers by swimming nude. She was known to have filled her fish tank with goldfish and Scotch and having dyed her cat green. When her husband William died in 1954, she renovated her Rhode Island home, installing eight kitchens and twenty-one baths. When her daughter survived several failed suicide attempts, she is reported to have said, 'How should she do it? Is there a chic way to go?' Her son counted the years he spent in prison amongst the happiest in his life.

After six weeks of yoga study with Iyengar, Rebekah claimed to be a yogi. 'You see,' she was famed to say, 'Money can buy anything.'

Iyengar lived with them for six weeks. In the house with twenty-one bathrooms. Though Rebekah was on her best behaviour when Iyengar was visiting, he could probably sense the self-indulgence, decadence and hedonism that characterized her life. 'I saw Americans were interested in the three Ws: wealth, women and wine,' he said. 'I was taken aback to see how their way of life conflicted with (life in) my own country. I thought twice about coming back.' After that visit Iyengar declared that it was the last time he would visit America.

Simultaneously, he began to tire of the circuit he was doing amongst the ranks of the rich and powerful. Something in him wanted to reach the ordinary man on the street. Maybe the house with twenty-one bathrooms had been the last straw!

YOGA BRINGS PEOPLE TOGETHER

After World War II, when the rest of the world was nauseated by racial discrimination and its possible repercussions, South Africa institutionalized apartheid. In 1948, the National Party won the national election on a platform of racism and segregation. With the protection of the law, apartheid created cruel and forcible separations between people. When people disobeyed, the state machinery would come down hard upon them, quelling all resistance.

There was physical segregation of races and many areas were declared only-white areas, where blacks and Indians were not allowed to hold property. The administration concentrated on eliminating what they called 'black spots' within white areas, moving the coloured inhabitants from their homes and land and shifting them to undeveloped areas outside the city. Besides this, coloured people were not allowed to vote.

Menuhin's Jewish roots left him very sensitive to discrimination of any sort. During the war, he gave 500 free concerts for the American and British troops. Once Hitler came to power, Menuhin refused all invitations from the Berlin Philharmonic. As soon as the war was over, he played two concerts for the recently liberated inmates of Bergen-Belsen and another camp at Bardowiek.

Menuhin visited South Africa in 1950, his skin already bruised by the horrors of the Holocaust. Intolerance and injustice of any kind abraded him to the core. Blacks were not allowed into his performances in South Africa, so he held a special performance for them. When his promotion agency threatened to sue him for these performances, Menuhin said he would publicize this widely in the London media, making the agency hastily back down.

This was a time when Indians were not allowed to visit South Africa. Menuhin, whose hackles rose against any discrimination, wrote a strongly-worded letter to an organization he was part of in South Africa, the International Arts Youth League. He suggested that Iyengar be invited. If they did not invite him, Menuhin threatened, he would withdraw his membership too. 'I cannot accept privileges for one race while permitting the exemption of other races,' he wrote.

A flurry of newspaper articles covered Menuhin and Iyengar's struggle against apartheid, lauding their courage. It was in 1979 that Iyengar finally stepped onto South African soil.

But the South Africans could not wait that long. In the 1960s, Swami Venkatesananda (disciple of Swami Sivananda), Joyce Stuart (a South African teacher of yoga), and a few other students who had taken classes from Iyengar in London invited him to South Africa. When this did not work, they arranged that Iyengar teach the South Africans in Mauritius, which was neutral ground. There were eleven students from South Africa in the first class, and every year the number increased.

Mauritius was still an undeveloped island, and most necessities had to be shipped in. According to Joyce Stuart, the first classes 'were conducted in hotel lounges, on beaches, flat concrete rooftops and even on an old tennis court'.[33]

During classes, the students got their dose of the Iyengar fire, and also his passion, as in the absence of his customary props 'a stack of biscuit tins...as well as a hotel couch (were) dismantled in a swirl of yogic zeal, (testing) the hotel manager's patience to the limit!'

Joyce Rensburg was a participant in the first workshop. She had never studied yoga with a teacher before. A trifle unsure, she tried to become inconspicuous by placing her yoga mat at the back of the hall. As she struggled to keep pace with Iyengar's instructions, she heard his footsteps padding firmly towards her.

'Who is your teacher?' asked the thundering voice.

'Sir, I have no teacher,' Joyce whispered, her heart filled with dread, 'only your book'.

Joyce held her breath, waiting for the explosion.

Instead, Iyengar said, nodding his head with approval, 'Yes! A good book is better than a bad teacher.'

---

33   http://www.bksiyengar.co.za/history.aspx

To compensate for all those months she had practised without a teacher, he said, 'You go to the front of the class and work under my nose.' Many of these early pupils went on to establish Iyengar institutes of their own, and Iyengar now has as devoted a fan following in South Africa as he does in most other parts of the world.

AND MEANWHILE IN RAMAMANI'S HOME

12 July 1961

Rama sat on the porch, plaiting young Savita's hair and singing the songs of her favourite composer, Purandharadasa...
'Narayana, ninna naamada smaraneya,
Sara amruthavenna naligeege barali.'
'Oh Narayana, the thought of your name,
Is the essence of nectar and let it come to my tongue.'
In the background were the sounds of Prashant practising his violin. The fragrance of fresh rice and drumstick sambhar wafted into the main room where Geeta was helping Suchita with her Marathi essay on Chhatrapati Shivaji. Iyengar was abroad, teaching, as had become the annual routine.

Sunita and Vanita came running into the house, their clothes completely drenched, their plaits dripping. Their shoes squelched muddy brown water onto Rama's spotless floor.

Vanita said, 'The waters are rising everywhere. They have stopped traffic from entering the city.'

'There were policemen all over, Aai. They told us to go home immediately. The first floor of Garware College has been submerged,' Sunita chimed in.

Geeta walked over to the Murphy transistor radio and tried to tune into the news. At first, the crackle of radio static came on. Then, the sweet sounds of Ali Akbar Khan's sarod flooded the room. Outside, the sound of rain was like distant drumbeats.

Rama tied the bow to finish off Savita's plait. 'Prashant, go to the neighbours and see if you can find out what is happening and come back right away,' said Rama.

Prashant returned with news that the army had been called in. The neighbours had all taken their precious possessions and were up on the terrace in the hope that the deluge wouldn't reach that level.

Rama shepherded her children upstairs. As soon as they were safe and dry, she started walking down the stairs.

Even before it was completed, Panshet Dam had begun developing problems. Despite better advice, the municipality was trying to fill it up in the monsoon of 1961. Cracks started developing in the dam and the army was summoned to take control of the situation, as Pune was in danger of flooding if the waters burst. The army jawans loaded the dam with thousands of sandbags, but managed only to delay the inevitable by a few hours. Instead of entering the city and drowning sleeping Puneites in the dead of night, the waters were held back till later in the day, when the city was awake and could be more prepared.

The uncontrollable deluge from Panshet broke the smaller dam at Khadakvaasla. Though some people were warned and started shifting out of their homes onto higher ground, there was no definite flood warning.

The low-lying areas were completely deluged, and water entered the old Peths and the Deccan Gymkhana area. All the bridges other than the Bund Garden Bridge were submerged. The Panshet Dam carried water enough for the city of Pune for a year. This was unleashed onto the city in hours. The worst part of it was the complete chaos. The electricity and water supply were cut off completely and phones were not working. The only thing that was working overtime was the rumour machine.

Rama hurried downstairs and rummaged around. The children were afraid. They wanted their mother to come back. 'Aai', they called plaintively.

She returned in a few minutes. Carefully wrapped up in her arms, she carried the Light on Yoga *manuscript. This was the condensation of her husband's work on earth so far, and she could not allow it to come to any harm. Her jewellery, money and other material possessions were all unimportant in comparison. The manuscript was second only to her children.*

The waters of the Panshet Dam rose and fell without harming the Iyengar home. But with Rama's unruffled clarity, Iyengar's manuscript would have probably survived any flood.

When Rama came to Pune, she could not speak a word of the local language, Marathi. She did not even have any broken English to fall back on like Iyengar did. In just a few years, it was she who helped the kids with their schoolwork, whether it was Math or Marathi. How she picked it up is difficult to say, but Geeta remembers her mother not only explaining Marathi poetry to her for school, but also reading novels in Marathi.

Geeta says that her mum in her first couple of years in Pune began to understand Marathi, but could not speak it at all. When she returned from Tumkur after Geeta's birth, she suddenly began to converse fluently, without making the typical mistakes with gender that most South Indian speakers make while speaking a Devnagari tongue. Like English, most of the Dravidian languages do not ascribe genders to objects, so non-native speakers find this a stumbling block. Iyengar often struggled to get his genders right, but Rama was a natural.

Though Rama was from a small town in traditional South India, she never passed judgment on the Westerners who visited them or on how they dressed. She encouraged Geeta and the girls to wear shorts while they practised yoga to aid mobility.

The Pune shorts were born of Rama and her friend Dhan Palkhivala's efforts to design a yoga costume that would make sense for the women in the Indian culture and climate. They came up with the Pune yoga shorts, which were essentially bloomers with an elastic band at the thigh to prevent them from riding up.

Though Rama never participated in the class, she would often come and assist, particularly during pranayama classes. Collie Dastoor talks about 'Amma', as the Pune pupils called Rama, adjusting her spine and straightening her back in pranayama and instructing her in sparse, but clear, English.

Very fond of music, Rama inculcated this into her children as well. Prashant played the violin and the girls learnt dance and music. Rama never pushed the children into doing anything. She did not insist, like most Indian mothers, that her daughters learn to cook. And yet learn they did. It was almost osmotic. Rama used to suffer from migraine headaches, which would leave her incapacitated. At times like this, not even her husband's yoga could relieve her pain. At these times the girls naturally took over the household responsibilities.

In the early days, Guruji was quite worried about Prashant and his seeming lack of motivation for anything besides the violin. Guruji would cite Dhan as an example and say look how strict she is with the kids and how well they are turning out, implying that Rama should be stricter with Prashant. But Rama was unconcerned with how anyone else brought up their children. She gave her children unconditional love and allowed them to discover themselves. She knew that, in the end, they would turn out right.

Geeta had nephritis when she was a young girl. She was in a coma for several days. The situation got so bad that Guruji actually began to feel that he might not be able to bear the endless expenses of doctors and hospitals. When she came out of coma, he told the doctors he wanted to take her home. Doctor Grant was the physician in charge. He refused to grant them permission to take her home. If Guruji wanted to take his daughter home, it would be at his own risk. Both Guruji and Rama felt this was a risk they were willing to take.

Geeta was brought home and put on a strict regimen of yoga. All medication was stopped, and despite this she began to get better every day. When they took her to the doctor for a routine check-up a few months later, the doctor found her much better and told them that they should continue with the medication she had been taking. Geeta was taking no medicine. Only doing the yoga recommended by her father.

Whenever Iyengar returned from a trip abroad, Rama would make a trip to Tirupathi and to visit Krishnamacharya, who had shifted to Madras after the closing of the Yogashaala. Rama felt that the family owed all they had to him.

Krishnamacharya stayed at the Iyengar home on three occasions – twice in 1962 and once in 1978. Despite his famous temper, Rama was never afraid of him. She knew how to anticipate his every need and made sure she always had everything ready for him before he even asked for it.

Ramamani's consideration was not reserved exclusively for the guru. Bhikubai was the domestic help at the Iyengar home. She had six children, all of whom called Rama 'Aai' (mother). Even in the days when the Iyengars did not have too much, Rama would cook enough so she could feed her children as well as Bhikubai's family. They remember her curd rice and tamarind rice and a special sweet of cashew and almond made every Thursday when Anna had a difficult practise session. Even without the arduous practise, all the rest of them got to share the sweet.

Tukaram, Bhikubai's son, remembers a theft occurring in the Iyengar home. The silver vessels that the family ate in went missing.

Aai, as they called her, refused to call the police. She knew that the finger of suspicion would automatically fall upon Bhikubai's family, and she trusted them completely. She would rather lose her possessions than subject her help to the ignominy of police questioning. The police later came in and asked whether they had had a theft in the house and requested her to identify the stolen objects. They had caught the thief who admitted he had stolen the family silver. Rama's faith was rewarded.

BELLUR BOY IN BRITAIN

The 1960s were years filled with promise and heartbreak for the western world. It was a decade of struggle. People were struggling for basic rights – civil rights, human rights, environmental rights and employment rights. People were fighting for the right to reclaim their sexuality – homosexuality was still illegal and punishable with imprisonment. Women were fighting for their rights – abortion was still considered a crime.

The world had been through two world wars in half a century. The senselessness of it all had already struck the masses. There was a ferment of disapproval over America's murderous war against the Vietnamese people. There was the fear of an imminent nuclear war. A short fuse in the head of someone in the Kremlin or the Pentagon and the nuclear war button could be pressed, signalling the end of the world as they knew it. In South Africa, they were fighting against apartheid. The Civil Rights Movement, though it would finally make the world a better place, made each city a potential powder keg. Consumerism went through the roof. John F. Kennedy and Martin Luther King, the icons of the age, were both assassinated. In 1966, *Time* magazine's cover story asked, 'Is God Dead?' The story described the guidelines for being a hippie:

'Do your own thing, wherever you have to and whenever you want. Drop out. Leave society as you have known it. Leave it utterly. Blow the mind of every straight person you can reach. Turn them on, if not to drugs, then to beauty, love, honesty, and fun.' – Timothy Leary

Iyengar at Mumbai airport leaving for Europe.
L-R: Sukhtankhkar, Dhan Palia, Freny Palia, Burzo Taraporewala,
Ramamani, Madhu Tijoriwala, Diana Mahalaxmiwala, BKS Iyengar, Dhan
Palkhivala, Dr. D'Souza, Sheila D'souza, Minoo Choi, Nellie
Kids in front: Diana Mahalaxmiwala, Ralph D'souza, Aadil Palkhivala,
Jehangir Palkhivala, Phiroze Palkhivala

The West, questioning its own morality, began to reach out to the Orient for direction. Yoga teacher Swami Satchidananda kicked off the Woodstock Festival, encouraging a crowd of 5,00,000 to 'let all our actions, and all our arts, express yoga.'

The Beatles discovered Maharishi Mahesh Yogi and Ravi Shankar. George Harrison began to play sitar and incorporate the tambura (a mandolin-like stringed instrument) into songs meant for mainstream consumption. Lennon's lyrics for their 1967 song, '*Across the universe*' were:

> *Words are flowing out like endless rain into a paper cup*
> *They slither while they pass, they slip away across the universe*
> *Pools of sorrow waves of joy are drifting through my opened mind*
> *Possessing and caressing me*
> *Jai guru deva om*

The song was inspired by their experience with Transcendental Meditation.

Pete Townshend of The Who not only gave up drugs because of his spiritual guru, Meher Baba, but also based many songs on his spiritual experiences. The song '*Pinball wizard*' from *Tommy* about the 'deaf, dumb and blind kid' who 'sure played a mean pinball', was seemingly based on Meher Baba's years of self-imposed silence.

A Native American quote symbolized the spirit of the time, saying 'Religion is for people who're afraid of going to hell. Spirituality is for those who've already been there.'

'The new approaches to the problem of God,' said *Time*, may (among other possibilities) 'lead to a more realistic, and somewhat more abstract, conception of God.'

The battered generation was ready to embrace the teachings of the East.

Silva Mehta was a Czechoslovakian émigré who came to England during World War II. She had married an Indian man and so lived in Bombay in the 1950s. Around that time she had an accident, which left her with a damaged spine.

Iyengar had already created a splash after having taught Menuhin. A friend offered to take Silva to Iyengar's class. He was due to do a lecture demo at the World Vegetarian Congress held in Bombay in November 1957. She dodged both the opportunities. To Silva, a Czech married to a Gujarati, the practise of yoga seemed too outré to take a chance on.

When her spine problem developed into osteoarthritis, the doctors predicted a lifetime in a wheelchair. The other equally painful recommendation was an operation to fuse several vertebrae. Terrified, Silva went to a naturopath she knew, who said the only cure for her was Iyengar.

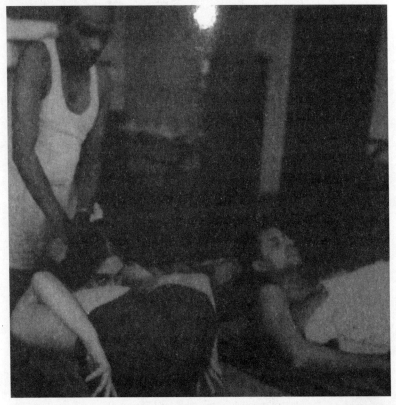

Iyengar adjusts Silva Mehta in Yoganidrasana. To their left is Behram Palkhivala

Within three weeks she was in the Iyengar class and taking additional private lessons with Martha Wartenburger, Iyengar's Jewish student in Bombay. Silva imagined that she would learn all she needed to in a few weeks. That was not to be. Though she divorced her husband and shifted to London, she remained wedded to Iyengar Yoga all her life. She never did end up in a wheelchair. In a year or two, she became capable of asanas that she would never have thought possible, even before her spinal injury. Silva ended up being one of Iyengar's topmost teachers in Europe.

Though Iyengar had already been teaching Menuhin and Krishnamurthy in England and Gstaad since 1954, the circle remained confined to the best musicians in Europe and some Krishnamurthy loyals. In 1960, Iyengar gave a spectacular lecture demonstration in Highgate, London. All 200 people in the audience were enthralled. The success of this demonstration prompted Menuhin, then the President of the Asian Music Circle, to arrange another demonstration at the Institute for Recorded Sound. On 16 June 1961, the *Daily Mail* carried an article with an upside-down Menuhin and 'India's foremost teacher of yoga', B.K.S. Iyengar.

The next day the Director of the Asian Music Circle, Ayana Angadi, posted an advertisement saying Iyengar would be teaching a specially selected group of ordinary people. The group that came together for this class consisted of three women, Angela Marris, who had already taken classes with Iyengar in Switzerland, Silva Mehta, who had recently visited India to learn with him, and Diana Clifton, who had been practising yoga from a book. When it was time for headstands, Angela and Silva, who had already been with Iyengar, knew the protocol. Diana, who had only done it from a book, asked if she could do it against the wall. Iyengar said, 'I'm better than the wall – I've got arms.' As soon as she had got her balance, he left her alone in the middle of the room, doing a Shirshasana without support for the first time in her life.

When the Asian Music Circle decided that the members would benefit from a regular class, this class grew in strength to include, in the morning class, a group of musicians and Beatrice Harthan. The evening class included Angela, Silva, Diana, Patricia Angadi, Eileen Moon and Daphne Pick. Many of them went on to be vanguards of the Iyengar Yoga movement in Europe.

Diana, like most of these women, engaged in active correspondence with her yoga teacher. What he could not teach her in person was done through correspondence, with Diana sending him photographs of her progress. Iyengar, who replied to every scrap of correspondence he received, once replied,

> I went through all the pictures and I remarked in the back. On the whole you have made a good progress. For your husband standing postures and twistings are good... Hope members of the yoga class are fine (Iyengar, 1962).

When Iyengar returned the next year, he really began attracting public attention. That year the BBC shot a documentary entitled *Yehudi Menuhin and His Guru*, which created ripples when it was telecast on August 21st 1963. Introduced by David Attenborough, this 30-minute film now had the boy from Bellur making his debut on the world stage.

After the film released, there was a clamour for the classes. Besides doing regular demonstrations, Iyengar now began teaching his first public classes outside India. Before he left for India, the demand had swelled to such an extent that Iyengar directed the ladies who had started learning from him just a couple of years ago to start teaching in pairs.

These first converts were also responsible for raising money for him to keep coming back every year. From the first class of three people, they had burgeoned into classes of 700. Finally, Iyengar was no longer dependent on wealthy patrons. The onus had shifted to the middle class. Iyengar had actualized his dream. He had reached the man on the street.

Or was it the woman? Though yoga classes were open to both genders, the preponderance of women taking to yoga was remarkable. Every class comprised of at least 70-90 per cent women. The improvement to their health and mental equilibrium was what kept them coming back in droves.

But was that all it was? In 1963, Betty Friedan's book *The Feminine Mystique* hit the stands and went on to spend six weeks on the *New York Times* Bestseller List. Credited with setting off the second wave of feminism, the book drew attention to the happiness quotient of the average housewife. Though the book has now attracted much flak for being both racist and classist, there is no denying that, at the time, it was instrumental in helping people rethink the traditional pigeonholes to which women had been relegated.

A yoga teacher did a survey amongst her pupils, largely housewives. She found 'monotony and lack of recognition, indeterminate pains and psychosomatic symptoms', amongst the most frequent complaints. She identified this as 'housewife syndrome'. There was now a plethora of women eager to develop an interest beyond the bondage of domesticity and to achieve some degree of status and financial independence.

Yoga seemed to provide them with better health, mental well being, a more effective way of coping with the world and a potential source of income. The cherry on top was that the profession left them the flexibility to still be good mothers and wives. Yoga teaching gave women the freedom and autonomy to finally be in control of their lives. Iyengar, it seems, was right in time to reap the benefits of this new feminist revolution.

Quite predictably, the British Adult Education System in the 1960s was swamped with a demand for yoga teachers.

Iyengar's only real competition at the time seemed to be Yogini Sunita.[34] This yogini had apparently been born Bernadette Bocarro in Bandra, Bombay. She described herself rather intriguingly as a Catholic Brahmin. Having escaped from Bombay at the prospect of an arranged marriage at sixteen, she joined a nunnery. In a few years, disillusioned by the persistent materialistic demands by the nuns and the rigours of the cloistered life, she returned to her parents' home. There, on a walk by the seaside, she encountered Narainswamy, her guru who had apparently cured leprosy and tuberculosis with pranayama. Practising his technique, she felt a return of equanimity and self-confidence, enough to enable her to start teaching the practices she had learned when she shifted to England after her marriage to Roydon Cabral.

She now attended press conferences dressed in her ochre saree, long silver earrings and sat on the floor to deliver her discourse. The transformation of Bernadette Cabral, the westernized Anglo-Indian to Yogini Sunita, the sari-clad teacher of pranayama, was complete.

Her most popular exercise was the 'slip second', which she spoke about in her BBC radio interview in 1961. This is a mental exercise, in which all those people and situations that require personal attention and involvement are brought to mind. Then one tries to let all of these attachments and worries go just for a second.

Yogini Sunita taught that Pranayama Yoga was a way of life, a way of concentrating one's complete attention on the thing at hand, with no anxiety about the past or future. In 1978, at the age

---

34 http://www.academia.edu/9574981/The_Institutionalization_
    of_the_Yoga_Tradition_Gurus_B.K.S._Iyengar_and_Yogini_Sunita_
    in_Britain

of thirty-eight, the yogini died, hit by a car as she crossed the road on foot. Her attention had wavered for a second.

Yogini Sunita's Pranayama classes were already being offered by the Inner London Education Authority (ILEA). With the publication of *Light on Yoga* in 1966 and its summary acceptance as the 'Bible on Yoga', Iyengar Yoga became a strong contender to become the main programme taught by the ILEA, which coordinated publicly funded classes from car mechanics to cake decoration.

Peter McIntosh, the chief inspector of Physical Education for the ILEA, was as open-minded as he was far-sighted. He was determined to bring yoga into the Physical Education curriculum in England. What Iyengar had been struggling so hard to achieve in his own country was being taken up by a total stranger in a foreign land.

The ILEA wanted to ensure that yoga became institutionalized, but in a safe way, with a teacher who was qualified and capable. While McIntosh looked high and low for his candidate, he was disappointed with the people presenting themselves as yoga teachers. A chance meeting with Hepzibah Hauzer, Menuhin's little sister, unearthed Mr Iyengar.

McIntosh then scheduled several meetings with Iyengar, where they discussed the issue of procuring reliable and competent yoga teachers to lead the classes. Finally, McIntosh found the person under whose capable hands the ILEA could have its crop of dependable yoga teachers. The ILEA declared in 1969 that 'gurus trained by Mr B.K.S. Iyengar, the author of *Light on Yoga*, a recognized authoritative book on this subject' would be qualified to teach yoga on public funds throughout inner London. This stamp of approval from the government mechanism imbued Iyengar Yoga with an aura of officialdom and inspired trust.

Iyengar had a very clear brief. He was explicitly asked to teach physical aspects of yoga and avoid discussions on religion or spirituality. He was to ensure that there was an emphasis on safety and avoiding physical injury to the students.

Thus, Iyengar's focus in these early classes was how to physically achieve basic asanas. These were the notes made by a pupil in a London class of 1974, which comprised only of anatomical instructions on how to achieve the perfect Virabhadrasana 1 (Warrior I) – 'Turn at the kidneys. Inner arms straight. Raise arms stretching from coccyx.'

When Iyengar was accused of concentrating too heavily on the physical aspects and ignoring the rest, he said, 'Better life can be taught without using religious words. Meditation is of two types, active and passive. I took the active side of meditation by making students totally absorbed in the poses.'

Iyengar was managing with his considerable charisma to wrap his British pupils around his little finger. The stiff upper lip and their lukewarm responses to the world seem to have been altered by Iyengar spewing fire and brimstone at them.

Though they carped about his firmness, they still kept coming back in droves. Undeterred by his heavily accented English and his famous temper, they were attracted by his magnetism, his immense knowledge of the subject, his wit, the passion in his eyes and the humour he imbued each class with.

Karin Stephan, one of Iyengar's early pupils, recounted an interesting story about the London class.[35]

Iyengar was teaching one of his early English pupils how to use a chair to support her shoulder stand. She was in her late sixties or seventies. Without blankets, the metal edges of the chair end up being very painful. But for Iyengar, it was always an all-or-nothing situation. As he tried to get her to straighten her back, her protests grew more and more animated.

Finally, she burst out, 'Mr Iyengar, Mr Iyengar, you're killing me, you're killing me!'

35 http://www.yogamacro.com/karin_profile/ks_writings/ memories/nmemories.htm

The yogi leaned over her and adjusted her one last time in the pose and said drily, 'That's all right. Do the pose first and then die! That way you'll go to heaven!'

The teachers were supposed to be first approved by the Senior Inspector of Physical Education. Since Iyengar came to London only once a year, they took classes with Silva Mehta in the interim and were approved by Iyengar on his annual visits as he watched them in class. Though they started with no set syllabus, within a few years Iyengar had created three graded sequences, each progressively more difficult than the other.

Iyengar's annual visits were emotional and stimulating events, where participants often found themselves buckling under the high standards their guru had set for them. The hall was often a scene of dramatic meltdowns and tears, as Iyengar unleashed his fury on the students.

'I am not slapping you,' he would say, 'I am waking the sleeping intelligence within you.' This would be accompanied with a swift, sharp whack on the unresponsive body part, which would not only jolt the student, but also everyone else around into renewed action. It was probably in these sessions that Iyengar earned the new appellation based on his initials, Beat Kick Slap Iyengar, instead of Bellur Krishnamachar Sundararaja Iyengar. But to Iyengar's mind, he had to teach them one year's worth in the space of a few days.

'He is a terror,' said a pupil in the USA about Iyengar and the classes held in London. 'People are shocked at his methods – shouting at students and knocking them around. But he is really in a class by himself. He is an absolute genius. If I had the money, I'd be in England with him right now.'

In his later years, with decades of allegations of physical abuse hurled at him, Guruji was questioned on an Indian talk show by the popular anchor, Prannoy Roy, about his propensity to raise his hands on his pupils. He responded with, 'My dear friend,' stressing all three words equally as he always did, 'I have been practising for seventy years. If someone makes a mistake, naturally, my hand goes there.'

In an unabashedly delightful Iyengarism which one of his French pupils, Noelle Perez Christian, has recorded in her book *Sparks of Divinity*, he is known to have said matter-of-factly in one of his classes, 'Don't sit too close to the wall, I may need to kick you.' The kick, then, far from being physical abuse, transmutes into an instrument for awareness and growth.

Ian Jackson, the runner-yogi and author of the book *Yoga and the Athlete* talks about the effect of a slap from Mr Iyengar. 'The blows sounded much worse than they were. They didn't actually hurt, but they made an unforgettable impression. Without the slaps...I would probably still be unaware of the tightness.'

Iyengar approached philosophy in a practical way, through the human body and his asana practise. Another pupil of these classes notes these words of Iyengar, 'The end of discipline is the beginning of freedom. Only a disciplined person is a free person. So-called "freedom" is only a licence to act and do as we like.'

It was not surprising, therefore, that many of the teachers who attended these classes reported remarkable personal transformations that they attributed to the sessions with Iyengar. Though he stuck to his brief of not introducing philosophy and spirituality in class, his students said, 'He simply led us, all unawares, into an altered state of consciousness and then called our attention to it when we were already there.'

In the later years, the ILEA tried to develop a system where people who applied to be teachers should have been practising yoga with an established yoga teacher for at least two years. While Iyengar was not personally involved with picking the teachers, he was involved with the syllabus and laying down the standards of assessment. Iyengar Yoga had now become an ingrained part of the

British system of adult education. The British adopted yoga with the same enthusiasm as they usurped the chicken tikka as their national dish!

Many of his later teachers in England emerged from the earlier classes with the ILEA. Clara Buck, who continued coming to visit Iyengar in her eighties, was a delightful woman who, as a young model, had her face plastered on the tin of Ovaltine. She went on to live an adventurous life in the French Resistance, serving as De Gaulle's interpreter in World War II. She discovered Iyengar Yoga rather late. 'In 1972, at the age of sixty, I was farming in Southeast England. One day a neighbour dropped in and asked me if I would like to go out with her to Hastings, Sussex – our nearest town – where an apprentice Yoga teacher needed "guinea pigs."[36] I said I would go anywhere just to get away from the farm for a while, since I worked all hours that God gave me. I was permanently tired and that day more than usual. After one hour of strenuous exercise I felt refreshed and decided to make further investigations. I enrolled in an adult education class and though I had to travel one hour each way, I never missed a lesson. One-and-a-half years later, I sold my farm and went to visit Mr B.K.S. Iyengar, in India, who is my guru. After five years he encouraged me to start teaching, and now, at the age of seventy, I have a profession that makes me feel younger than I felt when I was twenty,' she said. Clara, who began teaching at sixty-five, was soon offering two private lunchtime Iyengar yoga classes a week at ten pounds a month in the middle of London.

Women like Clara were Iyengar's ambassadors in Europe.

---

36 http://www.academia.edu/638080/A_Social_History_of_Yoga_and_Ayurveda_in_Britain_1950-1995

GURUJI'S GLAMOUR GROWS

In the meanwhile Guruji's Bombay and Pune classes were growing in strength. Besides the old brigade of teachers – Barzo, Dhan, Sam and Freny – now Madhu Tijoriwala had joined the class. Madhubhai was a Gujarati solicitor who gave up his daily badminton game and embraced yoga with ferocity. He soon became an indispensable part of Iyengar's life.

Much younger and still at least a decade away from becoming teachers were Jawahar Bangera, Aadil and Jehangir Palkhivala, the Motivala sisters (Anahita, Tina and Diana), and Collie Dastoor's daughter, Navaz.

Madhu Tijoriwala was instrumental in helping Iyengar acquire land for the Ramamani Iyengar Memorial Yoga Centre and was the one who went on to create the Light on Yoga Trust.

This early group of teachers and students often went out of town with Iyengar, on yoga vacations, to places like Matheran and Mahabaleshwar. Iyengar did not enjoy the heat, so he would try to get away in May and often it would be with these early pupils.

Iyengar in Mahabaleshwar with his Mumbai students

On one of these trips, when the pupils were trekking in the hills, they reached Kate Point, where a barricade prevented people from going any further. Guruji stepped over the barricade. With Jawahar and Birju, he went off to climb a sharp cliff in the distance. Guruji was not satisfied. Just above this was a rocky outcrop barely two feet by two feet in dimension. It was so tiny that Jawahar and Birjoo, who had climbed up the slope with him, waited at the lower point as there was barely enough place to accommodate Guruji on the rock. And for Iyengar, there was only space enough to stand. Iyengar, oblivious of the gasps and warnings that his pupils were shouting from lower down, went up slowly into Shirshasana. There was no place for him to do the traditional step back in the headstand. With only two feet available, there was just enough space for him to place his feet next to his elbows, and gracefully raise himself into a headstand. All around him was jagged rock and a fall of several hundred feet. His dhoti flew horizontally as he did the asana, as proof of how windy it was that day. Then he went on to do some other asanas, as his students watched him, terrified.

From the opposite cliff one of the pupils was taking photographs, and the 'American pupil with the dog' was screaming out to Guruji, 'If you fall you will only lose your life, but we will lose our teacher.'

His students remember that Kate Point in Mahableshwar, for many years after, had a plaque stating that this is where Iyengar had once done Shirshasana.

Iyengar nonchalantly does his asana practise at the edge of a cliff in Mahabaleshwar

When they got back to Pune, Aadil Palkhivala, who was witness to this breath-taking performance, asked him, 'Guruji, how did you do that? When you were out there in that small space, how did you do those extreme balancing poses?' Iyengar, who loved to talk in riddles, gave him this cryptic answer: 'Known. Unknown.' Aadil interpreted this to mean, 'Focus on what you know, and the unknown doesn't bother you.'

Barzo and Tijoriwala went with Iyengar on a trip to Amarnath in Kashmir in the 1970s. Sunoo Taraporewala, Barzo's daughter, remembers them packing like excited adolescents for this trip. Cadbury's had just introduced the Five Star bar, a chocolate bar filled with gooey caramel. They bought a giant box of Five Stars to sustain them through the journey. By the time they returned, they had all sworn off Five Star forever.

Iyengar in Mahableshwar with his Mumbai students.
Front row (l-r): Rati Unwala, Perin Cabinetmaker, western pupils, Sam
Mahalaxmiwala, Unknown
Top row: Dhan Palkhivala, unknown, Madhu Tijoriwala (standing) Iyengar,
Nergis Pesikaka, Anahita Mahalaxmiwala

When they were about to leave, Guruji realized he needed something from his bag. Unfortunately, he had put a strong stainless steel lock on his bag and had misplaced the key. Everyone was unsure of what to do, as there were only moments for them to leave. Barzo's son Irach saved the day by arriving on the scene brandishing his mum's hairpin. They all laughed at the inadequacy of his implement. Within moments, the young lad had picked the strong steel lock and placed it on Iyengar's palm. While Guruji guffawed, the family produced a new lock to replace the broken one and, perfectly armed, they were ready to set off on the great pilgrimage.

They flew into Srinagar and stayed on a houseboat for a few days. Despite the cramped space and the fact that they were on holiday, Iyengar would wake up early every morning to practise. So his students had no option but to wake up bleary-eyed at the crack of dawn and practise with him.

People normally embark on this yatra in the Indian month of Saawan (July/August) as a light rain begins to fall softly and mists envelop the mountains. Beginning at Chandanwari, 16 kilometres from Pahalgam, the road becomes steeper and steeper, till it can only be accessed by foot or pony. Getting to the Amarnath cave entails 30 kilometres of steep walking, and at the end of it Lord Shiva manifests to His devotees as a Shivling of ice.

On this long trek to Amarnath, while the rest of them had brought their old shoes, Iyengar had a new pair of shoes. Within the first kilometre he had terrible shoe bites. Despite this, Madhubhai remembers him always walking miles ahead of the rest. This time he was doing it out of choice, accompanied by people whom he liked. He probably thought often, and with gratitude, of his early days in Hubli and Dharwar, when he was forced to walk this distance every day just to earn a meal.

Iyengar in an asana at Kate point in Mahabaleshwar – you can gauge the ferociousness of the breeze by the flying lungi!

MR IYENGAR RETURNS TO USA

Mary Palmer was two years older than Iyengar. Born in 1916, she did not discover yoga till she was fifty-one. At the time, she suffered from depression, stuffed sinuses, bad knees, and other unidentified aches and pains, which she could not resolve with conventional medicine.[37]

She joined the local yoga class at the 'Y', and within two years, when the teacher left, she was called upon to teach. Mary, who was actually a pianist, had studied Music Theory at the University of Michigan where she still lived with her husband. If someone had told her in her youth that she would become a yoga teacher at some point in her life, she would probably have sniggered.

It was in 1968 that Menuhin visited the Palmers in their historic home built by Frank Lloyd Wright. It was a very unusual home, inspired by the form of the triangle. Mary headed the Ann Arbor Music Society, and often hosted visiting musicians. In this house, where even the bathrooms and kitchen were triangular, Menuhin first told Mary, who was teaching by now, 'You haven't done yoga unless you've studied with B.K.S. Iyengar.'

Intrigued, and keen to equip herself better since she was now teaching, Mary decided she would make a trip to Pune and study with Iyengar. After all, a recommendation from Menuhin could not be easily ignored.

Mary took a twenty-four-hour flight to Bombay, then the four-hour drive to Pune, before she reached Iyengar. The Iyengars were at this time still living in their two-room home at Subhash Nagar.

Iyengar took one look at her and asked her where she was from. Then he dismissively told her there was no space for her. It was

---

37 https://iynaus.org/yoga-samachar/remembering-mary-palmer-1916-–-2011

difficult for the family in those days – there was just the small room in front of the kitchen where Iyengar taught his students and the kitchen where Rama and the six children carried on with their lives. Occasionally a neighbour would give them space in the adjoining home for the group class.

Having no phone and no modern appurtenances to contact him with, many students like Mary would land up at Iyengar's doorstep only to be turned away. Mary was not one of those who would give up easily. She stayed on for three weeks, just standing by the sidelines and observing the classes, till Iyengar's obduracy was worn away by her own.

After three weeks he threw a challenge at her. 'Okay, I'll let you come to the class,' he told her, 'but if you come down from headstand before I say to come down, you will please go away and not come back.'

Mary had never been in a headstand longer than two or three minutes. Iyengar made her stay in headstand for fifteen minutes. Mary had determined she was going to study with him. Nothing would make her retract that decision. Fifteen minutes of Shirshasana was nothing compared to what she wanted from him, a lifetime of teaching.

She passed the test.

Mary spent hours in the front room of the Iyengar home, absorbing and soaking in the teaching till it was time to leave. She felt satiated for the moment. The black fingers of depression that had been pulling her down were replaced by an inexplicable feeling of well-being, like a little window that she didn't know existed, which had been opened up to let the light come flooding in.

The changes in her life and the lives of those she taught convinced her that she was onto a good thing. Thanks to the experience with Rebekah, Iyengar still retained a negative impression about Americans and the frivolity and lack of respect with which they treated the subject that was so close to his heart. It was Mary's assiduousness, and the seriousness with which she pursued what she had undertaken to do, that finally thawed his heart. Mary continued to go to Pune to study with Iyengar whenever she could, and would also travel to England, as Iyengar went there to teach every year.

In 1972, Joan White, one of Mary Palmer's students, was injured in a horse riding accident, and the prospects for recovery sounded dim. She had broken her back and had sustained severe spinal injuries, which left her temporarily paralyzed. When she called Mary to tell her the doctor's prognosis, Mary replied in her honey-glazed Southern drawl, 'Don't worry, sweetness. This will be the reason that I will get B.K.S. Iyengar to come back to this country.' And she did!

Iyengar had himself admitted that he had decided not to go back to the USA till 'a student came to my hometown and tempted me to visit.' Nine months later, convinced by Mary's devotion, Mr Iyengar was in the Ann Arbor 'Y', teaching a class of forty people. As usual, he veered between being tough and demanding and concerned and compassionate.

Mary Dunn, Mary Palmer's daughter, was part of that first class. Iyengar was directing them in Janushirshasana and Mary was anxious for her daughter to appear proficient to her Guru. She did not want her daughter to err and incur his ire. With frantic gestures of hands and face, Mary Palmer indicated to her daughter what she thought she should be doing. Her daughter was trying to shut her mother out and to concentrate single-mindedly on what Iyengar was trying to communicate to them. Mary Dunn realized that if her attention wavered for even a second, those fiery eyes and the smarting hand would be on her in a moment. She ignored her mother as best she could. But Iyengar, who has been famed for having eyes in the back of his head, caught the attempted exchange.

'Mary,' he told her mother categorically, 'outside class, she is your daughter. In class, she is my daughter.'[38]

Marian Garfinkel, who met him the first time at this workshop, remembers her first Iyengar moment. The night before the class, when they had met informally at the Palmer home, he had asked her what he could help her with in class the next day. 'I need some help with my headstand,' she told him innocently. The next morning in class, she was standing in front of him as they were about to begin the class, when he leaped down on her from the platform that he was standing on.

'You wanted to stand on your head?' he said ferociously. 'You can't even stand on your feet.' That is the way he was with his pupils, breaking them down to build them up. With Joan, who had just had her injuries, he was compassionate and caring. He gave her special attention, making sure she understood what she needed to do and what she needed to avoid. After eighteen years, America was feeling the fire and light of Iyengar's personality again. Mary Palmer remained one of Iyengar's most faithful pupils, till she died at the age of ninety-five.

---

38 http://iyengarnyc.org/wp-content/uploads/2012/08/Fit_Yoga_ Light_on_Iyengar.pdf

SHE LIVES IN HIS HEART

All the Iyengar children were devoted to their mother. Of all the children, Prashant was most the child of his mother. His calm and equanimity in the face of everything, his quiet acceptance of other people, his grace under pressure, his philosophical bent of mind, were all hallmarks of Ramamani.

Sundara, too, loved his wife with a passion that was tangible. Once on his return from abroad, Dhan had seen him envelop her in a rugby tackle with an intensity that belonged in a sports field. She was thrilled to find that he did not allow his guru status to stop him from showering his wonderful wife with the love she deserved.

Instead of being the kind of partner who railed against his spouse for being different, Sundara realized and appreciated the differences in their personalities. 'My impatient nature, speed, quick decisions and impulsiveness were counterbalanced by her soft voice and the quiet expression in her eyes.' Then expressing the romantic ideal of every wedded couple, he said, 'We lived without conflict, as if our two souls were one.'

Rama was on the one hand the epitome of love, but on the other, she had the capacity of being totally detached. She must have known that it would not be long. Soon the family would have to do without her.

When the first large group of students came in from abroad, Rama suggested that instead of hiring a space as they were forced to do, they should acquire a space of their own. The family was much more prosperous now. There was enough spare cash to invest in a piece of property.

In 1968, Iyengar had seen a plot of land that seemed like it might be good for their home and a small yoga centre. When he realized that the space was 20,000 square feet, he gave up the thought. He knew he would never be able to afford something so large. Mr Godinho, the owner, had been approached by a Christian organization who wanted to build a hotel on the property, but at the time he was not interested in selling it to someone for commercial purposes. When he needed to sell it a few years later, Godinho was approached by Mr Gera, a student of Iyengar and now an established real estate developer in Pune. An appointment was fixed for Iyengar and Godinho to meet. At the meeting, Godinho was very impressed by the man who had taught Menuhin yoga. He was now quite happy to sell it to Iyengar because he felt the space would be utilized for a good cause. Iyengar was going to share it with a friend, as he could not afford to buy the whole piece. Though Godinho had wanted to sell it for a higher price, he capitulated and sold it to them at a very affordable price.

For four years Iyengar would just go and look at the land. Having now exhausted all his capital, Iyengar could not afford to build anything. But they could afford to dream. The children wanted the home in front of the yoga space. Rama disagreed. No, the yoga space would be in front of the home. After all, it was yoga that had sustained the family and helped it prosper. Their home would have to be behind the yoga space.

Many years after they acquired the property, on 25 January 1973, they had a Bhumi Poojan, a ceremony to lay the foundation stone for their future home. The pooja entailed several hours of prayer and a ceremonial meal.

The exertion of the pooja left Rama weak. On 26 January, she was taken to a nursing home; she seemed to recover and feel better than when she was at home.

It was Saturday, 27 January. Iyengar always left for his yoga classes in Bombay on Saturdays. He asked Rama if he should cancel his trip. She asked him to carry on with the class. He left.

Sunita and Suchita had a sitar recital that evening. After waiting till the recital was over, Rama asked the nursing home to call their neighbour, Mr Prabhavalkar. They did not have a phone at home in those days. When Prashant and Geeta arrived it was late in the evening as they had not been able to find any public transport. Immediately, Rama sent them back, asking them to light the lamps at home and bring the other children. Prashant and Geeta went home and lit the lamps. They were unable to bring the other children to see their mother because they had no way of transporting them to the nursing home.

She saw them come back alone and asked why the others hadn't come. Then she told her two eldest children that her time on earth was coming to a close. She wanted them to shift her to the floor so she could be closer to Mother Earth, but the doctors would not allow it. So, sitting up, holding the hands of her children, she blessed them and told them that they would have to take care of the family now. As quietly and peacefully as she had lived her life, Ramamani passed away. It was 4 a.m. on 28 January 1973.

Barzo Taraporewala and Madhu Tijoriwala were the ones to bear the news to Guruji. Guruji, already having had a restless night, was up when they came knocking on his hotel door. They told Guruji that they had a message from Prashant that Rama was seriously ill. Iyengar, who had left her looking pretty well the day before, told them he would finish the Sunday class and then leave. When his pupils insisted that they leave immediately, Guruji began to fear the worst. But the pupils, wanting to reduce the impact of the shock, did not tell him about her passing directly. Freny Motiwala joined them on the journey to Pune. When they reached Pune, they took the road towards home instead of the nursing home, which was in the opposite direction.

When Guruji asked them why they were not going to the nursing home, they finally told him that Rama was no more and that she had been brought home. By the time they reached home, word had already got around and many students had come to pay their last respects.

Guruji greeted them all and comforted his crying children, never once showing any emotion himself. 'I am never separated from her for she is always in my heart,' he said. It must have made the parting easier.

Savita, Guruji's youngest daughter, feels her mother had a premonition about her death. She remembers that about a week before her mother's passing, a grapefruit had fallen from the neighbour's tree. The neighbours never ate the fruit but always gave it to the Iyengars, who relished it. When Savita began to peel the grapefruit, Rama said she would peel it for her. Savita did not want her to. Her mum had been looking tired and run down for a few days now.

'No, Aai. You need to rest,' she told her mother.

Rama said, 'Today, I am here to peel it for you. Tomorrow, who knows?'

In the last days Rama had confided in her children that she was unable to sleep. She felt like she was sleeping on thorns. She was hungry but was unable to swallow any food. But till the end she continued to do what she felt was her duty to her family.

The Iyengar family had a parrot, which they would ask innocuous questions to. 'Are you our grandfather from our mother's side or grandfather from our father's side, or grandmother from our father's side or grandmother from our mother's side?' And in answer, the parrot would pick a chit. A few days before her death, Rama wrote a question in Kannada and placed it in the parrot's cage. Then, when the parrot answered, she tore up the piece of paper into little fragments. The kids were very curious. They wanted to know what their mother had asked the parrot. 'We will put it together and ask Anna to read it,' they told her. Hearing that, Rama destroyed it so completely that no one could decipher it. Savita is sure that this question to the parrot had been related to her impending death.

Her girls had sometimes complained that Rama was the only one amongst all their relatives who had one gold thaali instead of two. She had always told her children that they would have to buy her the gold thaali that her husband had been unable to afford. They would have to give it to her on Iyengar's sixtieth birthday, when, according to tradition, the couple normally renews their marriage vows. She died five years before her husband's sistieth birthday, with only the thaali from her mother around her neck. Her husband's love, that had encircled her through her life, had more than made up for the lack of the thaali.

Self-effacing, and always putting her husband and his career before herself, Ramamani had not given her husband the chance to say goodbye.

Till the end, his pupils remember, whenever he saw something beautiful, whether it was a mountain, an opera, a painting, a home, a flower, or a road, the first thought that would come to his mind and his lips was, 'How Rama would have loved this!'

Clara Buck garlanding Iyengar on his seventieth birthday

The next week, Guruji was back in Bombay for his weekend classes. The students were disconsolate and gripped with a heavy melancholy. He took one look at his miserable class. 'Come on, come on!' he prodded them. 'Who has lost his wife; you or I?' The class could not but smile.

When Rama died three days after the Bhumi Poojan, some folks felt it didn't augur well for the future to use the land for any good purpose. Not Guruji. In his mind, the land had been blessed by his wife. He was determined that the new yoga centre and home be built on this land, as Rama had envisaged it.

THE EMPTINESS OF LOSS

The geometry of grief is capricious. Sometimes sharp and painful in its angularity, sometimes round and comforting in its circularity, it punches little holes into our beings, creating spaces misted over with memory and regret.

For Geeta, her mother's death meant abandoning the strip of colour at the end of her plain saree and taking refuge in the solace of pure white. For Prashant, it meant giving up the Indian violin that he had been playing passionately since he was a child. For the other children, it meant having to hold their grief within their hearts to avoid burdening their father. For their father, it meant throwing himself into his work with even more fervour than before.

Geeta, the oldest daughter, turned into the lady of the house, taking over her mother's responsibilities. She became surrogate mother to her siblings, took over the responsibilities of the home and helped her father with the yoga classes. Prashant gave up his dream of being a musician and came back to the practice of yoga with the tranquil, philosophical temperament that he had inherited from his mother. For all of them, Rama's death was like a painful surgery in which an essential part of them had been excised. After a while, the pain became a dull ache, but each of them experienced the emptiness in their own particular way. And despite the emptiness they sometimes experienced, life went on.

The Shankaracharya was visiting Pune in 1978. Guruji, always a rash driver, was setting out to meet him when he ran into a stone on the road. The scooter skidded, injuring him quite badly in the process. Fortunately, a rickshaw driver who knew him picked him up and brought him home. He was so disoriented that he kept telling the rickshaw driver to go further even though they had reached home. The rickshaw driver, who had probably brought scores of visitors to the Institute, knew exactly where he needed to drop him. Having established a connection with the family that day, the rickshaw driver still comes to yoga class.

Soon after, Guruji had another accident. He used to joke that he was now 'adjusted' on both sides. His injuries were so bad that doing his asanas every day became a monumental struggle. His spine was injured. His arm was limp. It was a struggle for him to even do simple things like Trikonasana. It was like starting at the beginning all over again. This was when he decided that he would not cut his hair till he regained his previous form. By the time he had regained his form, his long hair had become such an intrinsic part of his personality, that he couldn't get rid of it. After the second accident, at the end of 1978, the scooter was relegated to history. The Iyengars had their first car. An Ambassador.

By this time, Guruji's eyebrows were taking over as the most prominent feature of his face. Thick and bushy, they had begun to acquire a life all their own. They seemed to have their own particular way of communicating approval, disapproval, challenge and acceptance. Like fuzzy caterpillars, they dominated his face and animated his expressions, adding an extra dimension to Guruji's words and thoughts.

Dhan once told him that his eyebrows were looking very unruly and impertinently asked if she could trim them for him. Rather than the irritated response she expected, Guruji responded with a quiet, 'Let it be, Dhan.' As his eyebrows grew more unruly, his temper waned. His desire to change things within rather than on the outside became more marked.

When Guruji was seventy-eight, Doordarshan (India's government-sponsored TV channel) was at the Institute making a film on Guruji and his practise. As he was performing, he felt some discomfort in the left side of his chest. He was in the midst of doing a full split, Hanumanasana, an asana that came to him as naturally as breathing. Yet, there was a strange exhaustion, an unfamiliar constriction in his chest that he could not completely understand. He leapt up in full view of the cameras and went out into the courtyard and stretched his chest over a block, feeling his heartbeat race, his pulse uneven. He lay there a long while, trying to bring his breathing back to normal.

When Dr Manoj Naik reached Guruji's home, he ran an echocardiogram test and found that the heart was showing signs of having just undergone a myocardial infarction. The doctor insisted on the only remedies he knew: immediate hospitalization and a battery of drugs to bring the situation under control.

Guruji had worked with his body over a lifetime. He trusted his own methods more than he trusted the system of allopathy. He had overcome the after-effects of many ailments in the past. He would overcome this as well.

Within six weeks, he was back to his practise like the heart attack had been inconsequential, no more than a blip.

Within a couple of years, it decided to pay him another visit. He was eighty and this time it was a major heart attack. Very cordial with his doctor, he nevertheless refused to be admitted into hospital. Dr Naik was wringing his hands in despair. Guruji's age and stature made it difficult for Dr Naik to treat him like an ordinary patient. In this case, Guruji was determining the regimen and Dr Naik, despite his better judgment, was forced to agree.

When Guruji was later asked about his first heart attack, he said, 'There was no need for a doctor. It was the film I did. I collapsed. I was going non-stop in order to oblige.' 'Going non-stop' became the theme of his life.

AND LIFE GOES ON

The 1970s were a time when all essentials were in short supply in India; power, coal, cement, steel. The paucity of one fed the other. Infrastructure was in the hands of the State, including cement, so supply and price was manipulated by politicians.

A.R. Antulay, the chief minister of Maharashtra, extorted money from the Bombay builders in the form of donations to a trust he had established in exchange for receiving more cement than the quota allotted to them by the government. Cement, in the 1970s, had become a precious commodity.

Unfortunately, this was exactly when Guruji began building his home and yoga centre. Cement was what he would need the most.

Guruji was very clear about the design. He wanted a building that represented the eight paths of yoga, and had three tiers that symbolized the external, the internal and the innermost quest.

C.S. Sanghavi was one of Guruji's students. His daughter and daughters-in-law were regulars at the Pune class. Mr Sanghavi was given the contract to build the institute. The children of the Pune class remember him as the one who used to sponsor a glass of warm milk for each student who came to the pranayama class.

As they began the building, they encountered several problems. The expenditure seemed enormous and endless. On investigation they found that the good quality cement, which Guruji had so carefully procured from the Associated Cement Companies through the auspices of Nani Palkhivala, was being diverted and sold and in its place a substandard, low-quality product was being used. People accused Sanghavi and his son of being guilty of misdealings. There were stormy meetings in which both Geeta Iyengar and Dhan Palkhivala spoke fierily, demanding explanations from the contractor. When no explanations were forthcoming, C.S. Sanghavi's services were terminated. Soon after, he brazenly sent the Iyengars a bill for the 'free milk' he had provided to the students.

A new contractor, a cheery man called Ganpat Rao, took over the building. Till the Institute was completed, he could be seen perennially sitting outside the site wearing his Gandhi cap and sipping on his cup of coffee.

Finally, on the day of the inauguration, it rained like the heavens were falling down. The low-quality cement had allowed the entire roof to leak so badly that the top floor was deluged with water. Thankfully, eighty students who were visiting from South Africa chipped in – sweeping, swabbing, cleaning through the night, to make the place not only presentable, but gorgeous, with floral decorations and garlands.

The new nerve centre of yoga was ready to face the world.

But the home was missing something. Or so the children thought. As Indian as rhyming names, is India's cricket obsession. Guruji's children knew and used his cricket fetish to great advantage. As the youngest, Savita was always sent as a one-child delegation to make special requests and wheedle things out of their father that the other kids did not dare ask for.

It was New Year's Day of 1975. India had just won a test match against the West Indies by 85 runs. This was after two test matches in which the Indian team had been whipped by the West Indians. Indian national sentiments were running high. The highlights of the match were going to be telecast at 10.30 p.m. that night. Savita was requisitioned. 'Anna,' she said, 'they are telecasting the highlights of the cricket match between India and West Indies tonight. Don't you think we should get a TV so we can watch it?'

Guruji, whose life of deprivation made him very sensitive to his children's needs, at once agreed. And by the end of the day, a black-and-white Televista stood proudly in the living room.

The extended family had all come in from Bangalore and Mysore for the inauguration of the Institute.

That evening, when Guruji finished his classes for the day, he found a gaggle of female relatives all riveted to the Thursday evening Chaaya Geet programme. This normally featured a series of popular songs from Hindi films. Guruji expressed his displeasure at seeing the women of the house neglecting their domestic duties and instead watching cinestars cavorting around together on the TV screen. The TV was going to destroy their family life, he predicted.

After dinner, he was summoned for the highlights of the cricket match. His arguments against the TV immediately forgotten, he came down and delightedly watched India give the West Indies a drubbing in cricket.

BACK IN THE USA

By the early 1970s, Rama Jyoti Vernon, in California, had discovered the book that was about to change her life – *Light on Yoga*. She had experimented with many yoga teachers before this, but was looking for 'The One'. When she encountered *Light on Yoga* she felt she had found him.

Her husband and she went to India in search of the yogi in the book. After much searching, they were finally directed to Freny Motiwala, who was one of Guruji's early Bombay students.

Freny took them to Pune but with the warning that he lived in a small space and that there was a limited number of students he could take. They would not be able to participate in the classes, but they would be allowed to watch. Rama Jyoti and her husband were overawed. They were about to meet the great yogi himself. They were grateful for scraps.

They walked in through the narrow, tiled corridor to the small room where seven people were packed in, doing yoga with Guruji. Their imaginations had built him up into something larger than life. They were surprised to see a small man directing the class with such dynamism that the room seemed to crackle with energy. They watched him spellbound, while like a 'sculptor' he moulded the body into shape and like a 'conductor' he used arms, legs and body to orchestrate his little band of students. 'Your armpits have been lying in darkness,' he commanded imperiously, 'now open them to the light'. His thick accent made the word armpit sound like 'aurumpit' but the students apparently had no problem deciphering his words. Within moments, all the armpits in class became as noticeable as their noses. As they stretched in the forward bend Paschimottanasana, he clambered onto the back of the student at the furthest end of the room and then nimbly stepped from one back to the other, ensuring that each of them was performing to their maximum ability. As he reached the last student, the American moaning under the weight of Guruji, pushing down against a resistant spine and hamstrings, said, 'Oh Mr Iyengar, how I love to feel the pittypat of your little feet on my back.' The frown lines of concentration on Guruji's head evaporated and he laughed the signature Guruji laugh – head thrown back – emerging from the depths of his being. Slapping his impertinent pupil on the back with great affection, Guruji walked out of the room. The class was over.

Rama Jyoti and her husband waited for him to return. Photographs of Iyengar hung on the walls around them. Iyengar with Menuhin. Iyengar with the Queen Mother of Belgium. Iyengar with Krishnamurthy. When Guruji finally returned, he spoke about his wife Rama and her passing. He wanted to build a yoga centre dedicated to her. His eyes filled with tears as he spoke of her.

This was when Rama Jyoti asked him the question uppermost in her mind. She wanted Guruji to come to California and teach at her centre. Would he?

Guruji was unsure about California. He asked them to coordinate with Mary Palmer to make the arrangements for his trip. And that was how Guruji visited California in 1974.

This was his third trip to the USA. America, it seems, had atoned for Rebekah.

Judith Lasater, who attended the 1974 sessions in California, expected Guruji to be seven feet tall. She was surprised to find he was barely two inches taller than she was. Standing in the front row doing Tadasana, Judith concentrated hard to grasp at the meaning of his words under the thick glaze of his unfamiliar Indian accent. She tried to follow all his instructions, but however hard she tried, it felt like she could not please him. Feeling like this little man was picking on her, she felt the emotions rise. First anger and a 'How dare he? Who is this man anyway?' response melted into a 'Poor me! Why is he singling me out?' Then, in what she calls a 'blinding flash of the obvious', she realized that he was teaching her to recognize herself. She was learning how to examine her responses to the world, which, when things weren't going her way, always progressed from anger to self-pity. Filled with this understanding, she felt free. She looked into Guruji's piercing eyes and smiled. He smiled back at her, his eyes alight with compassion and comprehension. In her first class, he had taken her with a simple Tadasana on a journey into her inner being.

EVEN YOGIS PAY TAX

In 1969, India, to increase her depleting foreign exchange reserves, and to encourage people to bring back income earned abroad, introduced a new section under the Income Tax Act which allowed practitioners of any 'art' to bring back their earnings from outside India and be allowed a 70 per cent deduction on this income. Now that his income from abroad was increasing considerably, Iyengar felt that it would be a good thing to take advantage of this provision. He approached his student, Behram Palkhivala, one of India's best income tax practitioners at the time. To avail of the significant deduction, Behram had to prove that Iyengar Yoga was an art. The strongest argument that the state prosecutor had was the fact that Iyengar himself, in his book *Light on Yoga*, had continuously stressed the fact that Iyengar Yoga was a science. Behram's first argument was that just because Iyengar Yoga was a science, this did not preclude it from being an 'art' as well. He gave examples of many artistic pursuits that had science at their base: poetry had prosody, architecture had physics, painting had chemistry, sculpture had geometry, and music had notation. So yoga, though an art, he postulated, was like the other great arts, based in science.

He then presented the court with several photographs of the Iyengar daughters in dance movements that looked like yogic poses. But his final, clinching argument was based on straightforward photographs of Guruji doing his yogic asanas. 'Look at these pictures,' he said with an air of quiet drama, 'and after you peruse them, tell me whether on looking at this man you are prompted to say "What a great scientist!" or "What a great artist!" I rest my case.' Needless to say, he won.

Behram has a beautiful brass Ganesh that he received from Guruji as a token of gratitude. It sits on his interminable bookshelves as a reminder of Iyengar.

Behram was one of the early students to join Guruji's class in Bombay in the 1950s. He was at the time troubled with bouts of agonizing pain in the abdomen, which none of the many specialists he had consulted had managed to diagnose. When he joined the yoga class, the attacks of colitis and excruciating pain reduced in frequency, but did not completely disappear. The pain made its unwelcome appearance one night as Dhan and Behram were watching a Ravi Shankar concert with Guruji. It was so intense that they had to leave. The same intuition, that had helped Guruji choose the winning horse during his early days in Pune, came into play. 'How long has it been since your last meal?' he asked Behram. When Behram said it had been about seven hours, Guruji knew his hunch had been right. 'You must eat more often,' he told him simply. Following this advice, Behram managed to get rid of the pain that had troubled him for years.

Guruji, who had not managed to pass his school-leaving examination, had cracked what Bombay's most educated and experienced doctors had not managed to. After all, who would understand the anatomy of hunger better than Guruji, who had spent years on the brink of starvation!

Behram had been gifted with a magical metabolism which allowed him to eat copious amounts of food and never put on weight. His slimness made him much more capable and flexible than most other people in the Bombay class. There was one asana that Guruji used to be able to do as a youth, which he found he had lost the ability to do perfectly when Rama came into his life and food became a regular feature.

Paripurnamatsyendrasana entails an intense twist in the legs, spine, hips and ankles, while the arms and shoulders twist in the opposite direction to hold the shin and toes. Behram, with his forty-five-kilogram structure, was able to do it perfectly. When Guruji saw a photograph of Behram doing this pose so well, he took it from him and slid it under the glass of his worktable so he could be inspired by it. People had long criticized Guruji for his arrogance. How many teachers would have the humility and courage to display their own weakness and highlight a student's strength so openly?

HIS HELPING HANDS

One Guru Poornima, Geeta was speaking about her father's practice. She said, 'Guruji and his practise are two inseparable things. When he had no money, no food, no acclaim, he practised, when he had money and fame, he practised. When he was young he practised, when he grew old he practised.' Guruji himself said, after his wife's passing, 'I was married to Rama and yoga. Now yoga alone remains in my life.'[39]

His students would gather in the cool, dark and sub-terrestrial atmosphere of the Institute to watch him doing his asana practise. His sinuous movements were superimposed on the stillness of the asana, turning the air around him iridescent. The beauty and control in each movement made them hold their breath, gasp, and take furious notes.

Speaking to his granddaughter about his practise, he once said, 'Many a time, those who came to my classes were scholars or

---

39 https://balmainyoga.com/articles/evolution-practise-how-our-truth-changes-pixie-lillas-bks-iyengar/

pundits. If I erred, the blemish would have come on yoga and my guru. I could never take that. Hence, practise was, and is, always on. My practise involved awareness of what I am doing and sensitivity to what all is happening. I relied only on my experience and my primary duty was to share that in the form of teaching. So my practise never stopped and never will. I am a yoga sadhaka.'

On a day when he was not teaching, practise always began at 4 a.m., the Brahma muhurtha, with a shot of coffee, brewed just so. After his shot of coffee, he was ready for pranayama, which would be a one-and-a-half-hour practice. He would break for another coffee, bath, prayers and possibly a light breakfast. Then, after 9 a.m., he would continue his asana practice, which lasted for about three hours. This included half an hour of Shirshasana and one hour of Sarvangasana.

Guruji would say his asana practice was his spiritual practice. Often he would facetiously say 'Om Trikonasanaya namah', as he went into the position. He strongly felt that his physical asana practice, which involved and lit up every cell in his body, was much more spiritual than someone just repeatedly chanting mantras.

A light lunch would be followed by his correspondence, which was prompt and unfailing, and his newspaper reading, which could take an hour or two. If there was writing to be done, then he would do it at this time. If he was up to it, he would go back to the yoga hall for another session. As the orange evening light began to fill the Iyengar home, he would begin to wind up the day. After dinner was TV time for Guruji: the football world cup, or a cricket game, or his favourite Kannada soap opera. But the largest and most fruitful part of his day for Guruji was his practice time. This is when he would invent, create, discover and grow.

Faeq Biria, Iyengar's student from France, remembers a hectic trip to Oxford in the 1980s. After it was over, they were caught in a dreadful traffic jam and, by the time they reached their accommodation and finished dinner, it was past midnight. Guruji was allotted a room and Biria was supposed to be sleeping in the adjacent yoga studio. Exhausted by the exertions of the day, Biria fell off to sleep as soon as his head touched the pillow. In an hour or so, he sensed a dim light on in one part of the yoga studio. Through sleep-encrusted eyes, he could see Guruji in that corner of the studio. As Faeq drifted in and out of sleep for the next four hours, he saw Guruji going through a wide variety of yoga asanas. When Faeq scrambled to wake up at 4 a.m. to serve Guruji his morning coffee, he saw his guru emerging fresh and rejuvenated after his bath. Thinking he might miss his yoga practice in the morning because he was tired, Guruji had finished a four-hour practice at night. By 4 a.m. he was ready for a short nap. With a hint of schadenfreude, he told Faeq, 'Now I will have a yogic sleep and you will do sleepy yoga.'

A couple of months before he passed on, Guruji asked his granddaughter Abhijata to bring him the benches so he could do a variation of Shavasana. A couple of the younger students waited with Abhi to pitch in in case some help was needed. He waved them away, indicating that they should continue with their practice. After a while, when he opened his eyes, he found them still there. A flicker of irritation crossed his face. 'Why are you still standing here?' he asked. 'If you stand here like this, I will stop my practice.' The youngsters scurried away, feeling terrible to have upset him.

When he met one of them a few days later, he explained his irritation: 'Patanjali has said *abhyasa* (practice) has to be long, continuous, uninterrupted and with reverence. Only then will it be deep-rooted. First chapter, *Samadhi Pada*, fourteenth sutra.' Guruji was as respectful of other people's practice as he was of his own. All he wanted was for the youngsters to leave him alone and take their own practice seriously.

PROPS AND OTHER PARAPHERNALIA

In the 1940s, Guruji would cart back home large stones and other strange odds and ends that he found lying by the roadside to aid his practise. Much to the shock of passers-by, he would sometimes lie down over the wheels of a road roller on the street so that he could experience a more intense back bend. This dedication to his art earned him the label of 'lunatic'. Then he realized he could repurpose the water barrel at home for the same use. After experimenting with steel drums and round benches draped with blankets, the Viparitadandasana (supported back bend) bench evolved. This was based on the anatomical structure of the human body, and each person could use it differently, based on his structure or her flexibility.

In the early days, Guruji would cover long distances, often 25 kilometres or more each way across Pune on his trusty Humber bicycle. By the time he returned home at night after teaching through the day, he was exhausted. His legs trembled from fatigue. He would feel the tiredness right down to his nerves. He could not afford to just rest and allow his body to recover in the natural course, as he would have the same rigorous schedule to confront the next day. So every evening, he would lie with several rolled up blankets on his legs with a heavy water-filled drum on them to ease the nervous shiver. At other times he would have Rama or the children sit on his legs so that the warmth and the pressure could help ease the tremors.

When he later found students with nervous afflictions, debility, or anxiety that manifested in diverse ways, he extended this experience he had had with weights and pressure. He treated the students by tying their legs together with a soft cloth and then placing weights on them. He discovered that he could not only eliminate physical nervous tremors, but also nervous conditions that emanated from the mind. Both could be quietened, by lulling the nervous system into relaxation with weights. Modern science now conducts cutting edge research on simulating environments that recreate the atmosphere that we experienced as babies in our mother's wombs to rekindle the feeling of security we felt then. Guruji was achieving this instinctively with cotton blankets and a couple of weights.

Bricks or blocks were first used to aid people with their headstands and provide additional support. Now available in various shapes and sizes, they have become an essential part of the Iyengar Yoga practitioner's repertoire. And their applications are endless too.

When Guruji was in France in the 1960s, he first encountered the belts that were used on suitcases at the airport. His bag was secured with a belt, and when he got home, he found a myriad uses for it in his yoga practise. He found that using a belt could add resistance to any asana. This helped the development of form, flexibility and strength, depending on how it was used.

When he went back to France the next year, he thought he would pick up more belts, but because of the vagaries of the market, he found that they had been discontinued and were no longer available. He was left with no option but to find a local in Pune to replicate the belts. These then went on to become a ubiquitous part of the Iyengar arsenal.

Godrej used to make safes, cupboards, chairs and other steel appliances. They had established their reputation during the explosion at the Bombay Docks in 1944, when 800 people were killed and the whole area turned to rubble, but every Godrej safe in the offices of the merchants remained intact. They also made a chair that was a feature of most middle-class homes. Powder-coated stainless steel, durable and foldable, these chairs became staples at Iyengar Yoga classes. Used to support shoulder stands and to aid back bends, every feature of the chair, including the cross rung at the bottom, was used to advantage.

Using elements from his surroundings, he innovated to create features that were not only aids to people who found particular asanas difficult, but would also help to deepen and intensify the action in an asana for an evolved practitioner.

The wall ropes and ceiling ropes were adaptations of rural storage devices he saw in old homes in Karnataka that he felt could be used to advantage in his yoga practise, for supported work in inverted asanas. Using ropes that were used in village wells he improvised till he came up with the perfect aid for a headstand without any pressure on the head.

J. Krishnamurthy often spoke in his lectures of the alert passive mind. Iyengar knew that he had experienced this state often in shanmukhi mudra. Iyengar demonstrated to Krishnamurthy how the mudra could help one reach this state within minutes, which may require many years following other methods. They laughed over the story of Ramakrishna Paramhansa who was visited by some evolved yogis. The yogis told Ramakrishna that years of arduous sadhana (penance) had enabled them to walk on water and this was how they had crossed the river and come to meet him. Ramakrishna innocently said, 'Oh why did you take all the trouble and waste so many years? If you had given a boatman a few paise, he would have rowed you across!'

Guruji wanted to find some device that could be used to replicate the effects of Shanmukhi Mudra with a ubiquitous aid that would function like the boatman, enabling everyone to experience the alert, passive mind, without years of effort. He experimented for some years with the Hanuman chaddi, the famous tight-fitted underwear that left welts across the thighs. He had good results with it personally, but felt that the idea of using men's underwear over the eyes might be an idea that would lack popular appeal.

This is when the elastic band came into being. The alert and passive mind was now just an accoutrement away.

The *chumbal* is a soft cloth twirled into a doughnut shape that rural India uses to carry its heavy burdens. Its function is to pad the head and protect it while it carries heavy loads. Guruji earlier used blocks to raise the spine during Baddhakonasana and replaced these hard supports with two chumbals, one under each buttock, as they were anatomically friendlier.

Every few days, the Iyengar carpenter was summoned to create a new prop. He would measure the exact distance of Guruji's chest and buttocks from the floor and create a rough model. After Guruji had tested the sample on his own body, the final prototype would be created. Made of solid wood, these blocks, benches and props went on to populate Iyengar studios in every corner of the world.

In the West, they disparagingly called him 'furniture yogi', but Guruji did not let that deter him. He was concerned with helping people get well, and anything that furthered that purpose would be added to his arsenal.

When someone asked him why he did not patent his props, Guruji said, 'I designed props so people can benefit. Thousands are benefitting and will continue to benefit from them. Does God ever file a patent for his creation? Then what right do I, a mortal, have to do so?'

THE YOGIC PRIEST

Joseph Pereira was a young student at the papal seminary in Pune where Guruji and Geeta were invited for a lecture demonstration. With that first exposure, he was smitten. Father Joe was the person who was instrumental in helping Guruji find a space to teach in Bombay, a city where the prices of real estate are amongst the highest in the world. With Joe's assistance, Guruji was able to counter the resistance that Christian organizations had to renting out their premises for Yoga classes. The 'singing priest', as Joe was often called, was often summoned by Guruji to chant a Vedic incantation or sing a hymn.

According to Joe, Guruji had tremendous compassion for the challenged, and would often overexert himself in an effort to help people who were in need of his guidance, with little thought for his own health.

Guruji once held a retreat at the Moral Rearmament Centre in Panchgani, Maharashtra. After strenuous classes of intense yoga, the participants would gather in the common dining room at mealtime. As Joe sat down to eat a delicious bowl of mango puree, made from Alphonso mangoes from the red laterite hills of coastal Maharashtra, he heard Guruji's voice – 'Ay Joe! How many bowls can you eat? I will eat four times what you eat.' Joe ate four and Guruji ate sixteen. This was one of the few times the students saw him overeat. Otherwise, even the chocolate and the Mysoor pak that he so loved would be consumed in extreme moderation. No more than one small piece at a time.

At the retreat they heard that J.R.D. Tata, one of India's most respected industrialists, had passed on. As part of a memorial service to JRD, Joe sang his favourite hymn, 'Abide with Me', to the 200 people gathered there.

Later in class, when Guruji was unsuccessfully trying to adjust Joe in an asana, he said facetiously, 'Joe, you are good for nothing. You can only sing.'

In a few years, Father Joe's Kripa Foundation, now India's largest NGO, was to prove just how much good can be wrought by coupling noble intention with action. Inspired by Mother Teresa and Guruji, the singing priest has established a de-addiction and recovery centre that has helped former addicts and AIDS patients recover their lost lives. The Kripa Foundation Guruji Yoga Programme was formulated by Guruji, taking addiction treatment, which till then in the West had been largely psychospiritual and psychosocial, to a much-needed psychosomatic dimension. As Joe says, Guruji took this one step higher than Patanjali's 'Yogas chitta vritti nirodhah' to 'Yogas snahu vritti nirodhah'. A stilling of the oscillations in the cells, instead of just stilling of the oscillations of the mind, as Patanjali recommended.

'As it is in the cells, so it is outside,' was the dictum on which Guruji based the recovery. The programme helped convince the addict that the world outside was a reflection of the world within. Once they began a reformation at the cellular level, the world, for them, would never be the same again.

Much of the lure of alcohol and drugs lies in the fact that they are designed to create a surge of neurotransmitters which produce an extraordinary and compelling euphoria. This creates a dependence on artificial stimulants to recreate the euphoric feeling. According to Guruji, that was the perception that needed to be reversed. Those with dependency issues had to realize that the body is the temple of God's spirit. The shift to God takes place in the addicts when they learn to move from the periphery to the centre, from the sympathetic nervous system to the central nervous system. They finally reach the realization that the whole source of well-being is within them. Guruji poetically told Joe, 'We all have to realize our hearts are made of God. They will not be at rest till they rest in God.'

This was a time when the world was criticizing Guruji's yoga for being a purely physical form of exercise and Guruji himself was being criticized for his gross physicality and display of bodily prowess. He is just an acrobat, they said dismissively. When Father Joe was asked about Guruji and his concentration on the physical aspect of yoga, Joe had a simple answer.

'This is the man who taught me how to pray,' he said.

MANY FACES OF THE GURU

In 1978, Guruji turned sixty. The *Shastipoorthi* is the sixtieth birthday celebration, an important occasion in India. In Hinduism, it is considered a bridge between the householder's domestic concerns and the spiritual yearnings of the next stage of life – *Vanaprasthashram*. To celebrate the day, his students set up a special committee which was in charge of planning the events around the landmark birthday.

A book was released to commemorate the day – *Body the Shrine, Yoga thy Light*. It contained a mélange of articles about Guruji's past, his work, his family, and articles from people whose lives he had changed.

Since it is good to have one's guru's blessings on such a day, Krishnamacharya was invited to preside over the function. The guru was reluctant to visit the home after Ramamani's passing, as he felt that there would be no one to tend to his needs like she had done. But the family assured him that he would be looked after as well, if not better.

At the function to celebrate the birthday, Krishnamacharya was invited to give a speech. He sat ramrod straight on the stage and spoke continuously for two hours. In Sanskrit! He was ninety years old! The audience comprised hordes of Guruji's pupils from around the world. Across the hall, you could see people biting back their yawns and nodding off to sleep. They were all too polite to get up and leave.

In the second hour, Guruji spoke to Krishnamacharya in Tamil, possibly requesting him to stop. Krishnamacharya went on regardless.

Finally, Guruji took the mike from him and said, 'My guru is such a river of knowledge that he cannot stop flowing.' The audience clapped and cheered, more for this diplomatically-worded sentence than for the knowledge they had gleaned from the two-hour long Sanskrit speech.

Aadil Palkhivala, his pupil, asked him in the late 1970s, 'Iyengar uncle, can you describe your guru Krishnamacharya in one word?' Guruji thought for a moment and said, 'Selfish.'

'Why?' Aadil asked.

'Because,' Guruji answered, 'he died holding on to all his knowledge.'

'Krishnamacharya taught me nothing,' he was known to say. 'He told me to do Kapotasana. I did not know what it was. I had to find out what it was before I could begin to practise. As I did it, there was a pain in my belly. I felt an urge to urinate. When I went to the bathroom, no urine would emerge.' By the end of the day, he could not walk. At night, he crawled to his sister's part of the house. 'I am not passing urine. Something went wrong when I was doing the asana,' he told his sister and brother-in-law. Krishnamacharya told him harshly, 'Yoga is too much for you. Stop trying.' Guruji, however, knew nothing else. He persevered.

Faeq spoke of another such experience with Krishnamacharya. In the early 1980s Guruji showed Faeq his belly. He told Faeq that Krishnamacharya had made him practise Vrischikasana on his own for a week. This is a pose that requires an intensely flexible spine and much strength in the arms. After a week, he was asked to present the pose to his guru. Sundara was so stiff at this time that try as hard as he might, he just couldn't touch his feet to his head. But when he saw Krishnamacharya pick up the iron bar with which he used to beat him, he pushed himself so hard to touch his feet to his head that he felt something tear inside. Decades later, when he was doing inverted poses, he often had to leave the hall where he practised and come back after having thrown up food flecked with blood from this old injury. He had confided in his closest pupils, saying he felt that this injury would be the death of him. Despite this he kept working on it, till one day he called his pupil Biria to look at his abdomen in Shirshasana. He showed Biria how he had managed to heal the tear that had stayed with him for fifty years!

From his own experiences, he learned how to heal himself. His learning came from his own experimentation – his trials, his successes and failures.

All his life, Guruji was unable to reconcile the dichotomy between the unexpressed resentment he felt for the way he was treated by his guru when he was most vulnerable and the customary respect that is normally accorded to the guru in Indian culture.

'At least he gave me yoga,' he says charitably of Krishnamacharya.

LIVING WITH THE IYENGARS

Firooza Munawar Ali came to Guruji through Father Joe. After years of studying in the general class with Guruji, she decided to go to Pune to experience the fire a little closer to the source.

Firooza, like many of Guruji's pupils, was in total awe of her teacher. It was a strange double bind where on the one hand she was terrified of him and on the other loved to be around him. She asked

Guruji if she could come to Pune in her summer vacation when she was off from teaching Philosophy at a Bombay college.

He said, 'You will have to come when I call you.'

When he summoned her, it was possibly the worst time – the middle of the term at a teaching job that she had just taken up. When she asked for time off, the principal protested. To Firooza, it was clear. Her Guruji had called her. Firooza would leave whether she had permission from the principal or not.

So, with a twenty-year-old's faith that the Universe would look after her, she arrived at the doors of the Iyengar institute, with her bags and a 3,000-rupee scholarship that was to tide her over the month.

'Ah...so you have come,' said Guruji 'Where are you going to stay?'

'Here?' she asked tentatively. She had not realized she needed prior permission.

Informing her that she would have to pay to stay, he called out, 'Ay, Prashant open one room for her.' The family pitched in. Prashant opened the room, Savita ordered milk for her. They told her where she could go to buy vegetables.

Everyone who has ever stayed in those little rooms at the Institute has had their adventures with the gates that close at 8 p.m. One evening, as she was returning to the Institute, her dupatta (shawl) got entwined in the cycle wheel. Getting back to the Institute took much longer than she had anticipated it would. Finally, when she did reach, she was confronted by the locked gate. Most people who were late generally clambered over the gate. She would have to do that as well, but she couldn't leave her cycle unattended on the other side. So, with growing frustration, she struggled to haul herself and her unwieldy encumbrance, the cycle, over the gate. Even though she tried to keep it silent, it was a noisy operation. The clanging of the bicycle against the metal gate sounded loud and clear throughout the home.

She saw a shadow step outside onto the balcony. It was Guruji. She braced her tummy for the vitriol that would come her way for coming in late and adding to her misdemeanours by disturbing the family.

'Ay Prashant, open the gate,' Guruji said quietly, and walked away after he saw that she was safely within the environs of the Institute.

Firooza's days were long and peaceful, filled with intense sessions of yoga with Guruji and his family and short bicycle trips to pick up potatoes, onions, milk and bread.

Suddenly, on 31 October 1984, India erupted into unprecedented violence. Indira Gandhi, the prime minister, had been assassinated by her personal security guard, a Sikh. It was revenge for Operation Blue Star, where Indian commandos, ordered by Mrs Gandhi, had stormed the sacred Golden Temple in an attempt to flush out the terrorists who had holed up there. India, long brought up on tales of the 'loyal Indian soldier', was enraged. The guard, Beant Singh, had been one of Indira's favourites. When all the Sikhs on Indira's security team had been cursorily dismissed a few months ago, she had reappointed them all, saying she trusted them implicitly. One of these men, in whom she had reposed full faith, had killed her.

In the days that followed, Sikhs, conspicuous in their turbans, were hunted down and massacred in metros all over the country. Suspicion rent the air. Curfew was declared. People were not allowed to step out of their houses because violence was erupting indiscriminately. While India was trying to absorb these devastating events, Guruji thought of the young girl alone in her little room at the Institute. He went across to Firooza's room. 'What will you do for dinner?' he asked. She had not been able to step out to replenish her food supplies. She would be fine, she insisted. Guruji walked away. In a short while, Savita, Guruji's youngest daughter, appeared at the door of Firooza's room with a big bowl of bhel. The Iyengars shared their family dinner with her that day. Firooza was unearthing the soft heart under the leonine exterior. In that month she discovered that the Iyengar family love to feed people. Very often, after the umpteenth jalebi was thrust into her plate, Guruji would say, 'Eat one more, you can do more pranayama and wash it out afterwards.'

She remembers that one day in class, Guruji got impatient with an older man and, in an effort to make him intensify his asana, he slammed the man's head on the floor in dog pose. Soon, Firooza observed Guruji in dog pose, banging his head on the floor in contrition, trying to gauge how badly he had hurt the man.

Another day, he threw a new student, Jharna, out of class, saying she was not ready for pranayama. Jharna left the class, adjusting her contact lens that had been bothering her. Thinking she was crying, Guruji followed her out and told her, 'Don't worry, you can join next month.'

Guruji retained a particularly soft spot for the youngsters in his class. When a group of them created the first yoga t-shirt, Guruji, who had never worn a t-shirt till then, appeared in class the next day, flaunting it.

CHANNELLING GURUJI'S INNER CHILD

Through the 1970s, Guruji would always take the Deccan Queen to Bombay on Saturdays and return on Sunday afternoon. A Pune pupil who was travelling to Bombay told him he was taking his car and that he would drive Guruji to Bombay and back. Aadil Palkhivala, in college then, would, during his vacations, spend the week in Pune taking classes with Guruji, and return home to Bombay over the weekend.

So there were three of them in the car: Guruji, Aadil and the Pune pupil. In those days it was a tortuous drive up the Western Ghats on a narrow two-way road. One accident or breakdown on either side would cause a serpentine back-up in traffic that would often take hours and hours to clear.

They were driving along, chatting about this and that, stopping for the ubiquitous chai and batata wada along the highway, when they came across a traffic snarl. The highway was blocked for miles, as far as they could see. Traffic was at a complete standstill on the road towards Bombay. After half an hour of being stuck in the same place, Guruji said, sounding slightly perturbed, 'I am going to be late for class.' If there was one thing his pupils knew about him, it was that Guruji was never late. Now it seemed like God had taken it out of his hands.

There was no way the traffic could possibly clear so he could make it to class on time. Aadil quietly asked him, 'Guruji, with your permission, may I drive?'

'What can you do?' Guruji retorted sharply. 'Nothing is moving. Where can you go?'

'I could drive on the wrong side of the road,' said Aadil tentatively.

'You can do that?' asked Guruji. Before Aadil could even nod, he addressed his Pune pupil peremptorily, 'Hey you! Go to the back!'

Aadil took the wheel. He had to gauge when the other side was relatively free of traffic and drive at breakneck speed till he encountered a car and then try to merge with the traffic stream on the Bombay side. It was a tense and dangerous operation, as a slight misjudgement could cause a fatal accident. But every time he drove on the other side, pushing the accelerator to the ground, by his side was Guruji, laughing and clapping like an excited child. Needless to say, they made it to the class on time, with Aadil having witnessed a very different side to his otherwise dignified and sedate Guruji. One he would always treasure.

Besides a love for unexpected adventures, Guruji's other obsession was cricket. In the year 1983, when the economic growth rate in India was just 3.8 per cent, the demand for a colour television grew by 140.3 per cent. Many of the buyers were probably fathers like Iyengar, cricket aficionados, whose kids manipulated them into buying a colour television set. It was the year of the Cricket World Cup in Australia. It was the first time that Indians would be able to watch cricket up close from their living rooms, live and in colour.

Faeq Biria was in India, studying at the Institute. Guruji was helping a lady who just didn't seem to comprehend his instructions. He looked sadly around at his pupils who were practising around him and said, 'No one is learning anything or absorbing anything. No one is making any progress. Better to go and die.' And he turned on his heels and stalked off before anyone had time to react.

Biria, a devoted student, felt terribly guilty. The words 'Better to go and die,' kept echoing in his head. He had always felt that they as pupils were not worthy of their guru. And now Guruji had confirmed this by saying so himself. Biria took over the session that Guruji had been conducting, and helped the lady, all the while mulling over how he could work at becoming more deserving of his teacher. He was not in a mood for conversation after the class and he headed out as soon as it was over.

Hoping to catch a glimpse of Guruji and maybe apologize to him for having disappointed him, he glanced through the window to see if he could catch Guruji's eye.

There was no need for an apology. His teacher was in bliss. There, sprawled in front of the TV watching the World Cup cricket match was Guruji – looking very unlike someone who was making immediate plans to die.

India's fanaticism about cricket is exceeded only by her preoccupation with her cricketing heroes. The entire nation went through a collective paroxysm of pain when Sachin Tendulkar,

India's greatest batsman, developed an excruciating back problem in 1998. He found out about Guruji from other members of the Indian cricket team like Zaheer Khan, Anil Kumble and Rahul Dravid, who had all benefitted from yoga with Guruji or with one of his students.

Sachin's back had been giving him sleepless nights. For the first time, after his class with Guruji, he managed to sleep peacefully. With the discipline of a sportsman, he managed to follow the regimen created for him by Guruji assiduously. His backache reduced and slowly disappeared.

Almost a decade later, Sachin developed a problem in his foot, which caused him acute pain and discomfort. His physicians in London advised surgery. Zaheer Khan suggested that Sachin visit Guruji again. Guruji worked with Sachin's soles which he said 'were as hard as a rock.' When he returned to his London osteopath ten days later, the doctor said surgery was no longer necessary.

Thanks to Guruji's interventions, India's cricket fans could breathe easy again.

THE LIGHT SHINES BRIGHTER

Jawahar Bangera started yoga with Guruji in the late 1960s as a teenager. After a while he was asked by Guruji to start teaching at the Taj Health Club when Barzo, who was teaching there, had to give it up. Though Jawahar was an indispensable part of Guruji's retinue, it was only much later that he embraced yoga full time.

Birjoo Mehta was part of the Mehta family who joined Guruji's Bombay class in 1974, but he soon grew very close to him. He and his sisters, Aarti and Rajvi, though busy professionals in their own right, devote many hours of their lives to Guruji and the Institute. Rajvi, besides working full-time as a scientist, also edits the *Yoga Rahasya,* a magazine brought out by the Ramamani Iyengar Memorial Yoga Institute. Birjoo, who went on to become an electrical engineering graduate from the Indian Institute of Technology, started yoga with Guruji when he finished the tenth grade in 1974. Eight years after he started class, he was asked by Guruji to start assisting in the Saturday Bombay classes.

In 1984, Jawahar and Birjoo were asked by Guruji to accompany him as part of his entourage which was travelling to San Francisco for the International Iyengar Yoga Convention. There were several of Guruji's senior teachers accompanying him: Barzo Taraporewala, Dhan Palkhivala, Rati Unwala, Jasmine Sethna, Collie Dastoor and Dr Karandikar. Whilst the other teachers all had their own classes and were functioning relatively independently, Jawahar and Birjoo were assigned the task of being Guruji's shadows. They were more famously known as 'the boys'.

Fort Mason, where the first International Iyengar Yoga Convention was held in 1984, is set by the gorgeous San Francisco Bay. The space which was the venue of one of the largest yoga conventions in the United States was the unlikely setting of the World War II Pacific operations, having witnessed the shifting of 1.6 million troops and 23 million tons of cargo to the Pacific. The *New York Times* commented at the time: 'This port has one main commodity to send abroad. It is exporting war.'

Now it had been repurposed as a cultural centre. There were no traces of its grim history.

The 750 participants were divided into approximately twenty batches of 35-40 people each. At any point in time there were ten classes on, held in different sheds. Each batch would have two two-hour classes in the day. All through the day, Guruji (and his boys) would be on his feet, checking how the teachers were conducting the classes. Guruji would attend twenty classes a day – correcting, guiding, encouraging, chastising – to make sure everyone got the attention they needed. The boys realized that what they needed to do was provide the props, planks, ropes, bricks, anything that he required. They walked by Guruji's side and, almost before he could speak, they would present him with the prop he needed.

Birjoo recalls that when he reached one particular lady, Guruji stopped. 'What is wrong?' he asked. 'Nothing,' she said, 'I am fine.' He went to someone else and circled around and came back to her. 'What is wrong?' Again she said 'Nothing'. When he came back a third time, he identified the side that he felt had an imbalance. The lady finally said that she was a cancer survivor and had had surgery on that side. His softer, compassionate nature emerged. He began telling her what she should do and how she should do it. Birjoo noted that when an ordinary person sees someone limping, he knows something is wrong. Similarly, Guruji would be able to tell from the energy of someone that there was an imbalance deep within.

Lisa Walford was one of the people who were at the 1984 convention. She was attending a pranayama class taught by one of Guruji's senior teachers. The class was doing supported backbends over chairs, and from that position lifting up into Urdhva Dhanurasana to open the chest. The air felt different, as it always did, when Guruji entered the room in his bright red shorts. 'What are you doing?' his voice boomed. To the teacher, he said, 'You will do what you want when I am dead, but not while I am alive! Think of their nervous systems!' The rank disapproval in their Guruji's voice had by now turned every nervous system in the room into a mass of quivering jelly. He then demonstrated what he wanted done to quiet their nervous systems in readiness for pranayama. When he left the room, it still vibrated from the aftermath of his visit.

Ruth Fisk was a professional dancer before she started yoga. A bad fall had put an end to that career and yoga had put her on the road to recovery. There was still a persistent ringing in her ears that would not go away. At the convention in San Francisco, Ruth was summoned to the stage to help resolve this problem. Guruji put his fingers deep into her ears and then asked her if she was better. She shook her head to indicate a 'no'. Then, much louder than necessary she said, 'I can't hear you...Your fingers are in my ears.' Guruji's laugh echoed across the halls. Then he recommended some things that she could do at home. These helped her get better within the year.

The American tour was not all saffron and honey. There were moments that people in the Iyengar community would rather not revisit. Victor Van Kooten had first come to Guruji in a state of almost complete immobility and had with his help recovered full functionality. He had gone on to become one of Iyengar's premier teachers in Europe. Van Kooten was so grateful to his guru that he used to often donate a large portion of, or sometimes even all, his profits to the Trust.

At this convention, however, in one of the evening sessions, Van Kooten lashed out at Iyengar, accusing him and his demanding style of teaching for having caused irreversible damage to Kooten's back. Victor Van Kooten and Angela Farmer, both long-time Iyengar teachers, decided to break away from the system and go their own way, teaching yoga in a style evolved from their long studies with Iyengar and their own learnings along the way.

It was a bitter harangue, both unexpected and unkind. Iyengar felt hedged in. He felt hunted. He felt hurt.

Through the next few days, Guruji vented his unexpressed anger on his Indian pupils in various ways. The other Indian students also received an earful of their guru's wrath. They all accepted his fury as an indication of the fact that he considered them family. Who else can you express your disappointments and fears to but those that are closest to you? Even if they were couched in words of anger, the Indian mind understood it as a display of intimacy.

In a letter to Dhan more than fifteen years after the incident, the pain was still apparent. 'You were in San Francisco when the ruthless attacks on me went on for hours and not one student who accompanied me from India stood up to say the attack was wrong and uncalled for. Those who left me then still teach what they learnt from me and yet speak against me and my method of teaching, saying what they teach is right and not the one (the teaching) from me which (they say) is unfit for the West.'

For Dhan, the ire of her Guru was unwarranted. She wasn't present at the meeting when the bitterness spilled over. To clarify her stand she wrote to him telling him that she had not been present when 'the shameless attack was made on you by some of your ungrateful foreign pupils' saying 'I curse myself for not being there. I would never, never, never have allowed it to go uncontradicted.'

As the Iyengar community in the West grew in size, the rivalry, acrimony and conflict grew in the same proportion. Many of the early teachers who had trained under Iyengar in the 1950s and 1960s had already fallen away. Noelle Perez, who had claimed that Iyengar was God in 1959, had begun to denounce the non-spiritual Iyengar practise and had started her own yoga school called the Institut Superieur Aplomb. Dona Holleman met Iyengar in Gstaad in 1964. Deciding she wanted to be a yoga teacher at twenty-two, she went on to study in Pune with him and became one of his early European teachers. By 1980, she too had washed her hands off the Iyengar community claiming that it had 'lost that spirit which was present in the early days and (had become) commercially and politically oriented.'

From the standpoint of uninvolved bystanders, the Van Kooten outburst was anger directed at Iyengar, but stemmed not from his physical abuse of Van Kooten, so much as a slight to the Van Kooten ego. Only recently, Faeq Biria, the bullet-shaped man of mixed antecedents, had torpedoed his way into the heart of Iyengar and had become the favourite son in Europe. This elevation to power would have financial and emotional repercussions on everyone involved. The Iyengar organization had grown too large to be one happy family. Cracks had already begun to emerge on its surface. And these were causing pain to its patriarch.

The Van Kooten attack left Iyengar feeling vulnerable. His trust had been eroded. In the next stage of the tour, Guruji was not comfortable with Jawahar and Birjoo being relegated to staying

in another home, away from him. When he was told there weren't
spare bedrooms for them, he insisted that they would sleep in the
room with him. And they did. Happy to spend time with Guruji,
they would sleep on the floor, on the sofa, whatever was available,
and do their best to make him comfortable.

They knew exactly how he liked his morning coffee. The perfect
Iyengar coffee was made from steaming hot water poured into
freshly ground coffee beans to make a hot decoction. Once the hot
decoction was ready, it was never heated further. Instead, the milk
was heated to a high temperature and a half spoon of sugar was
blended in to give Guruji a steaming hot cup of coffee – a small cup
when he woke up and a slightly larger one when he had finished his
practise was, as Guruji said, 'his only vice.'

As soon as he had finished his pranayama and his morning
ablutions, one of them would hand him his cup of coffee. And then,
he would reminisce. These were precious times for both the boys,
and they count these talks as having been moulding influences in
their lives.

They had an opportunity to see him as a person. They saw him
change colours depending on the role he was playing. When he
was performing he was a consummate artist, when he was teaching
he was a scientist par excellence, and when he was practising he
became a philosopher.

When Guruji was practising at the institute in Pune, people
would often have to stand around him, guarding the space, so that
no one walked into him. The reason for this was that his practise
was so involuted and meditative, that he would virtually withdraw
into himself completely. That large, dynamic, public personality
that they knew would turn sage.

Later in the trip, Birjoo and Jawahar watched as he practised for
his upcoming performance at Marian Garfinkel's home. This was
an electrifying performance at the edge of Marian's pool, in which

Guruji went through every asana in *Light on Yoga*. They could see his aura growing larger than life as a performer, to captivate every person in the audience.

Guruji's sense of loyalty towards those he cared about was immense. Like most of us do with people we love very much, each of his pupils would want to have Guruji all to themselves. They would resent the presence of these young boys who were so close to Guruji, serving his needs and seeing to his comfort every moment of the day. When he reached Canada, he was told that there was no provision made for any additional people, only for Mr Iyengar. Guruji categorically told them that he had travelled all the way from India with the boys and unless they could come, he would not be coming.

Faeq remembers this same scenario playing out during the Europe tour when they were to go to the Netherlands. They informed Guruji that he would be welcome but Faeq would not. Guruji told them firmly, 'I travel everywhere with him. If he doesn't come, I don't come.'

Later during the trip, as they were floating down a river by moonlight, gazing at the star-studded sky, Guruji said, 'Hey Biria, you have read the *Mahabharata*. Do you know the story of Yudhishthira and his dog?'

Biria chuckled. He knew exactly what his guru was alluding to. At the end of the *Mahabharata*, when the Pandavas are making their way to heaven, they have a faithful dog that accompanies them on the journey. When he reaches the gates of heaven, Yudhishthira is invited into Indra's chariot. When he tries to enter with the dog, he is told that the dog is not allowed into heaven. So Yudhishthira says he will not enter heaven either, as he cannot desert his devoted companion. Hearing this, the dog reverts to his original form as Dharmaraj (The God of Righteousness, Yama) and blesses Yudhishthira who enters heaven in Indra's chariot.

Biria had just been complimented on his faithfulness. They lay there silently, guru and pupil, floating down the steel grey river, the stars smiling down on them. Biria was in bliss.

Besides his yoga classes, Guruji had a hankering after adventure of any type, so whether it was the fastest train or the tallest building, the scariest roller coaster or a helicopter ride over a volcano, he would make sure he experienced it.

They visited Disneyland and there was a sign on the roller coaster warning the public that it was not suitable for people above sixty. He looked at the sign and said, 'This is not for me.' He was above sixty then, so his companions were happy that he was not planning to tempt fate, when they saw him walk where the queue ended and calmly take his place in the line for the roller coaster. What he had meant was that the injunction was not for him. He was, after all, not an ordinary sixty-six-year-old.

When they were visiting the Grand Canyon, Guruji, who could never resist the edge of a cliff, went up into Shirshasana at the edge of a particularly dangerous looking one. He stayed up for quite a while, enough time for word to spread among the tourists that there was someone standing on his head at the edge of a cliff. When they came around looking for the person doing Shirshasana, he had come out of the pose, but with his usual sense of mischief, he played along. 'Oh is that so?' he said, 'Where is this person? Come on, let's go. I would like to see him too.'

One of Guruji's pupils had sponsored a private jet ride deep into the Grand Canyon. It was a tiny plane with just one passenger on each side of the aisle. When the plane began to bank to one side, Guruji called out to Jasmine, who was mildly overweight. He said, 'Hey Jasmine, the pilot says the plane is too heavy on your side. He wants you to shift.' Jasmine, not realizing that she was the butt of an Iyengar joke, meekly shifted to the other side of the plane as Guruji chortled like a mischievous child.

Faeq and Birjoo both spoke about Guruji's lightning fast left hand. Guruji was naturally left handed, but forced by the strictures of society, he used the right hand. Often when they were eating together and Guruji was served something that he was not very fond of, before anyone knew it, his left hand had transferred the offending article to one of his students sitting next to him even before the eye could register the movement. Then he would look at them, eyes twinkling mischievously and say 'Why can't you fellows finish what is on your plates? Look at my plate.'

EUROPE IN THE 1980s

When Guruji visited Europe in the 1980s, he was accompanied by Birjoo, Jawahar and Faeq. They sat in a centrally-heated car, devouring kilometres in seconds. Guruji showed them the place where he stayed and the amount he had to walk to get from his guesthouse to Menuhin's home every day. Guruji approximated that it was between 10-11 kilometres, each way. When they checked it on the odometer, they found it was exactly 10.7 kilometres. The boys were all moist-eyed. Not once did Menuhin or Krishnamurthy ask him how he made the journey daily. Not once was he offered an easier means of getting to his class. But Guruji swallowed his pride and accepted it all. He was doing it for his family. He was doing it for yoga.

Often, he had to go hungry because there was no vegetarian food available. There were days and days that he lived on bread and milk. Though for Guruji, Menuhin was his mentor and the one who introduced him to the world, Menuhin did not reciprocate the affection in the same unadulterated fashion.

In 1986, in a letter to Dhan Palkhivala, Guruji admits to feeling that the Europeans were taking advantage of him. 'I hate when people mistake my softness and use me as a thing,' he says.

'My crowded programmes in France and Belgium without my consultations have upsetted (sic) me a bit. They have not given time for breath.' And he concludes with, 'A fine exploitation with sweet words.' But he could not disappoint his followers across Europe, so despite the inhuman schedule he obliged.

There were demonstrations arranged across the continent and Faeq had volunteered to drive his guru to the various destinations. They travelled a distance of hundreds of kilometres across Switzerland, Germany, Holland, France and Italy. This is when Faeq began to see the compassionate and exuberant soul behind the stern façade.

Faeq recounts Guruji's deep-rooted loyalties to people whom he had adopted as friends. They were scheduled to be travelling to Rome for the next engagement. Guruji had, in the meanwhile, received word from one of his old pupils in Verona that he was ailing and unable to travel to meet Guruji. Could Guruji make some time to come and see him, he asked? Guruji put this to Faeq, who eager to accommodate his guru, chalked out the shortest route that would get them to Verona and then onwards to Rome. This was in the days of paper maps, before GPS irrevocably changed the way we travel. Faeq had not noticed that a short stretch of the journey would take them into Austria, at least not until the signs came up signalling the end of Switzerland and the border of Austria. When they reached the border, they had no visas for Austria, so the authorities at the border refused to let them pass through. 'Only 11 kilometres,' Faeq pleaded, but they were unyielding.

It was time for a conference with Guruji and a reappraisal of the original plan. Guruji said, 'He is waiting for us. We must go.' So they rerouted and travelled several hundred extra kilometres because Guruji wanted to keep his promise to his ailing student. They reached there late at night and Guruji spent a couple of hours showing him what he needed to do. With almost no sleep, they were back again, on the road to Rome, and to Guruji's next engagement – where hundreds of people awaited him.

Guruji was very fond of Vanda Scaravelli's son. The boy, Alberto, who was a mathematical genius, had allegedly been pressurized by Krishnamurthy to become a lawyer. Chafing under the restraints, the boy ran off and got on a ship to America. Krishnamurthy's wide circle of influence helped trace him before he managed his daring escape and, as he was still a minor, he was brought back to the family home. Though Guruji too had great aspirations for the boy and felt that he had the makings of a great yogi, Alberto ended up in a dead-end bank job, disappointing everyone who had pinned their hopes on him. Guruji had a wonderful relationship with Alberto, growing to be a father-figure to the sweet, sensitive boy. Every summer, till Alberto died rather prematurely, whenever he visited Paris, Guruji would invite him to the only Indian restaurant in the city, Natraj, and share an idli-sambhar with him.

An Italian TV crew wanted to cover Guruji for national TV. In charge of production was a very attractive Italian girl, Barbara, who was new on the job. The programme was being telecast live, so it had to be planned meticulously. It was to be a demonstration followed by questions from a phone-in audience. So Guruji, who was wearing just his bright coloured shorts for the demonstration, within moments had to change into his formal kurta and dhoti. At the best of times, the dhoti was a complex operation, but Guruji's dhoti, an amalgam of the Maharashtrian and South-Indian styles, was even more befuddling than either of these styles individually. The narrow backstage area and the short time available for the change made the whole operation look pretty near impossible. Guruji said he would be able to manage the change in the short time available if Biria helped him out backstage. After a short, intense demonstration, Guruji did a lightning change, and the programme seamlessly flowed into the question-answer session. As soon as the demonstration was over, the phones began ringing off the hook in response.

One of the questions put to him on the show was why Guruji was always claiming he was the best. With frank immodesty veined with characteristic humour, Guruji said, 'I have been looking for someone better for years so I could sit at his feet and learn, but I haven't found anyone yet.'

The programme proceeded flawlessly and ended exactly on schedule. The young production executive was thrilled that her first assignment had been completed so successfully. When she saw Guruji and Biria, she instinctively came towards them, arms outspread, ready to demonstrate her gratitude to Guruji with hugs and kisses. As she neared him, she probably realized that this may not be the most appropriate behaviour. Still, bubbling over with elation as she was, she had to display her joy in some way. She deflected her attentions to Faeq, who was by Guruji's side, and showered him with the kisses and hugs that she had meant for Guruji. Guruji silently watched this demonstration of affection. When they were having breakfast with Vanda Scaravelli the next day, she said, 'So it was a great show. Everyone loved it. But what did you think?' Guruji said, his eyes twinkling, 'I don't know. I sweated, and this Faeq got all the kisses from pretty girls.'

After Guruji's success in Italy, Faeq and he drove back to France. It was the night of Easter, but it felt like they were replaying the night of Christ's birth in Bethlehem. There were no rooms available anywhere. They drove around looking for accommodation for what seemed like hours. Guruji was unconcerned. 'This is life,' he said, 'on that side of the border I was a national hero and here we can't find a bed to sleep on.' Biria was getting more and more anxious. Finally, Biria stepped into the luxurious hotel that hosted the red carpet crowd for the Cannes festival. He asked for a single room. It was available, but at an astronomical price. He went outside and cheerfully told Guruji that they had a room. Guruji had seen the hotel from the outside. He had seen the grandiose entrance. 'And what is the price of the room?' he asked Biria. Biria told him that the price didn't matter because the next day they would go to one of his student's homes. Anyway, it could be charged to the Iyengar association that had invited them. Besides, it was just for the night. It was a long and arduous trip across Europe and, between demonstrations, Guruji really needed to rest. Guruji stopped his protestations midway. 'What is the price of the room?' he asked again. When Biria named the obscene figure, Guruji placed his palm softly over Biria's thigh. 'Listen to me son,' he said, 'I come from a country where millions of people sleep on the street on a newspaper. I cannot pay this price and sleep in this hotel. I am sorry.'

So it was decided that they would sleep in the car. They would not be allowed to park and sleep within the city limits, so they would have to drive into the outskirts of the city and park for the night. Before that, they needed to find a place where they could empty their bladders. By now it was 4 a.m. and everything was closed. It was impossible to find a bathroom. 'See, if we were in India, we could have stopped anywhere and relieved ourselves. You have made your lives so complex in the West,' said Guruji, grinning.

The only place open at that time of the night was a nightclub. Guruji said, 'At this kind of place we can't go in saying we need to use the bathroom. We will need to tell them we want a drink.'

So they went in. Guruji, in his traditional kurta and dhoti and the long red caste mark on his forehead, and his Sancho Panza, the short, stocky, Irani-Russian with a decidedly French accent, Faeq Biria, who had, to further confuse matters, begun sporting a caste mark of his own. The duo was, understandably, stopped at the entrance. What did they want? In the manner of the Phantom, they asked for milk. No, they were told, we have nothing for you. Could we use the bathroom please? They asked, coming to the point at last. No, they were told as they were led out of the establishment by the muscled guards. And thus, quite unceremoniously, ended Guruji's first visit to a nightclub.

Their mission was still unaccomplished, but after driving around some more, they finally found a café that was open, which would serve them some hot chocolate and allow them to use the bathroom.

They drove outside the city and found a space where they could sleep undiscovered by the police. Reclining the seats and covering themselves with shawls, they settled in for the night. Biria slept like a baby, waking up to the sound of crashing garbage cans around him. He found Guruji beside him already wide awake and doing some stretches in the car seat. 'Did you sleep well, Guruji?' he asked, concerned that he had made his guru sleep on the street through the night. 'How did you expect me to sleep?' said Guruji. 'From the moment you closed your eyes till this moment, you snored nonstop.' Biria's cheeks turned red with embarrassment. He was guilty of a double sin. Not only had he deprived his guru of a bed at night, he had also deprived him of sleep.

In the course of their tour of Europe, Guruji and Biria were travelling from Dover to Belgium. The designated driver reached late and they reached the ferry just as it was pulling away from the jetty. A collective cry of dismay emerged from the yoga group. Guruji was scheduled to perform and talk in Belgium that evening. They checked with the officials and found that there were no other ferries leaving for Belgium till the next day. Seeing this motley bunch of people, some very unusually dressed, all trying to negotiate the ferry timetables and looking quite confused, one of the officials decided to help.

'This ferry will go to the next port where it is scheduled to stop for ten minutes. You can drive there and request the person in charge to let you board. It is against the protocol, but that may be the only way you could get to Belgium on time,' he advised them.

The yoga party, including Guruji, were herded back into the car and driven at top speed to the next port. When they got there, they realized that it was not a passenger port at all.

They rushed into the huge industrial-sized elevators, struggling with their suitcases. In the melee, they seemed to have lost Silva Mehta, Guruji's English Yoga student. When she reappeared moments later with bags of food that she had picked up for the group, the rest of them did not know whether to be angry or grateful.

They reached a man at the counter. He had his head bowed, and he was busy reading something under the counter. He looked up in irritation at being disturbed from his reading.

Putting on their most pathetic faces, they implored, 'This is a great yogi from India, and he has to reach Belgium by this evening. There are a large number of people waiting for him there. We know that it is not normally done, but could you please do us a favour and let us board from this port?'

The clerk at the counter looked up at them. Then he stared at Guruji a moment longer than was polite. Still looking at Guruji, he slowly said, 'As long as he signs the book.' He placed the copy of *Light on Yoga* that he had been reading on the counter for an autograph. Smiles of relief flooded the yoga group as they absorbed the fortuitousness of discovering this Guruji fan in a cold British port.

On the ferry, some old Australian ladies, much taken with Guruji's regal silk kurta, dhoti and magnetism, asked the group if he was the

High Priest of some religion. When Guruji was told that the old ladies seemed fascinated with him, he dispensed with all formalities and graciously invited them to the Indian-style repast, sharing the food that Silva had taken so much trouble to buy the group.

Birjoo remembers an unknown man at an American airport coming up to Guruji and saying. 'Sir, I read auras and there is something very special about you. Who are you?'

In class he would intuitively pick up disturbances of energy fields and be able to identify problems without having to be told about them. Ruth Fisk left her nine-month-old baby, Tyler, with a babysitter and made her way to the Iyengar Yoga Convention in Ann Arbor in 1994. Ruth had already been teaching for years, but was on a break because of her baby. She was in one of the advanced classes being conducted by Patricia Walden in the racquetball courts. Guruji and his entourage were walking from one room to another, observing and correcting. He strode into the room, a little man with a giant presence. Frisson rippled through the room like a wave. As soon as he stepped into the room, his voice boomed: 'Why is that woman in Parshvakonasana?' He was bristling with irritation. He looked at Patricia, and said again, 'Why is this lady in this pose?' Walking up to Ruth, 'Can't you see she has just had a baby?' He had never seen Ruth before. Seconds after entering the room, he picked up from her energy that she had just had a difficult delivery. He swung into action, asking for a chair, a block and a bolster, making her as comfortable as he could. He gave Patricia rapid-fire instructions on what she was to do to put Ruth back on the path to wellness. As he helped her do inversions against a wall, he asked in a gentle tone, 'How is the baby?' Then, even gentler, 'And how is the mother?' At which point Ruth, who had only heard stories of Guruji's ferocity, was completely overwhelmed by his compassion and gentleness, and began to cry softly. After she had answered, he said 'Very good' in his clipped, accented English and stalked away to help someone else.

Doyse Royce was seventy-eight when he first encountered Guruji in class. He was trying hard to get a particular posture, but, in full view of the class, he collapsed and fell to the floor. Embarrassed beyond belief, he was all set to weep. He braced himself for Guruji's fury. Instead, Guruji came to him and said, 'Do not be disappointed, you made a good try.' Then, he turned to the class and said, 'That was the correct way to fall.' Royce, who a minute ago had been feeling the soapy taste of failure on his tongue, was exhilarated. His guru had said he did something well. How did it matter that it was falling from a pose?

AWARDS AND ALL THAT JAZZ

When the young ingénu, Iyengar, had first met B.G. Kher in 1949, the minister had predicted that Iyengar would receive government recognition later in his life. Even at that age, Iyengar's passion and proficiency caught the eye of the jaded politician. Kher was known to be an honest and sincere administrator, but he had the natural propensity of politicians to bestow favours more generously upon family and friends. Yet he could not fail to see the spark in the young yogi that he was sure would be recognized and rewarded some day.

It was finally as late as 1991, that Iyengar received national recognition from the Indian government. In 1991, he received the Padma Shri award, followed by the Padma Bhushan in 2002. In March 2014, just months before his passing, he was awarded the prestigious Padma Vibhushan.

If one is familiar with India's political history, one can read a pattern in this. Every national award that Iyengar received was when the BJP was in power at the centre. Detractors are quick to point out that these awards came Iyengar's way because of his connection with Murli Manohar Joshi, a prominent leader of the BJP and the minister for Human Resource Development. Joshi, whose daughter, Nivedita, had been a long-time follower of Guruji. Now a devoted Iyengar teacher, she had come to Guruji with an incapacitating spinal injury, which doctors around the world had not been able to remedy, but Guruji had healed.

The argument about national awards has a long and chequered history. The makers of the Indian Constitution had inserted article 18 (1), abolishing all titles, to bury the British system of handing out titles to people who supported them. This was aborted by the later introduction of the 'National Awards', which have become infamous for their association with political patronage and nepotism.

Governments at the helm favour their own political agendas. This has become as nondescript a fact as brushing one's teeth every morning. For the BJP, giving a yoga maestro an award is in line with their party agenda of Hindutva. Though yoga transcends religion and race, the propagation of this art by the BJP is an effort to reclaim it as essentially 'Hindu'.

It is possible that the BJP gave Guruji these awards to further their own ends and to show their gratitude to him for Nivedita's recovery. This is the way political parties function in most of the world.

The more important question to ask about Guruji and the awards he received is not so much which government finally gave him the awards, but whether he was truly worthy of the nation's highest honours. That he deserved them is a fact that no one can quibble with.

In fact, most people felt that the Indian government had been remarkably slow-footed in recognizing Guruji. It was only after he had earned accolades abroad that the Indian press and government finally recognized his work.

Iyengar Yoga was made part of the adult education system by the Inner London Education Authority (ILEA) as early as 1969.

Guruji's demonstration at the Haverford College in Philadelphia inspired an American sculptor, Robert Engman, to create a sculpture called 'After Iyengar', which has been displayed at the Morris Arboretum, a public garden in Pennsylvania. He said, after watching Mr Iyengar, 'It was absolutely the most incredible physical and mental expression I've ever witnessed in my life.'

In 1985, Guruji was invited by Jacques Chirac, then mayor of Paris, to the Festival of India in France.

In 2004, *Time* magazine declared B.K.S. Iyengar amongst the 100 most influential people in the world. The article said of Mr Iyengar, 'His philosophy is Eastern, but his vision is universalist.'

The Oxford Dictionary has an extensive research team that is continually monitoring words by checking recent writing, from song lyrics and popular fiction to scientific journals. Of the words that appear most frequently in the course of this research, they pick those that they consider most significant and which are not likely to evaporate with a change in trends. In 2010, one of the words included in the Oxford Dictionary was 'Iyengar'.

The noun 'Iyengar' is defined by the Oxford as:

'A type of hathayoga focusing on the correct alignment of the body, making use of straps, wooden blocks, and other objects as aids to achieving the correct postures.

Origin: Named after B.K.S. Iyengar, the Indian yoga teacher who devised the method.'

Two of the other words to enter the lexicon that year were 'chillax', which meant to calm down and relax and 'staycation', which meant a holiday at home. Comparing frequency of usage, 'Iyengar' won hands down.

By the end of his life, Guruji had yoga centres in seventy-two countries of the world. The Iyengar system, demanding alignment and awareness in the asana, is now said to be one of the foremost schools of yoga the world over.

The name that has become the most ubiquitous 'yoga brand' was not a name that he chose, but one that was thrust on him. Iyengar believed that yoga was too vast for individuals to claim it. But humankind loves to distinguish and label. We love to create walls where none existed. And so we did with Iyengar.

The word yoga derived from the Sanskrit root 'yug', which means 'joining', but has instead created infinite separations. The rivalry between yoga schools is on par with the hostility between opposing football or cricket teams. And there is not even the veneer of civility that surrounds sport. Yoga schools tear each other down based on minor differences in the names of asanas, the sequence of poses in the Surya Namaskar, the breathing that accompanies or does not accompany a pose, the misdeeds of the founder and the aura of spirituality attributed to the practice. Each school claims superiority and frowns on members of other schools and their practices. Rather than celebrating the unity of spirit in all of humanity, many of these sad, disillusioned people create walls between each other, shutting out people perceived to be from rival yoga groups.

By the 1990s, Hollywood celebrities had embraced yoga and conferred some of their starriness on the ancient discipline. People like Madonna, Sting, Sarah Jessica Parker and Christy Turlington were the new ambassadors of the art. People were converting to yoga more for what it could do to their bodies, than for what it could do to their minds. The yoga body was long, lithe and lean, and it seemed, suddenly, like everyone wanted it.

With every trip Guruji made abroad, the number of students grew. Guruji was now never asked to make way for people who were

more important than he was. Everywhere he went there would be
crowds awaiting him. Everywhere he went he would be recognized
by someone whom he had never encountered in his life. People
would suddenly approach him and fall at his feet. When he went
to airline counters and told the person his name, they would say
'As in the yoga?' and then be flabbergasted to know that they were
speaking to the great Yogi himself.

Just as the influenza had, at his birth, swept malefically across
every continent of the world, the salutary effects of Iyengar Yoga
now swept across the world, spreading wellness and health.

GROWING A COMMUNITY

In 2002, when Iyengar was awarded the Padma Bhushan, he visited Bombay before going to receive it, as that was the same time that Yogashray, the new Iyengar Yoga centre at Parel, had opened up. He was in Bombay after a long time and had a hectic schedule.

He had a long morning practise at Tijoribhai's home, then, at the request of the owner, he had breakfast at Swati Snacks, at the owner's request. His pupils had arranged for him to watch the film *Everest* at the Imax dome, a three-dimensional theatre. Since his grandchildren had accompanied him as well, they had booked tickets for the latest Harry Potter film. They asked Guruji, who had had a long day, if he would like to rest. No, no, he insisted, and went to watch the movie with them. After two movies back to back, they were invited to dinner by Tijori to felicitate Guruji for his Padma Bhushan. It was late at night when they finished with that. They wanted to take him home so he could rest. No, he said, the children have not seen Chowpatty. And off the group went to explore Chowpatty beach late at night. Guruji was eighty-four years old. He had packed into his day what most people his age would do in a week.

The next time he visited, Birjoo asked him what he would like to do. Guruji had fond memories of past visits to Bombay, and he wanted to explore the city. 'Don't take me to see temples,' he said. 'Everyone takes me to temples.'

Birjoo took him to Navy Nagar, a quiet, leafy, secluded part of town, reserved for offices and residences of the Indian Navy. He was delighted to be there because that was a part of Bombay he had never seen before. When they asked him if he would like to eat, he asked, 'What is good here?' They took him to have the sugarcane juice near the Taj, whose claim to fame is that it is 'untouched by hand'. Under the tough and demanding exterior, they discovered a little boy who was up for any adventure, and was not at all hard to please.

In 1998 the Light on Yoga Research Trust planned to have a spectacular celebration for Guruji's eightieth birthday. They had decided on Balewadi, a place slightly outside Pune, where the participants could stay in the hostel rooms of the establishment adjoining the space where Guruji would teach. These were not ready at the time, but would certainly be by the time the birthday came around, the authorities promised. Unfortunately, things went the way things always seem to go with the Indian government. The man in charge absconded with a large amount of money in bribes, leaving the rooms incomplete. Foreign students had already been charged $500, for both the accommodation and the teaching. Now that the hostel accommodation was not available, Guruji insisted that the participants be put up in hotels in Pune, which would drive the price up astronomically.

Still, Guruji said, we have promised them accommodation and we have to give it to them. By some quirk of fate, the rupee that was priced at thirty-five rupees to a dollar, got devalued to forty-five rupees to a dollar, and the money the Trust had received in dollars was worth much more than it was the previous year. This was not only enough to cover the extra cost of the hotel, but it was also enough to create a large corpus for the Trust. This later enabled the Trust to buy a piece of real estate in Bombay, which became Yogashray, the first Iyengar Yoga centre in the city.

Guruji was very keen that the centre, which the Trust had spent so much money acquiring, become a self-sustaining enterprise and, after a short while of tracking it, he realized it was doing well for itself. In fact, the fees for the yoga classes have not been increased since its inception to date. The idea is to make it affordable enough for families to attend classes. Guruji's focus was always the family. He made sure that the spouses of the teachers were always present on holidays and picnics, promoting the feeling of family.

MISCELLANEOUS MEMORIES

Navaz, Collie's daughter, talks about how Guruji returned from his trips to Europe, looking more and more fashionable. After one of the trips, he came back resplendent, in a sharkskin shirt and trousers, leaving his Pune pupils gasping. He had come a long way from the veshti and shendi.

As a child, she remembers walking past 'elephant eared' as the adults engaged in conversation, trying to pick up snippets of what they were saying. One particularly juicy exchange was when Guruji began talking to her parents about the way the women behaved in Europe after his wife had died. He was aghast at the way they kept throwing themselves at him. Though it was not apparent from the outside, he carried Rama in his heart till the day he died. It was very easy for him to resist their advances.

He later cautioned his pupil Aadil, who was going to be teaching in America and Europe. 'Be very careful about those women,' he said. 'When I went to Europe, they used to fall in love with me and wanted me to go with them.' Aadil could sense that his morality had been hurt by these advances. 'It is possible that his stern attitude towards them was also to put them in their place?' Aadil speculates. 'Maybe it affected his approach to teaching to an extent.'

Guruji was invited by the Government of India to teach at the festival in Rishikesh. He went there for three years, teaching absolute novices with the same integrity as he taught his students of decades. He had them all in headstand by the third day.

Bryan Legere, who teaches yoga in the USA, also earns a living from the 'yoga wall' that he creates for people. This wall consists of belts and ropes that look like they belong in a medieval torture chamber, but are actually de rigueur in an Iyengar Yoga studio anywhere in the world.

Bryan, who has travelled to India several times to study at the RIMYI in Pune was one of the Westerners who accompanied Guruji on his third visit to Rishikesh, then a part of Uttar Pradesh, in 1996. He remembers with amusement a political leader of the state coming up on stage, eulogizing Guruji and insisting that he return next year. Gracious as he always was, Guruji thanked him for the compliments, but said that as he was growing older, he was less inclined to undertake such strenuous workshops.

The politician returned to the stage and said that the teachings had been wonderful and it had left the students so elevated that he really wanted Guruji to return the next year. To which Guruji got up again and thanked him for his kind words and said that he had already come to the festival three years running, and that he wasn't planning to come back.

The politician got up for the third time, saying, 'Guruji, you must come back. I simply won't take no for an answer.' People who were watching this exchange from the audience were collectively holding their breath.

Guruji said, 'Sir, you are such an avid proponent of yoga, but I did not see you in any of my classes.'

The politician was embarrassed into silence. His aide walked out quietly, concealing his face with the collar of his Nehru jacket. Bryan was not sure whether he was trying to hide his mortification or his laughter.

YOGA OPENS UP NEW WORLDS

Yoga was spreading across the world in an unprecedented way. Tatiana Okunevskaya, one of the most famous and beautiful cinestars of the Stalinist period, said she had survived the 'Gulag' on a diet of carrots and yoga. In the early 1980s, yoga had become an underground activity in Russia. Groups practised secretly in private homes, and if they were discovered, they were likely to get arrested. In the late 1980s Russia suddenly became interested in non-conventional healing methods. Elena Olegovna Fedotova, a PhD student of psychology, was one of those exploring this field. She was sponsored by the Soviet Ministry of Health to travel to India and study changed states of consciousness. She visited ashrams and yoga schools all over the country and finally met Guruji. She was so elated that she invited him immediately to Moscow for the first National Conference on Yoga.

When the officials at the Russian consulate found out that their government had sponsored a 'yogi' to visit Russia, they became very curious about Iyengar. Everyone wanted to get a glimpse of this great man, who had been given a free ticket by the Russian government.

Fedotova received Guruji at the airport. On the morning of his arrival, it was raining heavily. When Guruji came out of the terminal, Fedotova threw herself down in *Shashtang Namaskar* in full view of the airport staff, completely oblivious that her knees were submerged in a puddle.

Though there were many in Russia who became convinced of the benefits of Iyengar Yoga, it was impossible to get the blocks, mats and belts that are such an important aspect of the practise now. The early students used earthen bricks, trouser belts and cotton blankets for their practise, but this did not deter them. Soon Iyengar Yoga centres were mushrooming all over Russia.

Guruji went to China in June 2011. He was ninety-three years old. He took two-hour classes that sometimes stretched to three-and-a-half hours, with 1,200 people attending. The hall was 60,000 square feet. Guruji kept walking up and down, supervising, teaching, and helping as many people as possible. Also accompanying him were his senior teachers: Birjoo and Jawahar, Manouso Manos, Patricia Walden and Faeq Biria.

Guruji had been warned by the Chinese government that he should not have a hint of the Hindu religion or spirituality colouring his classes. For the first couple of classes, he did not start with the traditional Om, but on the third day he asked the students to excuse him while he did his invocation to Patanjali before he started the class. Those of his pupils who knew the chant echoed it with him.

Manouso felt it was the best teaching he had ever witnessed. He later stated that he felt like it was the distillation of a lifetime's learning into pure crystals that could be easily assimilated. Guruji had always shared his teachings from the heart, generously and completely. But this time, he was giving off himself with an urgency and purity that was much more intense than ever before. At some level, Guruji may have known it would be the last time.

They were at Beijing's premier Indian restaurant one evening. Manouso sat with Guruji and they talked about nothing in particular. Guruji seemed tired, his voice subdued. Manouso felt that the conversation was unduly straining his guru. In a short while, someone came and asked whether Guruji was willing to talk to a reporter. As soon as the mike was placed in front of him, Guruji's vigour filled the room. He was on his favourite subject of all time. Nothing could dim his vibrancy, not age, not illness. Not when it came to yoga.

GURUJI'S GIVING GENE

Guruji's early life of privation had sown the seeds of generosity in him. Whether it was with his teachings, his time or his material possessions, he gave unstintingly and from the heart.

When he conducted the first American convention in Ann Arbor in 1973, he gave the money he earned to a leper colony, which did not have a mill to grind their grain. Having experienced being 'the outsider' first hand at so many points in his life, he empathized with the hardships they were suffering without the flourmill. He knew that no mill in the neighbourhood would be willing to grind grain for them.

During an earthquake in Gujarat in 2001, which killed about 20,000, injured 1,67,000 people and destroyed 4,00,000 homes, Guruji packed away trunkloads of the best things from their home in Pune to be donated in Gujarat. 'We have to give them our good things,' he said of the people who had lost their homes.

Bellur village is an hour-and-a-half away from Bangalore city. Driving past unruly traffic, untidy new settlements and burgeoning signs of industry, one reaches National Highway 4. Whizzing by

green fields, palm trees, and satellite towns for an hour brings one
to the nondescript turn towards Bellur village. A little sweet shop
with a faded plastic print of B.K.S. Iyengar's face, remnant of some
long-past celebration, indicates the left turn in the road towards
'Ramamaninagar'.

As you go down the little dirt road, you pass manicured,
multihued beds of lantana and cosmos blooms neatly arranged
outside a monolithic factory that makes lightbulbs. Shiny-faced
teenagers in blue and white pinstriped uniforms saunter in to
school. The girls with bright red polyester ribbons entwined in
their neat, twice-folded plaits and the boys, skinny and gangly, with
all the awkwardness of adolescence apparent in their gait.

Ramamaninagar, named after Guruji's wife, is home to the
Bellur Centre which has a multi-bed hospital, a senior school
and a degree college, where yoga is a mainstay. As you walk into
Ramamaninagar, you are first assailed by curious glances. Then the
braver amongst the children approach you and in broken English
try to find out why a stranger is here.

When Guruji lived here from 1918–23, the village had nothing;
just a haphazard collection of houses around three streets.
The ancient temple, they say, dates back to the period of the
Mahabharata. In fact, the village itself is supposed to be close to the
mythical city of Ekachakrapura, where the Pandavas escaped when
their jealous cousins, the Kauravas, burned their palace of lac to the
ground.

The home where Guruji was born now has ugly vitrified tiles
along the walls. It was originally probably a mud structure with a
clay-tiled roof. It has tiny rooms and miniscule windows. It was the
house of his father's aunt, where his mother Seshamma went to
give birth. It now belongs to strangers. Guruji's own home seems
an even more modest one-room affair, with dried palm fronds that
serve as a roof. The old lady who lives there just cannot fathom why

these strange-looking, strangely-dressed people keep coming there to peer at her home.

A few steps away is the primary school built by B.K.S. Iyengar from his first earnings abroad. Excited children stand outside, posing for photographs that they will probably never see.

When Guruji first thought of developing the village and trying to improve the lot of the villagers, they were suspicious. They were used to politicians who came in with election promises every few years, and then disappeared never to be seen again. If the government could not improve their lot, what could this Iyengar do to better their lives? Now, after seeing the school, college, hospital, free eye camps, reconstruction of their temples and the building of a huge water tank, suspicion has given way to reverence. When visitors come in from Pune, many villagers ask them for photographs of Guruji. They place the picture on pedestals, amongst the idols of Krishna and Ganesh, and perform a daily puja of this person who has touched their lives in so many ways.

Mr Govind Rajan began working at the Bellur centre, in Ramamaninagar in 2005. One night, after he had barely slept, he went to meet Guruji as usual the next morning. As soon as Guruji saw him, he said in Tamil, 'Yenna da? (What man?) Why are your eyes so bloodshot?'

He did not wait for an answer from Govind, but immediately draped him over the stone steps of the guesthouse, where they usually met to formulate the plans for the day. Not happy with that, he barked out some stentorian commands. The stern urgency in Guruji's voice made Govind feel that he was going to be smacked. Guruji led him into the guesthouse and arranged him over the wooden teapoy. Guruji then placed his fingers on Govind's eyes in shanmukhi mudra and continued to hold them in that position for about 8-10 minutes. At the end of ten minutes, Govind could physically feel the difference. The heat had vanished. He looked into the mirror. His eyes were perfectly normal, without a trace of redness.

THE POWER OF TOUCH

The world of yoga has come a long way from the time Guruji bicycled from door to door trying to popularize his teachings in Pune. Now it is estimated to be a 27-million-dollar industry with more than 20 million practitioners across the world.

Yoga practitioners are crawling out of the woodwork. In California, there is Bikram, who flaunts his mansion on Beverly Hills and his fleet of luxury cars. He is claimed to have said, 'I'm beyond Superman.' When asked how he can make such hyperbolic claims, he counters: 'Because I have balls like atom bombs, two of them, 100 megatons each. Nobody ***** with me.'

Whether it is Bikram, Rodney Yee, the poster boy of the modern yoga revolution, Amrit Desai of Kripalu Yoga, Kausthub Desikachar, or even many of Guruji's own pupils in the West, each of them has been implicated in sex scandals that have done nothing to abate their popularity. Bikram has a laughable defence. Alleging that he only sleeps with his students when they blackmail him with suicide, he says with a heartrending air of helplessness, 'What am I supposed to do? Sometimes having an affair is the only way to save someone's life.'

In comparison, Guruji's faults were miniscule. 'They call me angry and violent and say I am a tyrant...you know why, because they cannot point a finger at my character,' he is known to have said.

'Even when he slapped you, it was to aid the movement of energy,' said Ruth Fisk, who teaches in Michigan.

The Pune classes were upstairs in the hall of the Ramamani Iyengar Memorial Yoga Institute. Ninety-two now, Guruji was attending to a patient. He chided his grand-daughter, Abhijata, as she stood arms behind her back while he helped an old student with a back problem.

'You are all scared of touch,' he said to her. 'Without touch how can you understand somebody's pain?' He made her touch the person's back. 'The minute you touch the patient, you can feel the vibrations in his body. At that moment, you leave your body and enter the student's body. Nothing mystical.'

Guruji adjusted a blanket and placed it under the man's head. The frown on the man's head eased. 'You have to feel the pain and then find out how to solve the problem. By standing with your hands behind your back, you can never help anybody.'

By this time, Guruji had touched the lives of people in every continent of the world.

GOD CALLS HIM BACK

In July 2014, a month before Guruji's passing, Aditya Kapoor, a Delhi-based photographer, was assigned to take pictures of Guruji in what was to be the last photo session of his life. The photographs show a vibrant and sparkly-eyed old man, his legendary eyebrows now completely grey. In most of the pictures he is dressed simply in a veshti and kurta. Only when it is time for yoga, he wears his bright red yoga shorts. In one of the pictures, he is lying in Shavasana with eighty-five pounds of barbell plates on his thighs. Kapoor says, 'Once he started performing his yoga asanas, it was unbelievable. I have not seen people my age do the exercises he was pulling off. And you could tell he was enjoying it.' Ever the showman, when he did something spectacular, people would applaud, and 'he would crack a rare smile...it was beautiful,' said the photographer.

Guruji had told someone more than a decade before this, 'Now I am retiring. It took me ten to twenty retirings and I still haven't retired.' Then, eyes twinkling, he said, 'Trying to keep my body warm for the cameras.'

By 6 August 2014, Guruji was already walking in Yama's shadow. He seemed fragile and vulnerable. When Jawahar and Birjoo went to Pune that weekend, he called them in. The ninety-five-year-old man, who had given them so much, said softly to them, 'I wanted to thank you for all that you have done for me.' They realized that their time with their master was coming to a close.

As his health parameters worsened, he lost his appetite for solid food. Abhijata, ever the caring granddaughter, in an effort to tempt him to eat something, asked Biria to send some fruit he loved from France. In a few days a crate of fresh juicy peaches, plums and pears had arrived from Paris. By this time, Guruji was communing with his maker. The treasures of the world had lost their attraction. He did manage to taste the final offering of his student, but he was not in a position to appreciate it.

Now there was a swelling around his ankles, indicating kidney failure. The soul had decided it was time. The body had to find a reason. Though Guruji had been resisting going to hospital, in the last few days he surrendered himself to his family's will. He looked at the caring, anxious faces of his children and grandchildren around him. Occasionally, he would lapse into unconsciousness. 'There is some disconnect between my intelligence and life force. I am now within myself. You decide what you think is right,' he told his family.

He did not want them to feel like they had not done their best for him.

When they got to the hospital, the doctor was solicitous. He made it a point to explain to them the course of treatment and its possible repercussions. He also handed them his number in case an emergency arose. Guruji, gracious as always, raised his hands in a namaskar and said, 'Oh doctor, you are taking so much trouble for my sake...thank you...thank you.' He seemed resigned to the fact that the physical problems were but afflictions of the body. 'If the time has come to change the clothes, so be it,' he said serenely. 'Inside, I am quiet and peaceful.'

In hospital, Guruji was bathed in the love of his family. They took turns to sit by him as he lay in bed, his eyes closed, surrounded by the sounds and smells of the hospital. Students around the world were praying for him.

He opened his eyes and found Abhi by his side. He asked her if she thought he had completed all that God had sent him down to earth for. Abhi felt the tears prickle her eyes. This is not a conversation she wanted to be having with her precious Tatha (grandfather). 'I am telling God, if you have to get any more work done from me, keep me here.' Abhi did not want to imagine the alternative. As soon as the nurse arrived, she walked out of the room, so she could come to grips with her turbulent emotions.

In the 1960s, when he was vibrant in body and mind, someone in a question-answer session at Bristol had asked him, 'Why do you practise yoga?'

Guruji had thought for a few moments and then said: 'Because I want to have a good death.'

Almost a half-century later, at the age of ninety-five, Guruji had the good death he was hoping for.

At 3.15 a.m. on 20 August 2014, just a little earlier than he woke up every day for his yoga practice, Guruji left his body on earth.

He must have been perfectly in time to start his yoga practice in Heaven.